PRACTICING COMMUNICATION ETHICS

Practicing Communication Ethics: Development, Discernment, and Decision Making presents a theoretical framework for developing a personal standard of ethics that can be applied in everyday communication situations. This second edition focuses on how the reader's communication matters ethically in cocreating their relationships, family, workgroups, and communities. Through an examination of ethical values including truth, justice, freedom, care, integrity, and honor, the reader can determine which values they are ethically committed to upholding. Blending communication theory, ethics as practical philosophy, and moral psychology, the text presents the practice of communication ethics as part of the lifelong process of personal development and fosters the ability in its readers to approach communication decision making through an ethical lens.

Paula S. Tompkins is professor of communication studies at St. Cloud State University, USA.

PRACTICING COMMUNICATION ETHICS

Development, Discernment, and Decision Making

Second Edition

Paula S. Tompkins

Routledge
Taylor & Francis Group

NEW YORK AND LONDON

Second edition published 2019
by Routledge
711 Third Avenue, New York, NY 10017

and by Routledge
2 Park Square, Milton Park, Abingdon, Oxon, OX14 4RN

Routledge is an imprint of the Taylor & Francis Group, an informa business

First edition published by Pearson Education, Inc. 2010

Library of Congress Cataloging-in-Publication Data
Names: Tompkins, Paula S., author.
Title: Practicing communication ethics development, discernment, and
    decision making / Paula S. Tompkins.
Description: 2nd edition. | New York, NY ; Milton Park,
    Abingdon, Oxon : Routledge, 2019. | Includes bibliographical
    references and index.
Identifiers: LCCN 2018003146| ISBN 9781138243415 (hbk) |
    ISBN 9781138233942 (pbk) | ISBN 9781315277295 (ebk)
Subjects: LCSH: Mass media—Moral and ethical aspects.
Classification: LCC P94 .T65 2018 | DDC 175—dc23
LC record available at https://lccn.loc.gov/2018003146

ISBN: 978-1-138-24341-5 (hbk)
ISBN: 978-1-138-23394-2 (pbk)
ISBN: 978-1-315-27729-5 (ebk)

Typeset in Bembo
by Apex CoVantage, LLC

Visit the companion website: www.routledge.com/cw/tompkins

To my husband, Ed
For endings and beginnings.

CONTENTS

CONTENTS

PREFACE TO THE SECOND EDITION

Changes in the second edition. *Practicing Communication Ethics* keeps its focus on undergraduate students. It may be used as a textbook in courses on communication ethics or as a companion text in courses in interpersonal communication, small group communication, intercultural communication, or organizational communication. There are significant revisions to Chapter 2, "Developing a Personal Ethical Standard for Human Communication," that incorporate developments in moral psychology and moral development, the addition of honor to Chapter 4, "Six Ethical Values of Human Communication," and major revision of Chapter 8, "Communication Ethics and Digital Communication." There also is a new concluding chapter, Chapter 11, "Your Practice of Communication Ethics." All chapters have a new format where readers are asked questions about their *Everyday Communication Ethics* or to consider *Points to Ponder* that relate concepts and theories to a reader's individual experience. Each chapter concludes with both new and selected cases from the first edition. Writing and class activities are no longer in each chapter, but are available for instructors on a companion website.

Why study the practice of communication ethics? We have a general idea of what is the "right" thing to do, often guided by "gut feelings." Study of moral emotions in human development points to how emotions influence ethical judgment and action. Yet, when we rely *only* on emotions to guide our actions, it can be difficult explaining and justifying to others why we did what we did. Explaining or justifying how our actions are good, right, or virtuous is a practice of communication ethics that helps construct the ethical dimension of the social worlds in which we live. Communication ethics is concerned with practical problems of our everyday routines and interactions with family, friends, and coworkers, as well as life-changing decisions and events. As lived experience, ethics is not about "after the fact" judgments that debate "what-ifs" and "might-have-beens." When our ethical deliberations do not involve our everyday life, we risk becoming spectators that observe and judge others, instead of asking ourselves what we can do to make a difference. Our contribution to the ethical dimension of our relationships, workplaces, and communities begins to shrink.

Students of communication are familiar with the idea that communication is a practice. In ancient Greece, Aristotle defined rhetorical communication as the practical art of observing in any given case the available means of persuasion (24). The more recent concept of communication competence focuses on how competent communicators make judgments that appropriately apply communication theories, concepts, or rules in specific situations (Wilson and Sabee 8–9). A practice involves discerning how to apply knowledge and then implementing this discernment in decision making and action. Because communication is a practice that involves knowledge and skills of discernment, decision making, and action, it can be taught. Teaching communication has a long tradition from the ancient Greek teachers of rhetoric (Poulakis) to our communication classrooms today.

The idea that ethics is practical may be unfamiliar. For many, ethics involves reading abstract or complex philosophical theories that appear to have little practical relevance to daily life. *Practicing Communication Ethics*, in contrast, assumes that the practice of ethics is important for everyone, because practicing ethics affects the quality of your life and the lives of others.

When we grapple with issues of honesty and deception, fairness and justice, freedom and responsibility, care, integrity, or honor as we communicate, we are asking questions about what is good, right, or virtuous to communicate. By asking these questions, we are engaged in the practice of communication ethics. The goal of this book is to encourage readers to become more mindful of their practice of communication ethics and to develop their moral imaginations as means for improving the ethical quality of their relationships and communities. Practicing communication ethics is part of how we live our lives. Because communication is a process of creating meanings and relationships that constitute the worlds in which we live, how each of us practices communication ethics affects everyone involved in the communication process.

Practicing Communication Ethics presents an approach to ethical deliberation and decision making that readers may find helpful when facing a difficult decision about what to say, how to say it, or whether to say anything at all. It identifies common challenges to ethical decision making about communication, such as not recognizing or misunderstanding ethical issues and rationalizing unethical or ethically questionable decisions. Each chapter presents ideas and concepts that can help a reader address these challenges. Because the individual practice of communication ethics is a lifelong endeavor, ideas and concepts build upon a reader's current ethical practice of communication. I assume readers will continue developing their ethical practice of communication long after reading this book. The goal is not to change a reader's ethics, but to encourage her mindfulness and deeper understanding of her personal ethical commitments and how she can apply them in her daily life.

Practicing Communication Ethics is divided into three parts. Each chapter introduces concepts and theories important to the reader's individual practice of communication ethics.

Part I, Developing a Practice of Communication Ethics, encourages a reader to examine her individual practice of communication ethics. Chapter 1, "The Centrality of Ethics in Human Communication," introduces two ideas: 1) Ethics is central in communication, both as a process and in individual communication acts, and 2) Mindfulness is an important skill in practicing communication ethics. The constitutive nature of communication is discussed as a process comprising communication transactions that affect everyone involved in the communication process. This raises ethical questions about how individual communication acts and episodes are good, right, or virtuous for others. As communicators become more mindful and imagine the impact of their communication on others, their moral imagination is heightened and they become more aware of the ethical dimension of their communication.

The remaining chapters of Part I present ideas and theories that promote understanding of the ethical dimension of communication and skills for ethical discernment and deliberation. Chapter 2, "Developing a Personal Ethical Standard for Human Communication," discusses how the reader's ethical commitments are created through the process of moral development. Since publication of the first edition, child development research has identified three moral emotions critical for moral development—empathy, an equality bias, and disgust. This edition discusses communication's role in developing individual practices of ethics from this biological basis and the role of the communication act of acknowledgment in this process (Hyde; Tompkins). The chapter highlights how moral emotions influence the moral imagination and rudimentary understanding of the ethical values of care, justice, and honor. Readers are encouraged to think about experiences that influenced their moral development as part of articulating their personal ethical standard, and then to evaluate their ethical commitments using logical analysis or tests of experience. This understanding provides readers a baseline for exploring their practice of communication ethics as they read the remaining chapters.

Chapter 3, "Ethical Reasoning about Human Communication," introduces readers to ethical reasoning as a decision making process for discerning and deliberating about how to act, especially in ethically ambiguous, complex, or difficult situations. The second edition discusses how emotion and reason work together in ethical decision making, with emotion signaling what is important to think about, and reason critically examining and rigorously thinking about what emotion has identified as important (Nussbaum). Ethical reasoning is organized as a five-step process—recognizing an ethical issue, getting the facts of the situation to identify stakeholders and their interests, thinking about alternative ethical responses, evaluating alternatives from different points of view, and finally acting and reflecting on the decision. Chapter 3 introduces two concepts to aid recognizing the existence of ethical issues—rhetorical listening and ethical decision points in communication. Rhetorical listening encourages tracing relational connections created in the communication process to identify and imagine unrecognized stakeholders who may be affected by an ethical decision. These ethical decision points identify recurring questions of ethical communication practice that encourage nonpolarized thinking about communication ethics, for example to consider not only speaking or remaining silent, but also listening, turn taking, dialogue, debate, or other communication acts, as well as what to say and how to communicate.

A reader more closely examines the values of her personal ethical standard, as well as other values in Chapter 4, "Six Ethical Values of Human Communication." These ethical values affect the content and relational dimensions of the communication process. At the request of reviewers, the second edition adds honor to the communication values of truth, justice, freedom, care, and integrity. This edition points out how some moral emotions and ethical values are interconnected—justice to the equality bias, empathy and sympathy to care, and disgust to honor. Questions posed in *Everyday Communication Ethics* and *Points to Ponder* encourage a reader to examine more rigorously the values of her personal ethical standard and to consider how her practice of communication ethics would change if she included other values in her personal ethical commitments.

Chapter 5, "Applying Values and Principles in Ethical Reasoning," introduces a reader to three approaches for applying ethical values and principles—absolutism, relativism, and casuistry. The chapter explains absolutism using Kant's categorical imperative that ethical action involves applying an ethical principle as if it were a universal law creating a duty to act ethically. The discussion of relativism focuses on three forms of relativism—individualist, situationist, and conventional relativism—and highlights the importance of tolerance in ethical decision making. The second edition includes a discussion of the difference between political toleration and tolerance. Casuistry is discussed as a process for applying ethical values and principles that is responsive to the people and facts of a specific situation while maintaining commitment to ethical values and principles. The discussion of each approach identifies its strengths and limitations to applying ethical values and principles in ethical decision making.

Part II, Applying Ethical Theories to Human Communication, introduces a reader to six major ethical theories important to practicing communication ethics. Ethical theories provide ideas and concepts that can improve our ethical practice by challenging rationalizing tendencies of self-interest and poorly examined social convention. Ethical theories challenge a decision maker to develop and offer to others an ethical justification for discussion and critical examination as part of the process of deliberation. In addition, knowledge of ethical theories can stimulate the moral imagination, helping a decision maker think about ethical issues from multiple ethical perspectives.

Chapters 6 and 7 introduce key concepts of six ethical theories, followed with a brief discussion of strengths and limitations of each theory. Questions posed in *Everyday Communication Ethics* and *Points to Ponder* encourage a reader to think about how she might practice each theory, as well as how it supports or challenges her ethical commitments. Chapter 6 introduces traditional concepts of virtue theory, utilitarianism, and moral rights. The discussion of virtue ethics relies upon the ideas of Aristotle, who lived in the fourth century BCE. Communication ethicists are especially interested in Aristotle's theory of virtue, because he also is an early theorist of public or civic communication in his writing about rhetoric. The remaining two ethical theories discussed in Chapter 6 are moral rights and utilitarianism. These more recent traditional theories grew out of the work of philosophers beginning in the 17th century CE, the era known as the Enlightenment. Theories of moral rights and utilitarianism are associated with the modern era of Western culture.

Twentieth-century developments in ethics and philosophy have questioned modernist assumptions, challenging theories of utilitarianism and moral rights. To help the reader understand the importance of alternative approaches to modernist ethics, Chapter 7 begins with a brief discussion of modernist thinking. Chapter 7 introduces three theories that present alternatives of modernism—postmodernism, dialogue, and ethical care. The revised chapters include recent communication studies or scholarship in discussions of postmodernism's three common themes and dialogic ethics.

Part III, Four Contexts of Ethical Communication Practice, examines communication contexts in which the practice of ethical communication is vital at this historical moment—digital communication, community, intercultural communication, and the reader's individual practice of communication ethics. Because of the increasing importance of digital communication in our lives, the second edition moves digital communication to the first context in Chapter 8. While this chapter has been completely revised, incorporating both technological and research developments of digital communication technology, the chapter retains the focus of the first edition on how digital technology influences a communicator's experience of time, space, and physical reality, and of how digital filtering of data and nonverbal cues affects the communication process by augmenting a communicator's selective perception. There are new discussions of how digital technology affects individual communicators, including the moral development of children, and communication dynamics. Discussions of issues of truth/truthfulness and freedom in digital communication technology are updated.

Chapter 9 presents the second context for practicing communication ethics, the communities where the reader works and lives. Two dialectical tensions shape community life, the dialectical tensions of similarity and difference and of the individual and the community. The chapter explores how these tensions influence ethical issues of justice in relationships between community members and between community members and outsiders. There is an updated and expanded discussion of social capital and the metaphor of citizenship, the latter highlighting digital technology, organic public engagement, and civility as practices of civic behavior. Chapter 10 retains its focus on the dialectical tensions of intercultural communication competence, drawing upon the discussion of dialectical tensions of community in Chapter 9. Chapter 10 keeps its focus on ethical issues of negotiating cultural identity and the ethical and practical challenges of communicating about significant problems across cultural boundaries.

New to this edition is a fourth context and concluding chapter on the reader's individual practice of communication ethics. Beginning with a summary of what the reader has learned, the chapter discusses two additional challenges to practicing of communication ethics, special ethical temptations, and the rottenness of rigid perfection (Burke). The primary focus of the chapter, however, is not on challenges to overcome, but the reader's capacity to make a difference as an ethical communicator. In contrast to the rottenness of rigid perfection, the chapter introduces the excellence of perfection as an aspirational ethical goal. The reader's practice of communication ethics matters ethically as an act of hope. A communicator never knows how far the good she does will go.

Communication Ethics and Our Historical Moment

Ron Arnett suggests that the study of communication ethics may have special importance at our moment in history. The study of communication has addressed key communication challenges and tensions at critical historical moments. For the ancient Greeks, these were the challenges and tensions of speaking publicly during the infancy of democracy in Western culture (see Patterson; Poulakis). The challenge at the beginning of the 21st century is living in a world of increasing uncertainty and change. Since the first edition of this book, uncertainty has increased from multiple sources—increasing dependence on rapidly changing digital technology, economic uncertainty, climate change, war, and human migration. We are experiencing more social disagreement than consensus about the grand narratives of social life (Lyotard; MacIntyre). A growing realization that resources to support our lifestyles are limited sharpens our sensitivity to tensions and differences with others. The degree to which this historical moment of uncertainty, instability, and change will include ethics depends, in part, on the ethical practices of communicators who choose to respond with ethically responsive communication acts of hope, rather than cynicism. Our communication helps construct the worlds in which we live. If we do not practice communication ethics, there is less chance for it to characterize these worlds. Given this shared communication challenge, I offer this new edition of *Practicing Communication Ethics* in the hope that it will encourage the mindful and imaginative practice of ethical communication by individual communicators, like you.

References

Aristotle. *The Rhetoric and The Poetics of Aristotle.* Trans. W. Rhys Roberts and Ingram Water. New York: Modern Lib., 1954.

Arnett, Ronald C. "The Practical Philosophy of Communication Ethics and Free Speech as the Foundations of Speech Communication." *Communication Quarterly* 38.3 (1990): 208–17.

Burke, Kenneth. *Language as Symbolic Action: Essays on Life, Literature, and Method.* Berkeley, CA: U of California P, 1966.

Hyde, Michael. *The Life-Giving Gift of Acknowledgement.* West Lafayette, IN: Purdue UP, 2006.

Lyotard, Jean-Francois. *The Postmodern Condition: A Report on Knowledge.* Trans. Geoff Bennington and Brian Massumi. Minneapolis, MN: U of Minnesota P, 1984.

MacIntyre, Alasdair. *After Virtue: A Study in Moral Theory.* 2nd ed. Notre Dame, IN: Notre Dame UP, 1984.

Nussbaum, Martha C. *Upheavals of Thought: The Intelligence of Emotions.* Cambridge: Cambridge UP, 2001.

Patterson, Orlando. *Freedom: Vol. 1, Freedom in the Making of Western Culture.* New York: Basic Books, 1991.

Poulakis, Takis. *Speaking for the Polis: Isocrates Rhetorical Education.* Columbia, SC: U of South Carolina P, 1997.

Tompkins, Paula S. "Communication and Children's Moral Development." *The Children's Communication Sourcebook.* Eds. Thomas Socha and Narissra Punyanunt-Carter. New York: Peter Lange, *in press.*

Wilson, Steven R. and Christina M. Sabee. "Explicating Communicative Competence as a Theoretical Term." *Handbook of Communication and Social Interaction Skills.* Eds. John O. Greene and Brant Burleson. Mahwah, NJ: LEA, 2003. 3–50.

ACKNOWLEDGMENTS

The people most responsible for this second edition are my students. Innumerable discussions in and outside of class convinced me an updating was needed. There have been many invaluable discussions of teaching communication ethics with my virtual department—Bert Ballard, Pepperdine University; Leeann Bell McManus, Stevenson University; Lori Charron, St. Mary's University of Minnesota; Melba Vélez Ortiz, Grand Valley State University; Anette Holba, Plymouth State University; Spoma Jovanovic, University of North Carolina, Greensboro; Michelle Leavitt, William Jessup University; and Tammy Swenson-Lepper, Winona State University.

I am grateful for the helpful suggestions or comments of colleagues who reviewed the proposal for a second edition,

After a circuitous publication path, this book landed in the able hands of my editor, Nicole Salazar, at Taylor and Francis. Without her willingness to work with me as I juggled writing with aging parents, other family obligations, and teaching, this revision would not have been possible.

I must end by thanking my husband, Ed Lalor, without whose loving patience and support this revision would not have been completed.

Part I

DEVELOPING A PRACTICE OF COMMUNICATION ETHICS

1

THE CENTRALITY OF ETHICS
IN HUMAN COMMUNICATION

Once the conversation started, Taylor knew there was no going back. Mason was complaining about his roommate, Kelly. The three had been friends for years. Last spring, Mason and Kelly asked Taylor to rent an apartment together. Taylor said becoming roommates was one way to ruin two good friendships. Now, he is glad he is living elsewhere. Problems between Kelly and Mason were piling up because of Kelly's drinking. Alcohol had never been a big part of their lives. Their parents were occasional drinkers who allowed them a glass on special occasions. In college, they considered themselves different from students who went binge drinking. They told each other that they could walk away from alcohol, because they, not the alcohol, were in control. Things had changed. Kelly made new friends who went drinking after work and on weekends. "Kelly's been short of money. I had to cover the rent last month," said Mason. "I can't pay bills for two people. I'm not a bank. What will I do the next time Kelly can't pay the rent?" He then told Taylor how Kelly woke up in bed with no memory of driving home. Mason paused, "I'm worried. He's going to work, but I really don't know how he's doing. He could get hurt or hurt someone else. I could never live with that." The three of them were always honest with each other. When they asked for advice, they were always frank and open. What should Taylor say to Mason?

You may have found yourself in a situation like Taylor's, facing a choice about what to say in a difficult situation. If you are like most people, you want to say the "right thing" and help promote a good outcome for everyone involved. Taylor faces some difficult choices about honest communication in a friendship. Difficult communication choices raise ethical issues. **Ethics** is the study and practice of what is good, right, or virtuous. Practicing ethics involves discerning ethical issues and making decisions about how to act. **Ethical discernment** is the ability to recognize ethical issues and make ethical distinctions to formulate judgments about what is good, right, or virtuous. In **ethical decision making**, an individual uses those judgments to guide her decisions about how to act ethically. Practicing communication ethics involves discernment and decision making about what is good, right, or virtuous to communicate. The failure of decision makers to communicate ethically is evident around us. Media reports of deceptive or false statements by people in business, relationships, and politics are all too common. Controversy over digital fake news has brought greater awareness of deception in communication (Pew). Communication ethics, however, involves more than honesty and deception. Because communication can impact everyone encompassed in the communication process, communication ethics concerns everyone involved in the communication process. Practicing communication ethics involves discerning the proper weight to place on your self-interest to survive and thrive, relative to the self-interest of others in the communication process to survive and thrive, a weight that is good, right, or virtuous. When you have a question about whether your communication is fair, how to communicate care to someone, your freedom or responsibility to communicate, the integrity of communication, or question whether your communication is honorable, you face issues of communication ethics. Practicing ethics involves discerning the proper weight to place on your legitimate interests relative to the legitimate interests of others, a weight that is good, right, or virtuous.

You may have faced a difficult decision where you have questioned how you typically communicate, perhaps like the decision Taylor faces in his conversation with Mason in the chapter's opening case. Perhaps you decided what to say to someone or how to say it and then considered it a finished episode in your life, relying on what some call moral intuition (Hauser, et al.; Haidt). There are times, however, when you may wonder what is right or good to say, instead of what would be effective in meeting your personal goal or most efficient in completing a task. You may have wondered if a decision not to say anything was a good one, not just for yourself but for others. Perhaps you have listened to a friend's story about facing a challenge and then wondered what you would do if you faced a personal betrayal, a bribe to look the other way at work, or a request for personal sacrifice from a friend in grave need.

Points to Ponder

❖ *How do you decide what is good, right, or virtuous in a conversation with a friend or during a meeting?*

❖ *How do you decide whether to listen to someone you passionately disagree with or step back and let others speak?*

The idea of practice is not unique to communication ethics. You may be familiar with practice in sports or the arts. **Practice** is a method of learning that develops habits through repeated study, performance, and skill development. The skills an athlete relies upon during a game or a musician during a concert do not appear overnight. They develop as athletes and artists study to become skilled practitioners of their sport or art. A **practitioner** is a person who studies and develops skills for applying what she has learned in her actions. A practitioner uses knowledge, skill, and experience to make judgments about how to act in a specific situation. Society may use tests and licensing to limit the label of "practitioner" to persons who achieve a specified level of knowledge and skill development, such as licensing doctors, lawyers, or teachers. More generally, society recognizes the importance of practice for all of us in the idea that anyone can develop a skill by studying and applying knowledge through education. Practice is a method of learning that develops a person's knowledge and skill through study and systematic application of concepts and theories. Practice, however, does not guarantee success in every situation where knowledge and skills are applied. While athletes draw upon the same set of skills and knowledge whenever they play, each game presents different challenges in a unique combination of facts and circumstances for playing their sport, just as different pieces of music and concert venues present different challenges for a musician, or different patients and varying access to medical resources present different challenges in practicing medicine for a doctor. Practitioners draw upon knowledge, skills, and personal experience to make a judgment about the best—and sometimes a better—way to act in a specific situation. When judgments of practitioners do not work as expected, they take responsibility for their mistakes and learn from them.

Practice is essential in communication. Aristotle presents his theory of rhetoric as the practical art of observing in any given case the available means of persuasion (24). Rhetors draw upon their experience and knowledge of persuasion to make judgments about what to say in a specific speech. The tradition of teaching communication has a long history from the ancient Greek teachers of rhetoric, such as Aristotle and Isocrates (Poulakis), to our communication classrooms today. The ideas of practice and practicing help explain the present-day concept of communication competence. **Competent communication** involves applying knowledge and skills of communication appropriately, responsively, and ethically in a specific situation (Wilson and Sabee 8–9 and 38–9). One way to develop communication competence is by studying and applying communication theories. Competent communicators judge when to follow and not to follow guidelines of practice identified by communication theories, concepts, or rules. This requires that individual communicators discern and judge how to apply their knowledge and skills of communication appropriately and ethically in response to a specific situation. Competent ethical communicators use their judgments about what would be good, right, or virtuous to communicate, rather than relying only on judgments about what would be effective or efficient in meeting a communication goal.

Practice also is an important idea in ethics. There are different definitions of ethics and the related concept of morals. Before going further, it is important to be clear about how the terms "ethics" and "morals" will appear in this book. Some philosophers associate morals with society's expectations about how individuals ought to act toward others and ethics with how a person should live her life. Others consider ethics the philosophical study of what is good, right, or virtuous. Still others consider morals and ethics essentially synonymous (see Jaska and Pritchard 4–5). Both ethics and morals concern identifying and understanding what is good, right, or virtuous, whether it involves interacting with others in society, identifying habits and standards for living your life, or thinking about ethics generally. For simplicity, I will use "ethics" rather than "morals" throughout this book, except when a specific theory or ethicist uses the term "moral" to explain a key idea or concept.

This brief discussion of the different meanings of ethics, however, does not make clear how practice is important to ethics. The role of practice for ethics becomes evident in a second, alternative name for ethics—practical philosophy. **Ethics as practical philosophy** focuses on ethics as a practice for problem solving that applies concepts and theories about what is good, right, or virtuous in real world situations. An important feature of ethics as practical philosophy is that it addresses real world situations in ways that are local, timely, and responsive to the facts of a situation, rather than abstractly focusing on ethical issues and problems (Toulmin). If you used ethics as practical philosophy to think about Taylor's communication problem in the chapter's opening case, you would make a judgment about what to communicate as if you were Taylor in this situation, rather than only thinking abstractly or generally about how to communicate ethically with friends.

Becoming a competent practitioner requires time and commitment. A skillful violinist or competent basketball player does not develop overnight. Musicians and athletes use their skills of discernment and decision making to apply their knowledge and understanding in real world situations, and then reflect upon their actions. When they do this, they improve their practice as musicians and athletes. The same is true for practitioners of communication ethics. To practice ethical communication, a communicator must work to develop skills of ethical discernment and decision making to apply her ethical commitments as she communicates.

This is a book about developing a personal practice of communication ethics. This practice is not limited to specialists, such as philosophers, ethicists, or scholars of communication. Individual people practice communication ethics when their communication actions are guided by their ethical commitments. Research in moral psychology suggests that sometimes ethical action is more spontaneous than thoughtful, guided by emotions or intuition shaped by socialization and culture (Haidt; Greene). Other research suggests that when socialization of ethics is sporadic or does not occur, individuals may not recognize the existence of ethical issues or do not understand them even when they experience moral emotions. When individuals are not taught to think about or practice ethics, the ability to recognize ethical issues and act ethically may begin to disappear in their relationships, workplaces, and communities (Smith, et al.). This book can help you develop your personal practice of communication ethics, so ethics can play a more prominent role in your family, friendships, workplace, and community. If you are looking for an ethical checklist of "dos and don'ts" that would make you an ethical communicator, you will be disappointed. This book does not tell you what your ethical commitments should be. An important part of developing your practice of communication ethics is making your own ethical commitments and then being accountable and responsible for how you practice them. In the following chapters, you will read about concepts, theories, and skills that can help you develop your personal practice of communication ethics. Before you begin that task, however, it is helpful to understand how communication is important enough to matter ethically and, what counts for more, how *your* communication is important enough to matter ethically. The study and practice of communication ethics rests on the idea that individual acts and episodes of communication are important; they are not trivial. Your communication is important, not only to the individuals with whom you directly communicate, such as family, friends, and coworkers, but also to others who participate with you in the communication processes of the groups, organizations, communities, and cultures to which you belong. The idea that your communication is important enough to matter ethically is the basis of communication ethics and a primary reason for my writing this book.

Communication Matters

When a person says that communication is "just talk" or "empty words," she implies that communication is unimportant or makes little difference in the world. You may have had a conversation with someone who questioned whether it was worth your time or effort to talk about a problem, discuss an issue, or give a speech. She may have contrasted "mere words" with actions that have an observable result to encourage you not to waste your time communicating. Much communication, especially oral communication, is **ephemeral**, meaning it quickly disappears, often leaving no physical trace of its existence. Your words, for example, physically disappear after you speak them in a conversation with a friend. Unless your friend writes about your conversation in a personal journal or text or makes a digital recording of your conversation, your communication exists only in your and your friend's memories, perceptions, and expectations that the two of you created in your conversation. Because physical action is more visible and its results sometimes are longer lasting than oral communication, physical action seems more significant. Some people conclude that since oral communication "disappears" so quickly, it makes little difference what someone says; thus, actions appear to "speak louder" than words.

People may also trivialize communication by equating it with manipulation or deception. The ancient Greek philosopher Plato charged early teachers of communication with teaching techniques of flattery and deception that relied on mere appearance or opinion instead of the truth. This charge shadows the field of communication studies today (Dues and Brown). According to Plato and those who agree with him, many—if not most—acts of communication do not matter, because they do not rely upon the truth. When you consider most communication deceptive or trivial, you can ignore what people communicate and stop listening, essentially withdrawing from the communication process. The idea that communication is trivial has reappeared in recent arguments that most news is fake or that we are living in a post-truth world where distinctions between truthful and false statements disappear. Such arguments essentially claim that what a person says is irrelevant (Hannan xxiii), which makes both communication and communication ethics irrelevant.

The 20th century study of communication challenged the idea that it is trivial by claiming that communication is a type of action. Kenneth Burke argued that **rhetorical communication** is a form of action that uses symbols to promote cooperation by encouraging communicators to identify with one another (*Rhetoric* 43–6). He proposed that we study the different ways humans use symbols to encourage identification and promote cooperation. Communication theorist Dean Barnlund offered a different way to think about communication as a type of action. He proposed that communication is a complex transaction between communicators that affects everyone involved in the communication process. In **transactional communication**, each communicator participates in a complex process of creating shared meanings with other communicators that affects everyone involved in the communication process. Paul Watzlawick and his associates Janet Beavin and Don Jackson identified two dimensions of communication—the content and relational dimensions—that help explain how the creative process of communication transactions works. The **content dimension** consists of the meanings communicators create and share as they communicate with one another. These meanings influence communicators' perceptions and understanding of what they communicate. For example, when you and a friend talk about the qualities of a good friend, both of you share your personal meanings about what is a good friend. As the two of you talk, you begin to better understand what each other means by "good friend," or perhaps recognize that you do not understand each other very well. As you communicate, both of your personal understandings of friendship change a little, perhaps unexpectedly. You may become more committed to your understanding of what is a good friend or, together, the two of you may create a new understanding of your friendship. The impact of this understanding could extend beyond this friendship, influencing how each of you communicates with other friends.

The second dimension of communication transactions is the **relational dimension** which concerns how communication acts and episodes that cocreate meaning, simultaneously cocreate relational connections or links between communicators. Relational connections include expectations about how you and your communication partner will act. Continuing the example of your conversation about what is a good friend illustrates this interrelationship. As you and your friend create a shared understanding of what is a good friend, it is possible that how you act toward each other changes. This occurs because the meaning and shared understanding the two of you have constructed together also created new expectations about how you will interact as friends. Shared meanings are evidence of some form of relational connection, whether it is the intimate relational connection of a close, personal friendship or the looser relational connection of organizational or cultural membership.

A more recent claim for the importance of communication is that communication is constitutive. When communication is constitutive it symbolically creates the social worlds in which we live. John Stewart describes **constitutive communication** as a process in which our language use responsively creates meaning and relational connection with others and, so, creates social worlds such as our relationships, workplaces, and communities (119–24). The language we use when communicating is more than words and grammar; it is what we *do* verbally and nonverbally. Your communication creates relational contact and connection with others as a response to those communicators. Communication constitutes your world when your communication articulates meaning in such a way that you may be understood while others listen to you, and others communicate so that you may understand them as you listen. The content and relational dimensions of communication are interrelated and interdependent. Even brief conversations with a cashier at a checkout register can create fragile, yet important meanings and relational bonds that constitute the social world in which you live. For example, the husband of one of my friends died unexpectedly. The employees at his favorite coffee shop knew that something was wrong when he did not stop by for his daily cup. They inquired about what had happened. Brief, daily conversations create relational bonds that meaningfully link communicators to one another, creatively constituting our social worlds. Not only does your communication help constitute the social world in which you live, making your world more meaningful by connecting you with others in relationships, your communication acts affect others in your social world. Your communication connects you to people you know and those you do not, including people you may never meet.

Everyday Communication Ethics

❖ *Think of a time when your communication mattered and you did not recognize it. Would you change anything you said or did not say?*

Communication matters because the constitutive nature of communication transactions affects those involved in the communication process. Individual acts of communication (speaking, listening, turn taking, negotiating, etc.) are communication acts embedded or situated within communication networks and systems. Your communication consists of transactional acts and episodes that situate you between and among other communicators, cocreating, co-maintaining, co-transforming, or co-destroying meanings and relational connections that constitute your social world. A communication act matters ethically, because its impact follows the relational connections of communication networks and systems created by the communication process in which the communicator participates. The stronger the relational connection, the greater the possible impact of an individual communication act or episode within the communication process. Because communication (except perhaps for intrapersonal communication) affects others, it raises questions of ethics. The presence or absence of ethical qualities in your communication impacts others relationally connected to you in the communication process, whether you personally interact with them or not.

According to communication ethicist Michael Hyde, the construction of relationships and meanings of our social worlds begins in the communication act of acknowledging another person. **Acknowledgment** is a communication response of "Here I am" that replies to an Other's call "Where art thou?" This episode of call and response is transactional and constitutive, creating a foundation for future relationship and shared meaning between the acknowledger and Other. Hyde claims that positive acknowledgment is so important to human beings that without positive acknowledgment we would not exist (xiv). **Positive acknowledgment** involves openness and focus on another person that creates a relational syncing between the acknowledger and an Other. This syncing occurs when the acknowledger takes time and makes room for the Other in her life, attuning her attention and thoughts, without judgment, on the Other, "even if the Other is boring" (3–4). The creative energies of the transactional episode of acknowledgment are where we *begin* creating and constituting our relationships and shared meanings. How, what, and when the acknowledger and the Other continue to communicate will influence how a social world is coconstructed, including the ethics of that social world. In later chapters, you will read more about acknowledgment, especially in the discussion of the moral development of children in Chapter 2.

You still may not be convinced that ethics is important in communication. The chapter's opening case further illustrates its importance for communication. These friends value authentic communication. In the past, they frankly and openly communicated their thoughts and feelings with each other. **Authentic communication** is truthful, open, and clear. In Western society, people sometimes use truth as an ethical value to judge authentic communication as ethically superior to inauthentic, ambiguous communication (see Bok). An important factor in evaluating the ethics of authentic communication is how it affects others. When speaking authentically, Taylor provides Mason with a more accurate and reliable basis for shared understanding in their relationship than if Taylor's communication were inauthentic. Concluding that authentic communication is superior to inauthentic communication is an ethical judgment about communication in a relationship where people rely on each other. Because Taylor has a history of authentic communication, Mason can rely on the truthfulness of what Taylor says when making decisions. If, however, what Taylor says is not true, relying on Taylor's communication could harm Mason. Mason's expectation that Taylor's communication is authentic helps hold Taylor accountable to Mason and their relationship. Mason's expectation encourages Taylor to be truthful, while simultaneously helping maintain practices of authenticity in their relationship and social world.

Some people consider authentic communication a superior, ethical form of communication, because an authentic communicator is true to herself, honestly communicating what she thinks and feels to others. An authentic communicator chooses to be honest, rather than ambiguous or deceptive, even if it makes others uncomfortable or, perhaps, hurts others. Elaborating facts of the chapter's opening case can illustrate further the importance of honesty for trust in the relational dimension. Suppose Taylor has additional information about Mason that is not directly relevant to this roommate conflict. For example, Taylor may know that Mason's family is going through a crisis, such as a parent recently diagnosed with a life-threatening disease or losing a job. Mason may have a history of depression or self-destructive behavior such as threatening to commit suicide. In these circumstances, if Taylor communicates authentically to be true to himself, Taylor's communication has the potential to harm Mason. Because of close friendship, Taylor's communication has significant potential to affect Mason in some way. To communicate ethically, Taylor needs to recognize and be responsive to Mason's special set of circumstances in thinking about how to communicate in this situation. Thinking about this conversation as part of his ongoing relationship with Mason, for example, could prompt thinking about what is good, right, or virtuous for Mason, not just for himself. Taylor could discern the proper weight to place on his legitimate interest of being an authentic communicator, relative to Mason's legitimate interest to survive and thrive, a weight that is good, right, or virtuous. Taylor's practice of ethical communication with Mason is not limited to this single conversation, because it is situated within their ongoing relationship, raising ethical questions about what is good, right, or virtuous for each of them and their relationship.

Point to Ponder

❖ *Which is most important for authentic communication, honest expression of feelings or honest expression of ideas?*

Like Taylor, your communication raises ethical questions about what is good, right, or virtuous, because you are relationally connected with other communicators in your friendships, family, and work relationships. It is easier to visualize the consequences of a communication act for people you see on a regular basis. When you expand the context of your communication beyond an individual conversation or relationship to include the community where you live or the organization where you work, it is more difficult to trace the impact of a communication act or episode. If we never meet face-to-face the persons affected by what we say or post on social media, it is difficult to comprehend the impact of our decisions to speak or say nothing. In broad communication contexts such as your workplace, the neighborhood in which you live, or your campus, you are one communicator among many in networked communication processes that constitute these social worlds. Within these contexts, the impact of an individual communication act seems to disappear. Digital communications technology appears to further dilute the impact of individual communication acts as it expands communication networks, enabling you to communicate with more people than ever before, sending and receiving more messages faster than ever before. Your social media post or comment on an internet story could be one among many, perhaps hundreds or thousands, in a digital thread. When looking beyond your personal relationships, the impact and importance of your communication acts may seem small, even trivial in comparison. It is easier to understand how individual communication acts can matter ethically for people you know and interact with regularly, such as family and friends, than for people you never see.

The ideas of dialogical theorist Mikhail Bakhtin help explain how the communication of an individual person could matter ethically to others, even in a complex and message-saturated communication context such as a business, neighborhood, or digital culture. A common definition of **dialogue** is two or more people authentically communicating, face-to-face, in an open-ended and nonjudgmental process to understand one another (Johannesen 58–60). Bakhtin offers a different image of dialogue as a form of communication that is more complex and diverse (92–100). In **Bakhtinian dialogue**, communicators do not need to meet, or even know of one another's existence, to engage one another in an open-ended dialogue. Communicators are connected by their communication acts that link them to one another in a chain of communication about an idea, issue, or topic. While some communicators can meet face-to-face, others communicate at a great distance and may never meet. In fact, communicators may live at different points in history or at different places geographically, never knowing the existence of others who are linked to the chain of communication. One way to think about **Bakhtin's chain of communication** is that it is constructed by the messages that relationally connect communicators to one another. Bakhtin encourages us to think about dialogue as an ongoing conversation that has a past and a future that extends beyond individual communicators. When we communicate, we enter a dialogue that started before we knew about it and that will continue long after we finish communicating. Each person's communication act addresses others who are relationally linked in a chain of dialogic communication. You might imagine meanings moving along a chain of relational connections created by communication acts. Individual acts of communication matter ethically, as communicators consider and respond to messages sent by others linked to this chain.

Textbox 1.1

Dialogue—A Chain of Communication

Kenneth Burke presents a visual image of rhetorical communication that can help us imagine how individual communicators participate in Bakhtin's chain of dialogic communication (**Philosophy of Literary Form,** 110–1).

> Imagine that you enter a parlor. You come late. When you arrive, others have long preceded you, and they are engaged in a heated discussion, a discussion too heated for them to pause and tell you exactly what it is about. In fact, the discussion had already begun long before any of them got there, so that no one present is qualified to retrace for you all the steps that had gone before. You listen for a while, until you decide that you have caught the tenor of the argument; then you put in your oar. Someone answers; you answer him, another comes to your defense; another aligns himself against you, to either the embarrassment or gratification of your opponent, depending upon the quality of your ally's assistance. However, the discussion is interminable. The hour grows late. You must depart. And you do depart, with the discussion still vigorously in progress.

Bakhtin's idea of dialogue as a chain of communication helps explain how a single communication act, such as a conversation or a persuasive speech, can matter ethically, even in a complex and message-saturated communication environment where people will never meet each other, either digitally or face-to-face. A persuasive speech in a public speaking class can illustrate. The typical view of public speaking is that a single speech affects the speaker and the immediate audience. Sometimes, if the speaker or the occasion is important enough, the speech may reach a broader audience through media reports or internet posting. Bakhtin's idea of dialogue as a communication chain changes our understanding of what is a speech, as well as who the speaker and the audience are. A single public speech becomes a communication act or utterance that creates a link in a chain of communication on a topic or issue, such as immigration. The chain of communication includes communicators who have written or spoken about immigration in the past. The quality of a speaker's research reflects how she has listened to this dialogue about immigration. The ongoing dialogue also includes persons who will communicate about immigration in the future. In the communication transaction of public speaking, members of the audience also are communicators, not merely receivers of information and ideas from the speaker. After the speech, some members of the audience may think further about a provocative supporting material, story, or argument. They may internalize or appropriate these or different ideas from the speech and later communicate them to others, adding more links to the chain of communication about immigration. When a communicator gives a speech, even a classroom speech, she cannot be certain about how far the impact of her speech will travel along the expanding chain of communication to which she has linked herself and her audience. If we switch from the metaphor of communication as a chain to a metaphor of communication as water, we can think of a communication act as throwing a stone into a lake. The ripples created by the act of public speaking have the potential to travel along the relational dimension of the communication process beyond the audience seated before the speaker. Once audience members leave their seats, the arguments, supporting materials, and stories they internalize and appropriate may travel along the communication networks of audience members. The ripples created by a speech have the potential to affect people the speaker will never meet, beyond the horizon of the audience the speaker sees seated before her.

Everyday Communication Ethics

❖ *How far do your words or actions at work travel on the chain of communication.*

Communication matters ethically because communication acts impact everyone involved in the communication process. This includes persons that individual communicators may never meet, face-to-face or digitally. Because communication acts create meaning and relational connections that link each of us to seen and unseen others, communication matters ethically to everyone who coconstructs with you the social worlds in which you live. Answering questions about what is good, right, or virtuous to communicate is part of discerning the proper weight or proportion for your legitimate interests in relation to the legitimate interests of others in your practice of communication ethics. In later chapters, you will explore these and other questions as part of developing your practice of communication ethics. In this exploration, you will participate in an ancient Bakhtinian dialogue among great thinkers and average people who have searched for how to practice communication ethics in their efforts to live their lives as ethical communicators.

Developing a Practice of Ethical Communication

Unfortunately, understanding how communication matters ethically often is insufficient for discerning and deciding what is good, right, or virtuous in a specific situation. Deciding how to practice communication ethics involves awareness of your communication actions and how you make choices. This awareness is called **mindfulness**. When you are mindful, you are aware of what you say and do, of your surroundings, of the people around you, as well as how others and your surroundings affect you. In contrast, **mindlessness** is communicating with little or no awareness of what or how you are communicating, or how your communication affects others. When you communicate mindlessly, your communication is more automatic than thoughtful and aware. Research in communication and technology has shown that people often communicate mindlessly with technology. For example, people are polite to computers or treat a television set as if it were male or female (Nass and Moon; Reeves and Nass). When we communicate mindlessly, we thoughtlessly rely upon perceptual and communication habits. Our selective perception triggers a script of what to say or do that we follow automatically, without realizing what we are doing (Burgoon, Berger, and Waldron). We may laugh at people who say, "Sorry" to a digital device after dropping it, but who has not been embarrassed by mindlessly agreeing with a friend or family member when our thoughts were elsewhere? When we communicate mindlessly, it is easy to overlook important information or cues, and so we make mistakes. Sometimes our mistakes are ethically significant.

Point to Ponder

❖ *Is all mindless communication incompetent or unethical communication?*

Mindfulness is being fully present to what we experience, say, or do. When we are mindful, we are more open to new information, more aware of different perspectives and viewpoints, and more involved in what happens as it happens (Langer and Moldoveanu). One goal of this book is to help you become more mindful of your practice of ethical communication and how you use your ethical commitments in making communication choices. As you become more mindful of the ethical dimension of your communication, you become more aware of how your communication affects others involved in the communication process. As you become more mindful of your ethical commitments, you can become more intentional about how you practice communication ethics, including developing habits that encourage the practice of ethical commitments.

Sometimes the practice of ethical communication is understood as observable communication action, such as a specific speech or conversation, for instance Taylor's conversation with Mason that opens this chapter. Practicing communication ethics is more than the acts of speaking and listening. Practice of communication ethics includes how communicators recognize, understand, and make decisions about those issues. Discerning ethical issues and deliberating about alternative communication choices are important elements of a mindful practice of ethical communication. The remaining chapters in **Part I, Developing a Practice of Communication Ethics** introduce concepts and theories to help you become more mindful of your ethical commitments and how you make ethical choices about communication. Chapter 2 introduces you to theories and concepts of moral development that explain how children, adolescents, and adults acquire values and principles that comprise their personal ethics. One way to be mindful of how you practice ethical communication is to be aware of your ethical commitments and how they developed. Chapter 3 introduces a decision making process called ethical reasoning, a process for discerning and deliberating about ethically appropriate ways to act. Chapter 4 discusses six ethical values—truth, justice, freedom, care, integrity, and honor—that provide ethical insights into communication. You may decide to include one or more of these in your personal ethics, if you have not already. Chapter 5 discusses three approaches for applying ethical values and principles—absolutism, relativism, and casuistry. After reading about the strengths and weaknesses of each approach, you may decide to more mindfully use one of these approaches in your practice of communication ethics.

It is important to be prepared for roadblocks to your practice of ethical communication. While mindfulness is necessary, alone it is insufficient to overcome two common roadblocks, ethical nearsightedness and rationalization. **Ethical nearsightedness** is the inability to recognize and think about ethical issues. It is often caused by the perceptual habit of looking at issues only from your personal viewpoint. Developing your moral imagination can help overcome ethical nearsightedness. **Moral imagination** is the ability to recognize and consider ethical issues from different viewpoints, especially viewpoints that are different from your own (Jaska and Pritchard 12–3). In her study of ethical failures in business, Patricia Werhane identified the lack of moral imagination as a critical factor in ethical failures (10–3). Without a moral imagination, communicators are more likely to be ethically nearsighted. The human tendency to assume that others think as we do can hide the ripple effects of our communication on the communication networks that comprise our social worlds. Often our personal practice of communication ethics draws more upon our interpersonal experiences because these interactions are more prominent in our minds; however, many of the impacts and consequences of our communication practices move along networks of relational connection far beyond our daily interpersonal interactions. For example, a white lie that avoids an interpersonal conflict at one moment may have hurtful or harmful consequences for others in a family, a workplace, or a community; or it may be face-saving, creating a space for restoring a relationship. A well-developed moral imagination can help you think about potential consequences for telling white lies. The ability to recognize and consider different viewpoints affects a decision maker's ability to discern an ethically fitting decision that includes persons whose presence is not obvious. Without a well-developed moral imagination, it is difficult to discern and deliberate about what is good, right, or virtuous to communicate. In Chapter 3 you will learn about a technique called rhetorical listening that can help you identify the obscured or hidden persons who have an ethical interest in your communication decisions and actions.

Everyday Communication Ethics

❖ *Is there a conversation where your communication mattered but you did not recognize it at the time?*

The second roadblock to practicing communication ethics is the human tendency to rationalize decisions. When we communicate a decision to others, we explain it, providing reasons for it. These reasons are arguments. A **rationalization** is an argument that is based either solely upon personal self-interest or upon poorly examined social convention. Arguments based solely upon self-interest are not ethically responsive to what is good, right, or virtuous for others who are affected by your actions, relative to what is good, right, or virtuous for you. While arguments based on poorly examined social convention do include others, unless these arguments are ethically responsive in examining what is good, right, or virtuous for those affected by any decision made, these arguments are not ethically sound justifications. Rationalizations do not withstand critical evaluation by others, so we tend to keep them to ourselves, unless we are pressured to communicate them. When we do communicate our rationalizations, we try to find people who think like us and most likely will agree with our rationalizations. Ethical communicators offer justifications for their decisions to others for critical evaluation, including persons who may disagree with those decisions. Well-intentioned

17

decision makers who do not recognize the difference between rationalization and ethical justification are as likely to make unethical as ethical decisions. Overcoming the roadblock of rationalizing decisions is important for practicing communication ethics. The concepts and ethical theories you will read in Part II of this book can help you distinguish between rationalization and ethical justification in your decision making about communication.

Everyday Communication Ethics

❖ *What are the most common rationalizations your friends use? What rationalizations do you use?*

Part III explores three ethically significant contexts for ethical communication at this historical moment—digital communication, community, and intercultural communication. The final chapter focuses on your personal practice of communication ethics, based upon what you have learned.

Conclusion

Your communication matters. Your acts of communication affect everyone involved in the communication process in some way. Communication matters ethically because acts of communication affect what is good, right, or virtuous for everyone involved in the communication process. Communication ethics is more than an abstract theory or philosophy. It is a way of living that recognizes that our communication coconstructs the social worlds in which we live. When we practice communication ethics, we become more mindful of how we live our ethical commitments as communicators, searching for ways to harmoniously balance our legitimate interests to survive and thrive with the equally legitimate interests of others involved in the communication process to survive and thrive. If ethics is to be part of the social worlds where we live, it must also be part of our communication practices.

Vocabulary

Acknowledgment 10
Authentic communication 11
Bakhtinian dialogue 12
Bakhtin's chain of communication 13
Competent communication 5
Constitutive communication 9
Content dimension 8
Dialogue 12
Ephemeral 7
Ethical decision making 4

Case for Discussion

Directions: Identify the interests of persons in the case. Describe what you think would be good, right, or virtuous for each person.

1. *Whose Interests Matter?*

Jaylynn is getting ready for her second interview for a job at Sandstone, Inc. "I *have* to get this job. I need to leave Plymouth Corporation for my sanity. I can hardly tell from one day to the next if this new supervisor wants to fire me or keep me. She doesn't treat others in the department this way. No one in the department has supported me. They seem almost relieved it's me and not them that has the supervisor's attention." While reviewing notes from the first interview she thinks, "I just need the job at Sandstone for a year, while I look for a job to get me overseas. I've always wanted to work in another country." Jaylynn pauses for a moment, "Should I tell the interviewer than I only plan to stay with them for a year. Sandstone may not hire me if they realize I see this as a temporary job."

What should Jaylynn say during the interview?

References

Aristotle. *The Rhetoric and the Poetics of Aristotle.* Trans. W. Rhys Roberts and Ingram Water. New York: Modern Lib., 1954.

Bakhtin, Mikhail M. *Speech Genres and Other Late Essays.* Eds. Caryl Emerson and Michael Holquist. Trans. Vern W. McGee. Austin, TX: U of Texas P, 1986.

Barnlund, Dean. "A Transactional Model of Communication." *Foundations of Communication Theory.* Eds. K. Sereno and C.D. Mortensen. New York: Harper, 1970. 83–102.

Bok, Sissela. *Lying: Moral Choice in Public and Private Life.* 1978. New York: Vintage 1989.

Burgoon, Judee K., Charles R. Berger, and Vincent R. Waldron. "Mindfulness and Interpersonal Communication." *Journal of Social Issues* 56.1 (2000): 105–27.

Burke, Kenneth. *Rhetoric of Motives*. 1950. Berkeley, CA: U of California P, 1969.

Burke, Kenneth. *Philosophy of Literary Form: Studies in Symbolic Action*. 3rd ed. Berkeley, CA: U of California P, 1973.

Dues, Michael and Mary Brown. *Boxing Plato's Shadow: An Introduction to the Study of Human Communication*. Boston, MA: McGraw-Hill, 2001.

Greene, Joshua. *Moral Tribes: Emotions, Reason and the Gap Between Us and Them*. New York: Penguin, 2013.

Haidt, Jonathan. *The Righteous Mind: Why Good People Are Divided by Politics and Religion*. New York: Vintage Books, 2012.

Hannan, Jason, Ed. *Truth in the Public Sphere*. Lanham, MD: Lexington Books, 2016.

Hauser, Marc, Fiery Cushman, Lianna Young, R. Kang Xing Jin, and John Mikhail. "A Dissociation Between Moral Judgments and Justifications." *Mind and Language* 22.1 (2007): 1–21.

Hyde, Michael. *The Life-Giving Gift of Acknowledgement*. West Lafayette, IN: Purdue UP, 2006.

Jaska, James A. and Michael S. Pritchard. *Communication Ethics: Methods of Analysis*. 2nd ed. Belmont, CA: Wadsworth, 1994.

Johannesen, Richard L. *Ethics in Human Communication*. 5th ed. Prospect Heights, IL: Waveland, 2002.

Langer Ellen J. and Mihnea Moldoveanu. "The Construct of Mindfulness." *Journal of Social Issues* 56.1 (2000): 1–9.

Nass, Clifford and Youngme Moon. "Machines and Mindlessness: Social Responses to Computers." *Journal of Social Issues* 56.1 (2000): 81–103.

Pew Research Center. "Many Americans Believe Fake News Is Sowing Confusion." Pew Forum on Journalism and Media. 15 December 2016. www.journalism.org/2016/12/15/many-americans-believe-fake-news-is-sowing-confusion/. Date accessed: 1 July 2017.

Poulakis, Takis. *Speaking for the Polis: Isocrates Rhetorical Education*. Columbia, SC: South Carolina UP, 1997.

Reeves, Byron and Clifford Nass. *The Media Equation: How People Treat Computers, Television and New Media Like Real People and Places*. Chicago, IL: U of Chicago P, 2003.

Smith, Christian, Kari Christoffersen, Hilary Davidson, and Patricia Snell Herzog. *Lost in Transition: The Dark Side of Emerging Adulthood*. New York: Oxford UP, 2011.

Stewart, John. *Language as Articulate Contact: Toward a Post-Semiotic Philosophy of Communication*. Albany, NY: SUNY UP, 1995.

Toulmin, Stephen E. "The Recovery of Practical Reason." *The American Scholar* 57.3 (1988): 337–52.

Watzlawick, Paul, Janet H. Beavin, and Don. D. Jackson. *Pragmatics of Human Communication: A Study of Interactional Patterns, Pathologies and Paradoxes*. New York: Norton, 1967.

Werhane, Patricia H. *Moral Imagination and Management Decision-Making*. New York: Oxford UP, 1999.

Wilson, Steven R. and Christina M. Sabee. "Explicating Communicative Competence as a Theoretical Term." *Handbook of Communication and Social Interaction Skills*. Eds. John O. Greene and Brant Burleson. Mahwah, NJ: LEA, 2003. 3–50.

2

DEVELOPING A PERSONAL
ETHICAL STANDARD FOR
HUMAN COMMUNICATION

Julie is meeting Carol Marcus, her supervisor, to prepare a bill for a client. Julie had worked for three weeks at Everyday Events Corporation. So far, her first job after graduating is going well. A good letter of recommendation from Carol would be a plus when Julie moves on to her next job. Carol is making sure that Julie develops expertise in all phases of the event planning process, from negotiating a contract with small businesses or large corporate clients, to budgeting, purchasing, and running events. Carol told Julie that if her next job review is a good one, she would consider assigning Julie full responsibility for the company picnic for a large corporate client.

During the meeting, Carol uses an awards dinner to explain billing procedures. Carol shows Julie the list of charges for menu items. "What are these two sets of numbers?" asks Julie, pointing to charges for wine, beer, and mixed drinks. "Oh," says Carol, "we have an 'A' and 'B' list of charges for alcohol, depending on the client. This client is charged the 'A' list."

Over the next six weeks, Julie helps run three events. Although she works different jobs at each event, she always helps with set-up. At the third event, Julie notices that all three events have the same brands for soda, wine, beer, and mixed drinks. "How is the 'B' list different from the 'A' list?" Julie asks Dana, who is setting up drinks. Dana replies, "It's the same thing we serve for the 'A' list. It's different price lists for different customers."

What and how you communicate affects others. When you decide to tell the truth, keep a confidence, or disclose information, be direct yet civil in a conflict, or decide whether to speak or to listen to another person, your decision has consequences. In the opening case for this chapter, whether Julie decides to say anything about the two price lists for charging clients will affect Julie, her coworkers, her supervisor, and the clients of Everyday Events. When you think about how your communication affects others, you use your moral imagination. Moral imagination is important for recognizing ethical issues and thinking about those issues from different points of view. Deciding how to communicate ethically, however, involves more than your moral imagination. It also involves using ethical values and principles as you deliberate about your communication. In the opening case, if Julie is mindful of her personal ethical commitments, she would be better prepared to recognize and deliberate about issues of communication ethics at work.

A **personal ethical standard** consists of values and principles a person uses to make judgments and decisions about what is good, right, or virtuous. You might express a value or principle of your personal ethical standard as a maxim, such as "honesty is the best policy," or state that you believe in the value of truth. Examining your personal ethical standard is one way to become more mindful of how you practice ethical communication. It also develops your moral imagination. If Julie were mindful of her personal ethical standard, she would be better prepared to recognize and deliberate about issues of communication ethics at her job.

People express their personal ethical standard in different ways. If you say that justice, truth, or care is important to you, you identify ethical values of your personal ethical standard. If you say that you "never tell a lie" or believe that "honesty is the best policy," you state that an ethical principle of telling the truth is important in your decision making about communication. Maxims, proverbs, the Ten Commandments, and wisdom sayings of different cultures are all statements that describe practices for applying ethical values such as truth, justice, freedom, care, integrity, or honor. Many people use statements like these to describe their ethical commitments, while others have difficulty identifying or explaining the values and principles that comprise their ethical commitments. As you become aware of the values and principles of your personal ethical standard and its role in decision making about communication, you are better able to 1) critically reflect on how you practice your ethical commitments when you communicate, and 2) explain and justify your decisions and communication to others.

While private reflection is one way to examine your personal ethical standard, conversations about ethical values or principles with family, friends, coworkers, even strangers encourage you to think about your ethical commitments from different points of view. Discussing ethical issues or listening to what others say about an ethical issue or problem are practices of communication ethics that coconstruct the ethical dimension of your relationships and the communities where you live. In fact, such conversations play a critical role in how children, youth, young adults and even older adults develop and maintain their ethical commitments. Unfortunately, research indicates that for a significant portion of young adults, conversations that coconstructed their ethics occurred sporadically or superficially while they were growing up. As part of a long-term study following adolescents as they grew into adulthood, sociologist Christian Smith and his research team studied a stage of human development called emerging adulthood (ages 18–23). One focus of their research was how emerging adults understood what is good and bad in life, in other words their understanding of everyday ethics. The team found that a significant portion of emerging adults lacked the ability to recognize ethically relevant issues, think coherently about those issues, or provide a thoughtful explanation for their choices to others. The presence of ethics in the social worlds of these emerging adults was "thin and spotty" (62–5). This spottiness was an unintended consequence of interaction with adults who played significant roles in their lives, when these emerging adults were children and adolescents. Smith and his team argue that too many adults, especially those in public schools, used a conflict management strategy of sidestepping difficult issues to manage group tensions often created by diversity in academic ability, social class and status, or race. A strategy of avoidance, often a characteristic of dysfunctional families, does not provide children and adolescents models for practicing communication ethics—how to recognize and think critically about difficult or divisive issues, articulate personal thoughts so others understand them, or have their ideas and reasoning examined by others to identify strengths and weaknesses. These adults coconstructed social worlds with children and adolescents that obscured the presence of ethics and minimized learning knowledge and skills needed to practice ethical communication. In addition, Smith and his team found the lives of a significant portion of emerging adults were characterized by confusion and anxiety, self-obsession, emotional devastation, materialistic consumption, intoxication, sexual activity as a search for intimacy, and finally civic and political *dis*engagement. These findings converge with the study of the dark side of interpersonal communication (see Spitzberg and Cupach). For communication ethics, this profile is a negative example in support of how communication constructs the social worlds in which we live. For ethics to be part of our social worlds, ethics needs to be practiced in our daily communication. Without ethics as part of our daily communication, the presence of ethics becomes "thin and spotty" in our relationships and communities.

Everyday Communication Ethics

❖ *Growing up, who talked to you about the right and wrong thing to do?*

Adult conversations with children and adolescents are integral to their development, including their moral development. In the next section, you will read about theories and research that describe this process.

Moral Development

Moral development is the process of developing individual practices of ethical discernment, judgment, and decision making that guide action. It includes how people acquire and use values and principles in making judgments and decisions. Study of moral development has expanded beyond reasoning to include the role of emotions, particularly empathy. Study of the human brain by neuroscientists also provides a window on processes of moral intuition and reasoning. This section introduces you to research and concepts that describe the moral development of individuals from infancy into adulthood. These are part of the **descriptive study of ethics** that explains how existing practices of ethics develop. Descriptive ethics do *not* tell you what your personal ethical standard should be. In Part II, you will find theories that advise you on what your personal ethics should be. These are **prescriptive theories of ethics** that offer arguments about which values, principles, or practices *should* guide your discernment and decision making, so your actions can be good, right, or virtuous. Communication plays an important role in both descriptive and prescriptive ethics.

Moral psychologists have identified three **moral emotions** that influence how humans understand what is good or bad—empathy, an equality bias that promotes fairness, and disgust (Bloom). Researchers at the Yale Mind and Development Lab study infants and young children to understand moral development. Using duration of attention or eye contact as an indicator of interest, research shows that infants as young as six months show appreciation of the difference between what adults call good and bad behavior. Toddlers, who are able to communicate, identify who was good or bad, nice or mean. Because of empathy's key role in moral development and ethics, you will read about empathy first, then equality bias, and disgust.

Research shows that foundations for some ethical practices are biological or innate, especially empathy. Damage to empathic centers of the brain interferes with, even prevents, experience of feelings of remorse about harming others (Baird, Scheffer, and Wilson; Lough, et al.; Waters). Gene mapping research indicates that for some persons, absence of empathy may be related to the absence of genes associated with empathy (Baron-Cohen). Empathy plays an important role in **ethical sensitivity**, the capacity to recognize the existence of ethical issues and the impact of actions on others. Moral psychologists understand **empathy** as a biologically innate, value-neutral response to emotional distress that stimulates prosocial or cooperative behavior needed for human survival (Hastings, Zahn–Waxler, and McShane). Ethical practices that developed from empathy, and other moral emotions such as the equality bias and disgust, promote cooperation within groups. This created a social evolutionary advantage for survival of the human species (Bloom; Greene).

24

The biological basis for empathy appears early. Babies exhibit **automatic and reactive empathy** from birth, when they confuse distress of other infants as their own distress (Hoffman). If you have seen a baby start crying and then all the others started crying for no apparent reason, you have seen automatic and reactive empathy. Socio-neurobiology identifies mirror neurons in the brain as the biological foundation for empathy (Walter). **Mirror neurons** stimulate imitation of behavior, such as facial expressions or emotional expression. They create an automatic biological basis for emotionally understanding others, also called "mind reading" (Molnar-Szakacs; Shoemaker). Smiling (instead of frowning) to encourage positive feelings in work groups engages mirror neurons of coworkers to promote reactive automatic empathy. How an infant's innate capacity for automatic and reactive empathy develops influences how she understands others and eventually how she practices ethics.

Socio-neurobiologists call developed or *non*-automatic empathy, cognitive empathy. It engages other parts of the brain in the cerebral cortex. **Cognitive empathy** involves taking the perspectives of others and offering prosocial sympathetic actions. Cognitive empathy depends upon a child's developing capacity to distinguish between herself and another person, a capacity critical to her moral, cognitive, and emotional development (Davies; Vozzola). Perspective-taking and sympathy are found in more cognitively complex processes of ethical judgment, ethical reasoning, ethical action, and communication.

Empathy is a complex moral emotion. Sometimes you experience empathy as automatic, and other times your experience of empathy involves intentional thought and reasoning about how others are different and, yet, like you. Martin **Hoffman's four levels of empathy** help us conceptualize its developmental path. First is automatic and reactive empathy of infants explained by the brain's mirror neurons, discussed above. Second is egocentric empathy which occurs when a child comforts another person in ways that also reduce the child's own reactive empathic distress. An example would be a child comforting someone by patting his arm, while also patting herself to relieve her own distress. While self-comforting behavior of patting herself points to mirror neurons, patting the other person's arm points to the child's developing capacity to distinguish another person's distress from her own. The third level of empathy is when a child is cognitively capable of empathizing with a wide array of emotions and offers comfort to others in an increasing variety of ways. This requires cognitive recognition that others are different, so she employs her beginning skills of perspective-taking and drawing inferences about others' feelings and emotions that she may not reactively share. Hoffman's first three levels of empathy depend upon directly experiencing another person's distress. The fourth level of empathy relies even more on cognitive skills of perspective-taking, reasoning, and, importantly, imagination to share the feeling of distress of someone who is *not* physically present.

Sympathy is a moral emotion closely related to cognitive empathy. Both promote prosocial and cooperative behavior in differences ways. **Sympathy** does not depend on sharing or understanding a person's feelings of distress, while empathy does (Eisenberg; Eisenberg, Spinrad, and Sadovsky). Sympathy involves an actor's concern, sadness, or sorrow for a person's experience even when an actor's understanding of the feelings is limited, partial, or differs from the actual feelings of that person. A sympathetic response recognizes that "there is more to you than I can understand." Sympathy may be more important than empathy in promoting ethical sensitivity toward persons who are different or not physically present (Vetlesen).

At this point you may conclude that actions based upon empathy or sympathy are always good. Unfortunately, that is not the case. "Empathic morality should promote prosocial behavior and discourage aggression in cultures guided by caring and justice principles. But it does not operate in a vacuum, and in multicultural societies with intergroup rivalry, it might, calling to empathy's familiarity bias, contribute to violence between groups" (Hoffman 22). While creating a *capacity* for ethical sensitivity, empathy alone may be insufficient to promote ethical action. Yet, the importance of empathy is evident in brain research which shows that when empathic centers of the brain are damaged or lacking, the human capacity for ethical sensitivity is diminished or nonexistent (see Lough, et al; Baron-Cohen). Like empathy, the experience of sympathy does not guarantee ethical action (Eisenberg). Unexamined sympathy may create unintended harms, as in the inundation of Newtown, Connecticut with teddy bears after the Sandy Hook Elementary School mass shooting. The quantity of gifts from sympathetic outsiders required setting aside resources for storage, instead of using resources to heal the community (Riveria). Actions motivated by empathy or sympathy unexamined by reason, however well intended, may hurt or harm others.

Everyday Communication Ethics

❖ *How has empathy helped you? Has your empathy ever misguided you?*

Moral development research provides evidence for two other moral emotions—an emotional bias toward equality and disgust. The **equality bias** focuses on equality of outcome, creating a baseline sense of fairness or justice. By age 16 months, infants prefer equal or fair dividers of objects such as candy, stickers, or toys. At 19 months, toddlers appear to recognize social loafers who benefit from the work of others, but do not do their fair share of work (Bloom). An interesting research finding is that the equality bias does *not* necessarily include the observing toddler, who kept candy for themselves instead of offering it to a stranger. A different study showed child subjects frequently chose the option where *no* child received any candy to assure that they would not receive a lesser amount—"If it is not equal for me, then no one will get anything" type of thinking, or a less extreme solution—"If it assures that no one gets more than I do, everyone should get an equal but lesser amount of candy or stickers, including myself." The equality bias encourages a particular understanding of fairness, that relative disadvantage which involves *my* disadvantage is unfair. Although a focus on personal disadvantage promoted human survival in discouraging greedy behavior when distributing food in early human hunting and gathering tribes (Haidt; Greene), in today's social worlds the emotional bias for equality could interrupt experience of empathy, precluding acts of care and compassion for others. As toddlers develop the capacity to distinguish between themselves and others, they also confront issues of ethical practice faced by adults—discerning how to balance my self-interest to survive and thrive with the legitimate self-interests of others.

Disgust is the third moral emotion evident in children. It differs from empathy and the emotional bias for equality, in that disgust is learned. It is the opposite of empathy, leading to repulsion instead of compassion, making us indifferent to the suffering of others, even promoting cruelty and dehumanization (Bloom; Haidt). Disgust is an evolutionary adaptation to avoiding bad food or sources of disease, such as human waste. Studies show when persons experience even subtle reminders of cleanliness, such as standing next to a hand-sanitizer dispenser or seeing a sign asking to keep an area clean, they rated themselves as more politically conservative and were disapproving of actions than persons not exposed to these reminders of cleanliness. Adding disgust for a person or group to the similarity bias of empathy, strangers are to be feared as a possible source of contamination. Just because we initially experience empathy toward a person's misfortune does not mean that we will act toward him with compassion or kindness. The moral emotions of disgust or fairness based on the equality bias can interrupt automatic or cognitive empathy for a person, dampening ethical sensitivity and diminishing the likelihood we will act with care or compassion, especially for those who are different.

Moral psychologists Jonathan Haidt and Joshua Greene argue that disgust is important for understanding ethical practices that are not WEIRD—Western, educated, industrialized, rich, and democratic. Haidt points out that disgust plays an important role in the value of honor, which will be discussed in Chapter 4. Greene argues that the importance of disgust, once we account for disgust for biological carriers of disease, is less about individual human development than it is about unifying a specific group or community to compete with other groups. Practices based upon disgust have played an important role in the evolution of human culture. Greene argues these three moral emotions—empathy, the equality bias, and disgust—are the foundation of commonsense ethical practices that promote cooperation within groups that facilitate their survival. Yet, commonsense ethical practices can undermine, even prevent, cooperation between groups, laying the ground-work for intergroup conflict that leads to war.

Caregiver Communication and Moral Development

Although biology provides a standardized starting point, how adults communicate and interact with children significantly influences their development, including their moral development (Schumacker and Heckel; Baron-Cohen). Theories of child development focus on biological and cognitive development, language acquisition, and social development, often centering on deficiencies (see Kagan) without providing a clear picture of communication's role in child development. According to the US National Scientific Council on the Developing Child, the foundational interaction for child development, "**serve and return**," begins in infancy. This tennis metaphor describes how actions of a caregiver sync in response to the infant, to return the infant's initiating action or serve. "If adult response is not in sync, engaging the child in responsive, complementary behaviors, the child's learning process is disrupted with negative implications for later development" (cited in Shonkoff and Bales 26). The foundational interaction of "serve and return" parallels the **communication episode of call and acknowledgment** presented in Chapter 1. A crying infant calls "Where art thou?" to a caregiver who responds "Here I am." The caregiver focuses her attention and consciousness on the infant in acts of caring communication. Acknowledgment is a foundational communication act for human survival and thriving (Tompkins).

The importance of acknowledgment to human development becomes more apparent when we consider its role in coconstructing relationships and social worlds (Hyde). At birth, the call of infants and acknowledgment of caregivers begin coconstruction of human relationships and social worlds that will extend throughout an infant's life. The quality of these relationships and social worlds affects her survival and thriving (Tompkins). The significance of the life-affirming nature of positive acknowledgment becomes apparent in child development theories of attachment, where a child's sense of relational attachment to an adult as secure or insecure influences her language, cognitive, emotional, behavioral, and moral development (Baron-Cohen; Brownell and Kopp; Davies; Schumacker and Heckel; Vozzola). Positive acknowledgment of a caregiver—responding "Here I am" to a child's call "Where art thou?"—begins construction of a social world that supports a child's survival and thriving as she grows.

Adult acknowledgment of a child stimulates her growing brain, engaging her mirror neurons. It also lays a foundation for a child's imitation of adult acknowledgment, as well as other adult behaviors. When adults recognize and encourage developmentally appropriate communication practices, such as touch, asking questions, verbalization of ideas and feelings, listening, turn taking (sharing), etc., they promote a child's understanding that other persons and objects are different from her, as well as communication practices of recognition and positive acknowledgment. This encourages a child's curiosity and openness to the world around her. It also promotes her recognizing the partial nature of her understanding of others and the world, all of which stimulates development of cognitive empathy, sympathy, and moral imagination.

This discussion of the role of communication in moral development highlights the importance of face-to-face (f2f) interaction of a child with caregivers and family. Child development research shows that children whose parents are empathetic towards them and encourage them to consider how other children feel or think, show evidence of greater empathy toward other children who are upset (Zahn-Waxler and Hastings 42–4). Psychologist Sherry Turkle argues that the attractiveness and ease of digital communication technology, especially social media, has caused adults and increasingly children to use it alongside or as a substitute for f2f communication in ways that disrupt the emotional, moral, and social development of children. Chapter 8 will discuss further the impact of digital technology, especially cell phones, for the development of empathy and communication skills.

Point to Ponder

❖   *What happens to you, when you are acknowledged by another communicator?*

Everyday f2f communication routines and practices, such as sharing, truth telling, or turn taking provide opportunities for an adult to encourage a child's moral development, to think about how someone else feels when a toy is not shared, a lie is told, or a turn is skipped. These are opportunities to help children imagine the viewpoints of others, recognize the existence of ethical issues, and apply ethical values and principles in age-appropriate ways (Turiel 875–9). When your parents or a caregiver explained to you the importance of taking turns or thinking about how another child felt when you took her toy without asking, they encouraged your moral development in two ways. First, they prompted you to experience empathically the emotions of another child to help you understand the viewpoint of that child. This stimulated ethical sensitivity, recognizing that taking something that does not belong to you is wrong. Second, after helping you recognize this ethical issue, they encouraged you to practice justice in an age-appropriate manner. As a child, whenever you imagined how you would feel if your toy was taken without asking, you reasoned with the ethical principle of reversibility, a principle discussed later in this chapter. This reasoning prompted you to ask for a toy, instead of taking it.

Communicating with peers and in broader social or cultural communication processes also is important to a child's moral development. When messages outside the family are consistent over time with those communicated within the family, children tend to be committed to the family's values and principles (Damon). When the messages outside of the family are not consistent, children have the opportunity to learn alternative viewpoints and perspectives that may influence their personal ethical commitments.

Peers

Interaction with friends and peers significantly influences a child's moral development. Differences in power and status, particularly differences between a child and parents, create unequal patterns of communication within the family. In contrast, communication with peers is perceived as equal, so communication between peers would more likely engage the moral emotion of the equality bias, as well as empathy. Questions and issues of fairness occur frequently when children play. In f2f play, children explore what is equal or fair in practices such as turn taking and distributing treats, as well as practices of care and concern when a playmate is sad or hurt. In f2f play, children are better able to see and hear nonverbal signs of sadness or pain, than in digitally mediated play. Communicating with other children may be more important than communicating with family members in influencing how a child balances the needs and interests of others with her needs and self-interests (Turiel 899). Your experiences communicating at school, with friends, playing on a sports team or in a music group, or membership in children's or youth organizations served as a testing ground for figuring out how to address questions of status, power, fairness, rights, duties, and care and concern in friendships and social groups. Face-to-face communication with friends and peers gave you a chance to exercise your moral imagination, empathize with children who did not think as you did, understand their points of view, and, perhaps, recognize ethical issues not present in your family. You had an opportunity to test your developing ethical standard of what is good, right, or virtuous, as you discovered practices that reinforced ethical values and principles you learned in your family and some that did not.

Adults continue to influence moral development in later childhood and adolescence, though not as prominently as in early childhood. Besides acting as role models, adults suggest and guide ethical and communication practices, especially in groups. Sometimes adults intervene, typically when potential or actual harm is involved. Well timed and thoughtful communication by adults that engages and models ethical practice is important in helping children and adolescents develop their personal ethical commitments and practices. Conversations with adults that highlight ethical values, principles, or practices can help a child or adolescent navigate a difficult situation at a particular moment—whether to break a promise, violate a confidence, tell the truth, confront a bully, or reach out to a socially isolated child. If you can recall a conversation with a parent, grandparent, teacher, or coach that helped you understand what was right or wrong, good or bad, important or unimportant, and especially if you consider that advice important today, you are recalling a **memorable message about ethics** (Waldron, et al.). These messages coconstruct the ethical dimension of a child's or adolescent's social world, promoting ethical sensitivity and commitment to ethical values and principles. Memorable messages about ethics could help explain Smith et al.'s finding that the prominence of ethics in the lives of many in emerging adulthood was "thin and spotty." These emerging adults may have had few memorable conversations about ethics with adults while growing up.

Everyday Communication Ethics

❖ *What is your most memorable message about ethics, whether positive or negative?*

Culture

Culture is a multifaceted influence on moral development. Cultural symbols, values, and rules create a web of meanings that connect members to one another. This section will briefly present three arenas of culture that influence moral development—religion and spirituality, the marketplace, and popular culture. Think about how your experiences in these arenas engaged your moral emotions and moral imagination, influencing your personal ethical commitments.

Religion and Spirituality. Increasing worldwide human migration highlights religious and spiritual diversity. Wherever you live, you are more likely to have interacted with people from different religious or spiritual traditions than your parents did.

Textbox 2.1

Global Religious Landscape

Christian 31.2%	Buddhist 6.9%
Muslim 24.1%	Folk Religion 5.7%
Unaffiliated 16%	Other 0.8%
Hindu 15.1%	Jewish 0.2%

To examine the religious profile of different countries, visit the 2017 The Changing Global Religious Landscape Report online at the Pew Research Center for Religion and Public Life, www.pewforum. org/2017/04/05/the-changing-global-religious-landscape/.

While the US is predominantly Christian, its religious diversity is changing. Between 2007 and 2014 religious affiliation of US adults dropped from 83% to 77%, while religiously unaffiliated adults rose from 16% to 23%. In 2016, US adults were 70.6% Christian, 1.9% Jewish, 0.9% Muslim, 0.7% Buddhist, 0.7% Hindu, 1.8% other world religions or faiths, with 15.8% "nothing in particular," 22.8% religious "nones," and the remainder atheist or agnostic (Pew "US Less Religious"). Increasing numbers of immigrants to the US identify no religious affiliation (Pew "US Immigrants").

Because religion and spiritual traditions influence ethical practices, increasing religious and spiritual diversity will influence ethical practices in families, communities, and nations. Huston Smith argues that there are fundamental differences between Western Abrahamic religions of Judaism, Christianity, and Islam, the Hinduism of South Asia, and the East Asian religions of Confucianism, Taoism, and Shintoism (4–11). These differences produce culturally different ways of understanding the world that can influence ethical practices. Making what he admits are broad distinctions, Smith argues that Abrahamic religions are more conscious of nature and a person's relationship with nature in understanding the world. Abrahamic religions assume, for example, that a person can understand truth, including the truth of God's existence, by using his or her senses to observe the world. In contrast, Hinduism achieves understanding of truth by turning away from nature toward the human mind and consciousness. Hinduism assumes that the senses are not reliable in discovering truth, so a person must discipline the mind using practices such as meditation, to make the mind a more reliable observer of truth. The East Asian religions of Confucianism, Taoism, and Shintoism understand the world in yet a different way. East Asian religions focus on social relationships, especially a person living a relationship harmoniously and well. The truth of human existence occurs in the harmonious quality of relationships, rather than individual actions. These different ways of understanding the world influence how each of these religious traditions answers ethical questions about what is good, right, or virtuous. Whether you believe that it is possible to understand the truth by relying on your senses, or that a disciplined mind is more reliable than your senses in understanding the truth, would influence the values and principles of your personal ethical standard and what you would consider good, right, or virtuous to communicate. Similarly, whether you believe the focus of a good life is on the individual or on harmonious relationships would influence your personal ethical commitments and communication practices. While Smith encourages us to notice broad similarities in specific religions within the Abrahamic, Hindu, and East Asian religious traditions, we should also be sensitive to the significant diversity in doctrine and approach within each religious tradition. Differences in religious doctrine and approach can significantly influence ethical practices, as well as be a potential source of conflict within a religious tradition (see Sacks).

Communicating with people who practice different faiths or spiritual traditions, or no spiritual tradition at all, provides you with opportunities to understand alternative viewpoints and value commitments. Understanding alternative ethical viewpoints challenges you to exercise your moral imagination and perhaps consider alternative values and principles in your deliberations about communication.

The Marketplace. "The marketplace" is complex. It is more accurate to talk about different, interconnected marketplaces ranging from local, national, to global. Local marketplaces reflect local geography and community in locally owned businesses, small shops, and farmers' markets. One attraction of travel is visiting local marketplaces to experience cultural differences in cuisine, lifestyle, even how you make a purchase. What is fair in one local marketplace may not be fair in another. A challenge to international business is how to adapt to culturally different business practices. For example, is giving a piece of art or jewelry to a business partner's wife respecting the position of the business partner, or is it a bribe? Gift giving is a practice of respect in many cultures but not for US government officials and employees of the US executive branch. Rules for gift giving and receiving prevent bribery, which is unethical in US culture (U.S. Office of Government Ethics). Differences between marketplaces can influence what a culture considers good, right, or virtuous.

Your experience of the marketplace also varies depending on your role as a consumer or employee. For a consumer in Western nations, the economy presents a vast array of consumer choices from breakfast cereals, digital devices, to personal services. Choice allows customization to individual preferences. While non-Western consumers may have fewer choices when buying breakfast cereal, the international reach of corporations such as Amazon and Apple globally extend consumer choice, so more consumers expect to customize their purchases to their individual preferences. Consumer customization combined with the business maxim "the customer is always right," implies that consumers have *a right* to products that reflect their individuality. Understanding the marketplace as a place for expressing our individuality hides the fact that businesses do extensive marketing to sell mass-produced "personalized" products. Personalized consumption encourages us to think that what we purchase is good, right, or virtuous when it communicates our individuality.

For employees, the marketplace presents a complex range of experiences. For example, many Americans believe in the American Dream and its related notion of fairness, that individual initiative and hard work is recognized by personal reward. Gallup Polls from 2007 to 2015 offer a different picture of perceptions of the workplace, with almost a third of Americans rating the honesty and ethics of business leaders as low or very low (see Gallup). There is an interesting split in ratings of confidence in big versus small business. Small businesses, which operate in a more localized marketplace, inspire greater confidence and, arguably, are more honest and trustworthy. Big business is not to be trusted. This is no surprise, as news of unethical business practices of large corporations have become commonplace, from charging customers for false accounts (Corkery; Picoult) to raising prices of drugs well beyond the capacity of the average patient to pay (Thomas). The global reach of the marketplace also is represented in unethical business behavior. The falsification of pollution control testing and misrepresentation to consumers by the German corporation Volkswagen (Ewing and Tabuchi) affected consumers worldwide, as has the global sale of unsafe airbags by the Japanese corporation Takata (Tabuchi). Despite efforts to promote corporate responsibility (Kimmel; Pribble), unethical conduct calls into question the ethics of business practice.

Point to Ponder

❖ *Are your personal ethical commitments influenced more by your experiences at work or as a consumer?*

David Callahan, in his book *The Cheating Culture* argues that cheating has become a reliable way for a person to make short-term profits in the US. The international business examples noted above indicate that the US marketplace is not alone. When cheating for competitive advantage becomes an accepted business practice, it replaces marketplace practices of hard work, quality workmanship, or an organizational mission of improving customers' lives or contributing to society. Such practices are not limited to working-age adults. Using the brain's mirror neurons, children learn by imitating adults. Cheating can become a lifelong habit—cheating in class, in sports, getting into the "right" schools, and later getting a job and keeping it. The prevalence of deception in the marketplace pressures us to view cheating as ethically neutral, if not ethically acceptable. Chapter 4 will look at the implications of deception for both individuals and society, in the discussion of the ethical value of truth.

The influence of the marketplace on our personal communication practices and ethical commitments varies with personal experience. Your experience in the workplace and as a consumer, as well as that of your family and friends, influences your commitment to the principle "initiative, hard work or quality workmanship are rewarded" or that cheating and deception are ethically neutral or acceptable.

Popular Culture. Adults have been concerned with the effects of popular culture for over 2,000 years. Plato argued for censorship of music and stories because of their powerful effect on the young (*Republic*, Book III). Today, parents are urged to select carefully stories and media for their children, because of what they teach (Puka). Digital technology has made this gatekeeping more challenging than in earlier ages of print, radio, and television.

Mobile devices offer easy access to vast media collections, gaming, and digital conversations. Parents who monitor media use cannot presume their children will not access violent games or sexually explicit programming at a friend's home or on a mobile device at the playground. While hardware and software technology may block access to specific media, parents cannot presume that their children will not bypass digital watchdogs. Ease of access makes digitized popular culture seemingly if not actually pervasive, especially if parents do not personally supervise the media their children watch or use. Some parents, including executives of technology companies such as former Apple CEO Steven Jobs, have chosen to severely limit their children's access to digital devices to promote their healthy development (Fleming), long before Turkle's analysis of the impact of digital technology on children's development mentioned earlier in this chapter.

Digital technology also allows us to customize the popular culture we access. We can choose to receive popular culture messages on most any topic from most everywhere in the world. While we may intentionally access popular culture by customizing a digital playlist or video queue, customized access also occurs without our action or knowledge with software algorithms that filter digital messages (Gillespie). Digital customization of popular culture, like customization of the marketplace, expresses our individuality. It also can limit our access to alternative viewpoints, reinforcing what we already believe and understand (Pariser). This limits our moral imaginations. Generalizing about how popular culture influences moral development is difficult. When popular culture is digital, it is easier to learn about different people, ideas, and cultures. However, digital technology makes it easier for intentional and unintentional customization of messages. Digital technology has the potential to expand the moral imagination by offering access to alternative viewpoints, or to limit the moral imagination by digital filtering of alternative viewpoints. Chapter 8 will discuss further ethical issues of digital communication, including digital filtering.

Point to Ponder

❖ *What form of popular culture did you use as a child? What values or principles did you learn?*

When we look at theory and research in moral development, we better understand how our communication is important ethically. Beginning at birth, the communication practices of family, friends, peers, and culture influence the moral development and ethical commitments of children and even adults. You may have concluded that how others communicate with you determines your values and ethical commitments. How others communicate with you is important, but so is how you interpret your experiences and the choices you make based upon your interpretations (see Schrag).

The next section introduces you to two approaches for evaluating ethical qualities of values and principles you have learned through your moral development.

Evaluating Your Personal Ethical Standard

You apply values and principles whenever you decide to communicate—to keep or disclose a confidence, to tell the truth or a "white" lie, or how to confront a difficult person at work. Applying values may be an unconscious habit, until you wonder if a principle you were taught as a child, such as "never tell a lie," is the best guide for your communication choices in a situation. For centuries, philosophers and ethicists have asked themselves questions like this one about lying, to distinguish between decisions that are ethically justified and decisions that rationalize self-interest or poorly examined social convention (Nussbaum). Asking questions like these encourages you to exercise your moral imagination, to think about your interest to survive and thrive alongside the interests of others to survive and thrive. This section introduces two approaches for evaluating a principle or value for its ethical qualities—logical analysis and testing by experience. You may use some combination of the methods outlined in this section in deciding whether to include a value or principle in your personal ethical standard, as well as in your deliberations about how to communicate.

Logical Analysis

Logical analysis uses standards of logical reasoning to evaluate values and principles. Key criteria are consistency and coherence. When you apply these criteria, you aim to achieve harmony within your personal ethical standard in two ways. First, in how you practice your ethical commitments. Second, by avoiding or minimizing contradictions between the values and principles of your personal ethical standard. When you apply ethical principles and values with **consistency**, you apply them in the same or comparable manner in a wide variety of situations. The more often you tell the truth, even when it is not in your best interest, the more consistently you apply the ethical principle of honesty.

There are two additional criteria of consistency: reversibility and universalizability. When you use **reversibility**, you engage your moral imagination to picture yourself as a person experiencing the consequences of applying a specific ethical value or principle, to test whether you make exceptions in how you would apply your principles and values. Imagine a situation in which you had the choice to tell the truth or a lie. If circumstances were reversed and you were the person hearing the lie, would you think it is ethical to lie, or tell the truth? In the case that opens this chapter, if the company provides different service for different prices, there is a reason for the different prices for the same products. Julie could use the principle of reversibility to judge whether such a practice is ethical. Reversibility helps us check whether we are granting ourselves an exception in applying an ethical value or principle because it would benefit our self-interest without consideration of the interests of others.

Universalizability is a second criterion for evaluating consistency in ethical values and principles. Universalizability asks us to imagine what would happen if an ethical principle were applied to everyone, instead of just an individual or one group of people. What would happen if everyone told the truth? How would business practices change? Universalizability is another way to check whether we are granting ourselves an exception in applying an ethical value or principle because it would benefit our self-interest, and so apply an ethical value inconsistently.

Textbox 2.2

Evaluating Your Ethical Standard

Logical Analysis

- Am I consistent in applying a value or principle, or do I make exceptions?

    o   If roles were reversed, would I expect this value or principle to be applied to me in the same manner I would apply it to others (*reversibility*)? What is my practice?

    o   What would happen if this value or principle were followed by everyone, not just one individual or group of people (*universalizability*)?

    o   Am I being consistent for the sake of being consistent, or because it contributes to my legitimate interests and that of others to survive and thrive?

- Is there coherence between my values and principles within my ethical standard?

    o   Are there tension points where I must seek a balance between different values and principles? How do I typically manage these tensions? Are there exceptions? Why? Why not?

Testing with Experience

- What are beneficial or harmful short- and long-term consequences of applying this value or principle?

- Can I use this value or principle across a wide range of situations, or is it limited to a specific or unique set of circumstances?
- What would happen if this ethical value or principle became a habit for me? For others?
- Do others, especially those who sometimes or often disagree with me, find this value or principle ethically acceptable?
- Is this value or principle meaningful to people with different cultural experiences?
  - o If it is meaningful, is there a similar understanding of what this value or principle means?
- Am I willing to argue for or defend this value or principle as an ethically responsive communicator?
- Am I willing to be held accountable if I fail to practice this value or principle?
  - o Am I willing to argue for holding others accountable if they fail to practice this value or principle?

The second criterion for logical reasoning is coherence. **Coherence** encourages us to consider relationships among ethical values and principles in our personal ethical standard. Coherence encourages us to consider whether some are more important than others, how they complement or are in tension with each other. Coherence asks how we balance and prioritize what is important to us. Honesty can illustrate. If we are convinced that being honest is more important than the chance that our honesty could harm another person, it is ethically coherent to be honest. If we consider doing no harm as important as truthfulness, there is a tension between these ethical principles. Sometimes, points of tension develop into a contradiction, creating an ethical dilemma that requires you to choose which value or principle is more important. Points of tension do not automatically make your ethical standard incoherent. They can be a signal to be thoughtful and mindful in discerning and deliberating how to practice your personal ethical standard. Ideally, your ethical values and principles are coherent, with clear priorities or complementary relationships. In the everyday practice of communication ethics, commitments to values like truth, justice, and not doing harm can be difficult to prioritize or balance. In such situations, you use your moral imagination, experience, and ability to reason ethically to discern what is ethically important and make a judgment about what would be ethically responsive communication.

Testing by Experience

Testing by experience uses your experience and observation of others to think about the practice of a value or principle. The first test of experience is asking questions about the short- and long-term **consequences** of applying ethical values or principles about the interests of persons to survive and thrive. Thinking about potential consequences of your communication choices recognizes the transactional nature of communication, that communication acts and episodes affect others involved in the communication process. You ask questions about who would be harmed, who would benefit, which rights would be ignored or recognized, or who would be silenced. Telling the truth is a recognized ethical standard of communication because its consequence of respecting the rights of others as decision makers is a foundation of trust that benefits everyone involved in the communication process (Bok 18–22). It is important not to limit the scope of the test of experience to a single situation or category of experience, such as truth telling in your family. Do you tell the truth to friends, acquaintances, or strangers in the same way you tell the truth to family members? Why or why not? Using your moral imagination to think about how your communication can affect people beyond your immediate personal relationships is an important part of thinking about the consequences.

Many of the remaining tests of experience discussed below challenge us to think about both intended and unintended consequences of applying an ethical value or principle in a range of situations. The second standard of testing by experience considers usefulness—can the practice of a value or principle work across a wide range of situations? "Honesty is the best policy" is useful because it respects the rights of others to make choices and builds trust between people in a wide variety of situations including friends, acquaintances, coworkers, and strangers. A third test of experience is considering what would happen if an ethical value or principle became a habit. A habit is a practice you rely on without a second thought, as if it is automatic. This test asks you to consider whether the practice of a value or principle could be an ethical baseline or foundation of your actions. If, in your experience, the habitual practice of a principle or value has beneficial consequences, this is additional support for including a value or principle in your personal ethical standard. A fourth test of experience is the degree to which a value or principle is ethically acceptable to others. At first, this test might appear to be a rationalization using poorly examined social convention—do it because others are doing it. However, this test allows others to *critically* evaluate the practice of an ethical value or principle. It is one way to check the human tendency to rely solely on self-interest or poorly examined social convention instead of being open and ethically responsive to the interests of others to survive and thrive (Bok 91–4).

Point to Ponder

❖ *What value or principle of your personal ethical standard is the most important to you? How did you decide it is the most important?*

The last two methods for using experience to test a value or principle are the most difficult. The fifth test is the challenge of identifying principles or values that transcend cultural differences. Such principles or values would serve as a basis for intercultural discussions and problem solving about issues that transcend cultural boundaries, such as poverty, war, disease, and climate change. There is skepticism, however, about whether ethical principles and values can be shared in a meaningful way across diverse cultural boundaries, if they do exist. The principle of "honesty is the best policy" illustrates this challenge. Communication ethicist Vernon Jenson argues that truth and trust are interdependent, transcending cultural boundaries. However, practices of truth telling culturally vary as different cultures place different ethical priority on truth telling or understanding truth in different ways. In the US for example, truth telling is valued as a cultural ideal in personal and political life, even if the truth is embarrassing or shameful for the communicator or others. Truth is valued in itself, implying a right for others to know the truth, whatever the consequences. The principle "honesty is the best policy" illustrates this cultural understanding. In Japan, however, the ethical standard of truth telling is carefully balanced with the values of harmony and respect for the dignity of others, the truth that relationships are important for human survival and thriving. If the truth shames another person, it may be ethical for the truth to remain unsaid or ignored by face-saving communication practices of indirection or avoidance. Both cultures are committed to the principle of truth telling, but understand and practice truth in different ways. Chapter 10 will explore further the question of whether or how ethical values and principles transcend cultural boundaries.

The final test of experience, arguing for or defending a value or principle as an ethically responsive communicator, involves engaging others in an interdependent process of critical evaluation and deliberation (see Makau and Marty 10–1). When you argue for and defend values and principles of your personal ethical standard, you offer your reasoning to others for examination and discussion. This test requires an openness to be persuaded by arguments of others who disagree with your reasoning, combined with a simultaneous commitment to argue for the importance of these values and principles. You are committed to your values and principles, but remain open to the possibility that you could be mistaken. Such experiences can be important in developing your moral imagination.

When you use logical analysis and tests of experience to examine values and principles, you evaluate whether or how their practice is good, right, or virtuous for others, as well as yourself. Your evaluation may convince you that an ethical value, such as care, or principle, such as "honesty is the best policy," has earned your personal commitment. You may even conclude that a single value or principle is more important than any other value or principle. Alternatively, you may conclude that consideration of two or more values or principles is critical to your practice of communication ethics. As you read later chapters in this book, you will be introduced to different values and principles for you to consider for inclusion in your personal ethical standard of communication. Even if you decide not to include a particular value or principle, learning about different values and principles can clarify your personal ethical commitments and help you explain their importance to others. Ethically responsive communication about your personal ethical commitments helps make the ethical dimension of your relationships clearer to you and others.

Expressing Your Personal Ethical Standard as a Code or Credo

Groups and organizations sometimes make public statements about their ethical commitments or practices in the form of a code of ethics or a credo. A **code of ethics** consists of statements that identify ideals of ethical practice, as well as what the group considers the minimum standard of ethical behavior (Johannesen 181–205). When a code identifies minimum standards of ethical behavior, they function as rules or laws that govern the behavior of members. Codes help identify standards of behavior in ethically difficult or confusing situations. Some organizations have a process for enforcing their code and punishing members who break it. As a set of enforceable rules or laws, it is important for a code to be internally consistent. Professional organizations, for attorneys the US American Bar Association or the UK Bar Standards Board and for physicians the American Medical Association or the UK's General Medical Council, have professional codes of conduct and processes of enforcement to discipline members who violate these codes. Some critics of ethical codes argue that when codes are enforced as a minimum standard of ethical behavior, people search for ways to stretch the rules or make exceptions. When this occurs, enforcing rules of an ethical code is emphasized rather than mindfully practicing the values or principles on which the code is based.

A different type of public statement of ethics is a credo. A **credo** is a statement of principles and values that reflects ethical commitments of an individual, group, or organization. The statements of a credo are not legalistic rules to govern conduct, but a statement of commitments that guide practices of ethical discernment and decision making. A credo does not provide rules for enforcement. In fact, it is possible for statements in a credo to be in tension with one another, and in specific situations to be in conflict. Tension or contradiction indicates that two or more values or principles are highly prized but cannot easily or always be practiced simultaneously. Ultimately, how or whether a value or principle is practiced depends upon the discernment and decision making of the communicator in her consideration of the facts and circumstances of a specific situation. The purpose of a credo is to provide guidelines to stimulate thoughtful discernment and deliberation about how to act ethically, not to provide a set of rules enforced by punishment.

Two scholars of communication have publicly communicated their ethical commitments about communication, Roderick Hart and Wayne Booth. Hart, in his essay "The Politics of Communication Studies: An Address to Undergraduates," urges students of communication, like yourself, to recognize their responsibility to communicate in ways to promote the right of others to communicate. Communication is not for the educated few, but is every person's right. Although Hart calls the communication practices he advocates political, they are practices of a democratic ethic of communication that applies values of justice and freedom. Rhetorical communication scholar Wayne Booth urges communicators to be attentive to the quality of their rhetorical communication and how it affects others. He argues that the complexity of problems and ethical issues raised by "rhetrickery" must be addressed with an ethical practice of a listening rhetoric (127–8). Both Hart's and Booth's statements of their ethical commitments are credos rather than codes of ethics. They urge each of us to make a personal commitment to specific values and principles, rather than enforce a set of ethical rules.

As you think about your personal ethical commitments, consider whether you think of them as a code or a credo. Is your personal ethical standard a set of ethical rules you follow; do you expect some negative consequence when you violate a rule? Or is your personal ethical standard a set of principles or commitments that stimulate and guide your thinking about what is ethically important when you communicate? You may find that your personal ethical standard contains elements of both a code and a credo. The National Communication Association has two policy statements about communication ethics that you may find useful in thinking about your personal ethical commitments. Both statements take the form of a credo rather than a code.

Conclusion

Developing your personal ethical standard of communication is part of your lifelong practice of communication ethics that began when you were a child. Thinking about and evaluating your personal ethical commitments helps develop your moral imagination. It also can sensitize you to ethical issues and prompt you to mindfully deliberate about your communication choices. Your personal ethical standard, however, does not dictate your decisions. The nature of a practice is that you cannot be certain what you will decide until you face an actual moment of decision. If you have thought carefully and rigorously about your personal ethical commitments, you are better prepared to discern and deliberate about your communication choices and put your personal ethical standard into practice.

Textbox 2.3

National Communication Association (US): Credo for Ethical Communication

Preamble

Questions of right and wrong arise whenever people communicate. Ethical communication is fundamental to responsible thinking, decision making, and the development of relationships and communities within and across contexts, cultures, channels, and media. Moreover, ethical communication enhances human worth and dignity by fostering truthfulness, fairness, responsibility, personal integrity, and respect for self and others. We believe that unethical communication threatens the quality of all communication and consequently the well-being of individuals and the society in which we live. Therefore, we, the members of the National Communication Association, endorse and are committed to practicing the following principles of ethical communication:

Principles

- We advocate truthfulness, accuracy, honesty, and reason as essential to the integrity of communication.
- We endorse freedom of expression, diversity of perspective, and tolerance of dissent to achieve the informed and responsible decision making fundamental to a civil society.
- We strive to understand and respect other communicators before evaluating and responding to their messages.
- We promote access to communication resources and opportunities as necessary to fulfill human potential and contribute to the well-being of families, communities, and society.
- We promote communication climates of caring and mutual understanding that respect the unique needs and characteristics of individual communicators.
- We condemn communication that degrades individuals and humanity through distortion, intimidation, coercion, and violence, and through the expression of intolerance and hatred.

- We are committed to the courageous expression of personal convictions in pursuit of fairness and justice.
- We advocate sharing information, opinions, and feelings when facing significant choices while also respecting privacy and confidentiality.
- We accept responsibility for the short- and long-term consequences for our own communication and expect the same of others.

Source: National Communication Association, www.natcom.org/ethicalstatements/. Reprinted with permission from the National Communication Association. All rights reserved.

Textbox 2.4

National Communication Association (US): Credo for Free and Responsible Communication in a Democratic Society

Preamble

Recognizing the essential place of free and responsible communication in a democratic society, and recognizing the distinction between the freedoms our legal system should respect and the responsibilities our educational system should cultivate, we members of the National Communication Association endorse the following statement of principles:

Principles

- WE BELIEVE that freedom of speech and assembly must hold a central position among American constitutional principles, and we express our determined support for the right of peaceful expression by any communicative means available.
- WE SUPPORT the proposition that a free society can absorb with equanimity speech which exceeds the boundaries of generally accepted beliefs and mores; that much good and little harm can ensue if we err on the side of freedom, whereas much harm and little good may follow if we err on the side of suppression.
- WE CRITICIZE as misguided those who believe that the justice of their cause confers license to interfere physically and coercively with speech of others, and we condemn intimidation, whether

by powerful majorities or strident minorities, which attempts to restrict free expression.

- WE ACCEPT the responsibility of cultivating by precepts and example, in our classrooms and in our communities, enlightened uses of communication; of developing in our students a respect for precision and accuracy in communication, and for reasoning based upon evidence and a judicious discrimination among values.
- WE ENCOURAGE our students to accept the role of well-informed and articulate citizens, to defend the communication rights of those with whom they may disagree, and to expose abuses of the communication process.
- WE DEDICATE ourselves fully to these principles, confident in the belief that reason will ultimately prevail in a free marketplace of ideas.

Source: National Communication Association, www.natcom.org/ethicalstatements/. Reprinted with permission from the National Communication Association. All rights reserved.

Vocabulary

Automatic and reactive empathy 25
Code of ethics 41
Cognitive empathy 25
Coherence 38
Communication episode of call and acknowledgment 28
Consequences 39
Consistency 36
Credo 41
Descriptive study of ethics 24
Disgust 27
Empathy 24
Equality bias 26
Ethical sensitivity 24
Hoffman's four levels of empathy 25
Logical analysis 36
Memorable message about ethics 31
Mirror neurons 25
Moral development 24
Moral emotions 24

Cases for Discussion

Directions: Identify the interests of the persons in the following cases. Discuss what each ethical actor should do. How would you use your personal ethical standard in these cases?

1. Moral Development

The youth league basketball season is half over. Joel wishes it were finished. For the past four years, he has been assistant coach for his son's team and coordinates referees. His son's team has a new head coach, Mick. He had a reputation for being a passionate coach who won tournaments.

Joel does not think that Mick is a good role model of sportsmanship, playing your best even after a loss or "bad" call by a referee. Mick does not accept "bad" calls. Every game he argues with referees until receiving a technical foul. Sometimes referees throw Mick out of the game. Some parents think this shows Mick cares. Other parents told Joel that Mick's behavior is unsportsmanlike. This is not what they want their sons to learn from basketball. These parents have asked Joel to talk to Mick. Joel said he would think about it.

What should Joel do?

2. Personal Ethics at Work

It is 7 p.m. and the report is due at 9 a.m. tomorrow morning. Sharon, an assistant team researcher at Miller Financial Research, wants to use this report to show her abilities as a research analyst. Miller Financial Research made its reputation providing clients accurate and high quality financial information. Sharon interned with Miller the summer after her junior year, but had not worked with this research team. This team analyzes the technology industry, especially companies developing new technologies. This is her biggest assignment so far, drafting a section of the team report analyzing virtualization technology. Bill, her supervisor, told her last week that he is impressed with her work. He implied that if Sharon does well on this report, he would consider recommending her promotion to financial researcher.

Sharon thinks, "I could turn in something by 9 a.m., but it wouldn't be the quality to convince Bill that I am ready for promotion." She reads a report released late that afternoon from Smith Financial Research. She quickly sees data and analysis that she could use in her report. Several sections present almost exactly the information Bill assigned her to research. There is no way she can write anything as detailed as the Smith report, at least before 9 a.m. tomorrow. Perhaps she could use the Smith data and analysis to meet her 9 a.m. deadline. Her report would impress Bill if she did.

What should Sharon do?

References

Baird, A.D., Scheffer, I.E., and Wilson, S.J. "Mirror Neuron System Involvement in Empathy: A Critical Look at the Evidence." *Social Neuroscience*, 6.4 (2011). 327–35.

Baron-Cohen, Simon. *The Science of Evil: On Empathy and the Origins of Cruelty.* New York: Basic Books, 2011.

Bloom, Paul. *Just Babies: The Origins of Good and Evil.* New York: Crown Publishers, 2013.

Bok, Sisella. *Lying: Moral Choice in Public and Private Life.* 1978. New York: Vintage Books, 1989.

Booth, Wayne C. *The Rhetoric of Rhetoric: The Quest for Effective Communication.* Malden, MA: Blackwell, 2004.

Brownell, C.A. and Kopp, C.B. *Socioemotional Development in the Toddler Years: Transition and Transformation.* New York: Guilford Press, 2007.

Callahan, David. *The Cheating Culture: Why More Americans Are Doing Wrong to Get Ahead.* New York: Harcourt, 2004.

Corkery, Michael. "Wells Fargo Fined $185 Million for Fraudulently Opening Accounts." *The New York Times.* 8 September 2016. www.nytimes.com/2016/09/09/business/dealbook/wells-fargo-fined-for-years-of-harm-to-customers.html?action=click&contentCollection=DealBook&module=RelatedCoverage&region=Marginalia&pgtype=article. Date accessed: 4 March 2018.

Damon, William. "The Moral Development of Children." *Scientific American* 281.2 (August 1999): 72–9.

Davies, D. *Child Development: A Practioner's Guide.* New York: Guilford Press, 2004.

Eisenberg, Nancy. "Empathy and Sympathy." *Handbook of Emotions.* 2nd ed. Eds. M. Lewis and J.M. Haviland-Jones. New York: Guilford Press, 2000. 677–91.

Eisenberg, Nancy., T. Spinrad, and A. Sadovsky. "Empathy-related Responding in Children." Killen and Smetana, 517–50.

Ewing, Jack and Hiroko Tabuchi. "Volkswagen Scandal Reaches All the Way to the Top, Lawsuits Say." *The New York Times.* 19 July 2016. www.nytimes.com/2016/07/20/business/international/volkswagen-ny-attorney-general-emissions-scandal.html. Date accessed: 15 November 2017.

Fleming, Amy. "Screen Time v. Play Time: What Tech Leaders Won't Let Their Own Kids Do. *The Guardian: US Edition.* 23 May 2015. www.theguardian.com/technology/2015/may/23/screen-time-v-play-time-what-tech-leaders-wont-let-their-own-kids-do. Date accessed: 17 November 2017.

Gallup, "Honesty/Ethics in Professions." *Gallup Historical Trends.* http://www.gallup.com/poll/1654/honesty-ethics-professions.aspx. Date Accessed: 15 November 2017

Gallup. "Confidence in Institutions." *Gallup Historical Trends.* http://www.gallup.poll/1597/confidence-institutions.aspx. Date accessed: 15 November 2017.

Gillespie, Tarleton. "The Relevance of Algorithms." *Media Technologies: Essays on Communication, Materiality, and Society.* Eds. Tarleton Gillespie, Pablo J. Boczkowski, and Kirsten A. Foot. Cambridge, MA: MIT Press, 2014. 167–93.

Greene, Joshua. *Moral Tribes: Emotions, Reason and the Gap Between Us and Them.* New York: Penguin, 2013.

Haidt, Jonathan. *The Righteous Mind: Why Good People Are Divided by Politics and Religion.* New York: Vintage Books, 2012.

Hart, Roderick. "The Politics of Communication Studies: An Address to Undergraduates." *Communication Education* 34.2 (1985): 162–5.

Hastings, Paul D., Carolyn Zahn-Waxler, and K. McShane. "We Are by Nature Moral Creatures: Biological Bases of Concern for Others." Killen and Smetana, 483–516.

Hoffman, Martin. *Empathy and Moral Development: Implications for Caring and Justice.* New York: Cambridge UP, 2001.

Hyde, Michael. *The Life-Giving Gift of Acknowledgement.* West Lafayette, IN: Purdue UP, 2006.

Jenson, J. Vernon. "Bridging the Millennia: Truth and Trust in Human Communication." *World Communication* 30.2 (2001): 68–92.

Johannesen, Richard L. *Ethics in Human Communication.* 5th ed. Prospect Heights, IL: Waveland, 2002.

Kagan, J. (2013). *The Human Spark: The Science of Human Development.* New York: Basic Books.

Killen, Melanie and Judith G. Smetana, Eds. *Handbook of Moral Development.* Mahwah, NJ: LEA, 2006.

Kimmel, Barbara B. "Leading for Trust." *Corporate Responsibility Magazine.* 24 August 2016. www.thecro.com/topics/business-ethics/opinion-leading-for-trust/. Date accessed: 23 October 2017.

Lough, Sinclair, Christopher M. Kipps, Cate Treise, Peter Watson, James R. Blair, and John R. Hodges. "Social Reasoning, Emotion, and Empathy in Frontotemporal Dementia." *Neuropsychologica* 44.6 (2005): 950–8.

Makau, Josina M. and Debian L. Marty. *Cooperative Argumentation: A Model for Deliberative Community.* Prospect Heights, IL: Waveland, 2001.

Molnar-Szakacs, I. "From Actions to Empathy and Morality—A Neural Perspective." *Journal of Economic Behavior and Organization* 77 (2011): 75–85.

National Communication Association. Credo for Ethical Communication. www.natcom.org. Approved by Legislative Council November 1999. Date accessed: 4 March 2018.

National Communication Association. Credo for Free and Responsible Communication in a Democratic Society. www.natcom.org. Adopted by Legislative Council 1963; revised 2011. Date accessed: 4 March 2018.

Nussbaum, Martha C. "Why Practice Needs Ethical Theory: Particularism, Principle, and Bad Behavior." *The Path of Law and Its Influence: The Legacy of Oliver Wendall Holmes, Jr.* Ed. Steven J. Burton. Cambridge: Cambridge UP, 2000. 50–86.

Pariser, Eli. "Beware Online "Filter Bubbles." *Ted: Ted2011.* 2 May 2011. www.ted.com/talks/eli_pariser_beware_online_filter_bubbles. Date accessed: 18 April 2017.

Pew Research Center. *The Changing Global Religious Landscape, 2017,* 5 April 2017. www.pewforum.org/2017/04/05/the-changing-global-religious-landscape/. Date accessed: 10 December 2017.

Pew Research Center. *US Public Becoming Less Religious.* 3 November 2015. www.pewforum.org/2015/11/03/u-s-public-becoming-less-religious. Date accessed: 30 June 2017.

Pew Research Center. *Growing Share of US Immigrants Have No Religious Affiliation.* 19 May 2015. www.pewresearch.org/2015/05/19/growing-share-of-u-s-immigrants-have-no-religious-affiliation/. Date accessed: 30 June 2017.

Picoult, Jon. "What Went Awry at Wells Fargo? The Beaten Path of a Toxic Culture." *The New York Times.* 8 October 2016. www.nytimes.com/2016/10/09/jobs/what-went-awry-at-wells-fargo-the-beaten-path-of-a-toxic-culture.html. Date accessed: 23 October 2016.

Plato. "Republic." Trans. Paul Shorey. In *Plato: The Collected Dialogues, Including the Letters.* Eds. Edith Hamilton and Huntington Cairns. Bollingen Series LXXI. Princeton, NJ: Princeton UP, 1961. 575–844.

Pribble, Paula T. "Making an Ethical Commitment: A Rhetorical Case Study of Organizational Socialization." *Communication Quarterly* 38 (1990): 255–67.

Puka, Bill. "Character Education and the Young Child." Van Haaften, et al. 83–104.

Riveria, R. (5 January 2013). "Asking What To Do With Symbols of Grief as Memorials Pile Up." *The New York Times.* www.nytimes.com/2013/01/06/nyregion/as-memorials-pile-up-newtown-struggles-to-move-on.html?_r=0. Date accessed: 14 June 2016.

Sacks, Jonathan. *Not in God's Name: Confronting Religious Violence.* New York: Schocken Books, 2015.

Schrag, Calvin O. *The Self After Postmodernity.* New Haven, CT: Yale UP, 1997.

Schumacker, D.M. and R.B. Heckel. *Kids of Character: A Guide to Promoting Moral Development.* Westport, CN: Praeger, 2007.

Shoemaker, W.J. "The Social Brain Network and Human Moral Behavior." *Zygon: Journal of Religion and Science* 47 (2012): 806–20.

Shonkoff, J.P. and S.N. Bales. "Science Does Not Speak for Itself: Translating Child Development Research for the Public and Its Policymakers." *Child Development* 82 (2011):17–32.

Smith, Christian, Kari Christoffersen, Hilary Davidson, and Patricia Snell Herzog. *Lost in Transition: The Dark Side of Emerging Adulthood.* New York: Oxford UP, 2011.

Smith, Huston. *Essays on World Religions.* Ed. M. Darrol Bryant. New York: Paragon House, 1992.

Spitzberg, Brian H. and William R. Cupach, Eds. *The Dark Side of Interpersonal Communication.* 2nd edn. New York: Routledge, 2007.

Tabuchi, Hiroko. "A Cheaper Airbag, and Takata's Road to a Deadly Crisis." *The New York Times.* 26 August 2016. www.nytimes.com/2016/08/27/business/takata-airbag-recall-crisis.html. Date accessed: 2 December 2017.

Thomas, Katie. "Painted as EpiPen Villain, Mylan's Chief Says She's No Such Things." *The New York Times.* 26 August 2016. https://www.nytimes.com/2016/08/27/business/painted-as-a-villain-mylans-chief-says-shes-no-such-thing.html

Tompkins, Paula S. "Communication and Children's Moral Development." *The Children's Communication Sourcebook.* Eds. Thomas Socha and Narissra Punyanunt-Carter. NY: Peter Lange, *in press.*

Turiel, Elliot. "The Development of Morality." *Handbook of Child Psychology.* 5th ed. Vol. 3 of *Social, Emotional and Personality Development.* Eds. William Damon and Nancy Eisenberg. New York: Wiley, 1998. 863–932.

Turkle, Sherry. *Reclaiming Conversation: The Power of Talk in a Digital Age.* NY: Penguin, 2015.

U.S. Office of Government Ethics. "Standards of Ethical Conduct for Employees of the Executive Branch Final Regulation Issued by the U.S. Office of Government Ethics." Codified in 5 C.F.R. Part 2635 As amended at 81FR 81641(effective January 1, 2017). https://www.oge.gov/Web/OGE.nsf/All%20Documents/076ABBBFC3B026A78 5257F14006929A2/$FILE/SOC%20as%20of%2081%20FR%2081641%20FINAL. pdf?open

Van Haaften, Wouter, Thomas Wren, and Agnes Tellings. Eds. *Moral Sensibilities and Education: The Preschool Child.* London: Concorde Publishing House, 1999.

Vetlesen, Arne Johan. *Perception, Empathy and Judgment: An Inquiry into the Preconditions of Moral Performance.* University Park, PA: Penn. State UP, 1994.

Vozzola, E.S. *Moral development: Theory and applications.* NY: Routledge, 2014.

Waldron, Vincent, Joshua Danaher, Carmen Goman, Nicole Piemonte, and Dayna Kloeber. "Which Parent Messages about Morality Are Accepted by Emerging Adults?" *Moral Talk Across the Lifespan: Creating Good Relationships.* Eds. Vince Waldron and Douglas Kelley. NY: Peter Lang, pp. 35–54.

Walter, H. "Social Cognitive Neuroscience of Empathy: Concepts, Circuits and Genes." *Emotion Review* 4 (2012): 9–77.

Waters, T. "Of Looking glasses, Mirror Neurons, Culture, and Meaning." *Perspectives on Science,* 22 (2014), 616–9.

Zahn-Waxler, Carolyn and Paul D. Hastings. "Development of Empathy: Adaptive and Maladaptive Patterns." Van Haaften, et al., 37–60.

3

ETHICAL REASONING ABOUT
HUMAN COMMUNICATION

Ben nodded as Titus described the concert last night, "I'm glad that Krystal suggested we go. I've wanted to hear this band for more than a year. It's easier when the person you're with likes the same things you do." "Oh," said Ben, "I didn't know that you and Krystal were spending much time together."

"I've been seeing her for about three weeks," replied Titus. "It's easy with Krystal. We like the same things. She asks what I think and treats me like I'm important. It's nice to be with someone who isn't mean and hurts you . . . like Shaley." Titus and Shaley had dated for about two years. Everyone thought it was serious, until about three months ago. The breakup was messy, with mutual friends picking sides. "I think I may have found someone who's good for me," said Titus. "Oh, Krystal mentioned that she knows you."

"Yeah . . . well, my cousin dated her a couple of years ago," replied Ben. That was not all Ben knew about Krystal. He knew why his cousin, Carl, broke up with Krystal. Carl said that at first being with Krystal was great, because she made him feel important. Then she began to monopolize all his time. It started with asking, then demanding. Titus interrupted Ben's thoughts, "Was it your cousin Carl? You two are close. So, what did he tell you about her?"

An important idea in the study of communication is that competent or effective communication involves appropriately adapting your communication in a specific situation. As a communicator, you are challenged to adapt your speaking and listening by responding appropriately to ongoing changes in your role as a communicator, your relationships, and the facts

51

and circumstances of a situation. Competent communication also includes communicating in an ethically fitting manner. Sometimes what is ethically fitting to communicate is clear.[1] When a friend asks your opinion about a movie or song, you answer honestly. If a friend asks your opinion about a new romantic interest, as Titus does in the chapter's opening case, what do you say if you are unimpressed or concerned about your friend's emotional welfare? Sometimes it is less clear what is right to say, a good way to say it, to whom you should say it, or whether anything should be said at all. Making decisions like these involves ethical discernment. **Ethical discernment** is the ability to recognize ethical issues and make ethically relevant or important distinctions. It begins when you notice something that engages your moral emotions. Seeing someone upset or hurt engages empathy. Unequal distribution of goods, such as breaks or job responsibilities at work, triggers the emotional bias toward equality. Seeing extreme neglect of a child or an animal triggers the moral emotion of disgust. Ethical discernment stimulated by moral emotions is important for ethical deliberation and decision making, because emotion gives direction to understanding and reasoning (Nussbaum). Moral emotions identify what is important for you to think about in ethical reasoning. Moral emotions also can motivate you to act on decisions you make in your ethical reasoning. This chapter introduces you to ethical reasoning as a process of deliberating about ethical issues and problems, so you can decide how and when to communicate.

Before deciding about how to communicate ethically, you must discern or recognize that an ethical issue exists. Your moral emotions and moral imagination influence your ethical sensitivity (Tompkins 63–6). Discerning the existence of an ethical issue is a critical first step in ethical reasoning. **Ethical reasoning** is a problem-solving process of discerning and thinking critically about alternative responses to a situation to identify the most ethically fitting response. You may find ethical reasoning helpful when your moral emotions conflict, choices seem unclear or confusing, or the situation is ambiguous or complicated. You already have some experience in reasoning ethically. Whenever you think about an action or situation and conclude that something was not right and begin to think about what should be done instead, you have begun to reason ethically. You can improve your ethical reasoning by becoming familiar with concepts and practices discussed in this chapter.

Steps in Ethical Reasoning

There are **five steps in ethical reasoning**—recognizing an ethical issue, getting the facts about the situation, thinking about alternative ethical responses, evaluating alternative communication responses from different ethical viewpoints, and, finally, reflectively acting on your chosen response. Ethical reasoning is a problem-solving process of searching for the most ethically fitting way to act in a situation.

Step One—Recognizing an Ethical Issue

An **ethical issue** is a question or conflict about what is good, right, or virtuous. We notice ethical issues most often when something does not work as we expect. Our moral emotions are stimulated, so we respond to what is happening in some way. When relationships, procedures, or systems break down, our moral emotions may stimulate our thinking about how to solve the problems our emotions have identified. Breakdowns provide opportunities to recognize that some people or institutions benefit from how a relationship is defined or how procedures or a system is organized. We may notice that others receive little or no benefit or may be harmed by a relationship, procedures, or a system, such as the procedures for recognizing who may speak. When everything is working, our lives appear normal or neutral. We may be unaware of the ethical dimension of the organizations we belong to, the relationships we are part of, the procedures we follow, or our communication practices. When things do not go as planned, we feel uncomfortable or upset. Our emotions prompt us to wonder about the right or wrong of what we are a part of and what we do or say.

We may also notice ethical issues when our routines change, because we are more mindful of what we do and say. Once change becomes routine, we have greater difficulty recognizing ethical issues in our daily activities. The regularity of our relationships, procedures we follow, and communication rituals we perform provide "proof" that our routines are how things *should* be done. Communication routines, and the episodes or systems they maintain, can interfere with our ethical sensitivity.

Point to Ponder

❖ *What routines of the marketplace or digital communication interfere with ethical sensitivity?*

A starting point for discerning ethical issues is to ask questions of who will potentially benefit or be harmed in a situation. Questions of benefit and harm lead us to ask questions about what is good, right, or virtuous for persons involved in a situation. Answering these questions helps us identify the interests of stakeholders to survive and thrive. Individuals or parties whose interests are affected by a decision's short- or long-term consequences are called **stakeholders**. Stakeholders may be persons, groups, organizations, or communities. Ethical issues typically involve incompatible interests regarding the benefits, harms, duties, rights, goals, or outcomes that affect a stakeholder's legitimate interest to survive and thrive. In the chapter's opening case, Ben faces an ethical issue about telling his friend Titus what his cousin has confided to him about a former girlfriend. Telling or not telling what he knows has the potential to benefit, hurt, or perhaps harm several people, including friends and family members. Different stakeholders would be affected in different ways by Ben's decision whether to disclose what he knows about Titus's new girlfriend, Krystal.

Identifying stakeholders and their interests is important for discerning ethical issues you face when communicating. There are three common types of ethical issues—an ethical problem, an ethical dilemma, and an ethical tragedy. An **ethical problem** is a conflict between two beneficial outcomes, specifically between a person's immediate self-interest and what should be done. If you find a wallet with cash and credit cards, do you pocket the cash and then return the wallet, or do you return the wallet with all the contents to its owner? If you recognize this as an ethical problem, you might imagine how you would feel if someone returned a wallet you had lost with the money removed. Reasoning with a principle such as the Golden Rule, treat others the way you would like to be treated, would lead you to decide to return the wallet with all the contents to its owner, even if you first consider keeping the lost cash. Reasoning with the Golden Rule critically evaluated your initial emotion of happiness as misplaced, stimulating your moral imagination by engaging empathy or sympathy in losing a wallet. The ethical problem this situation poses is a conflict between an immediate personal benefit of keeping found money and returning this property to its rightful owner.

Textbox 3.1

Communication Routines and Obscured Ethical Vision

Social psychologist Philip Zimbardo (*Lucifer Effect*) argues that systems, including communication systems and routines, can create evil people. Zimbardo is known for the 1971 Stanford Prison Experiment (SPE), in which male college students were randomly assigned to role-play prison guards and inmates. Zimbardo designed the study to last several weeks but suspended it after six days. (Student) guards harassed, dominated, humiliated, and demeaned (student) prisoners both verbally and physically. Young men became evil people who committed unethical acts against their fellow human beings. Not until 2007 did Zimbardo publish a comprehensive discussion of the SPE. Much—if not most—evil, he argues, is caused by communication routines and systems, not by personality traits or individual dispositions. Zimbardo screened college student volunteers for psychological or other disorders, so participants were psychologically healthy. The language, communication routines, and systems of the prison setting obscured and hindered moral imagination and ethical discernment of these students and the researchers, including Zimbardo. Good communication practices turned into unethical ones. For example, a (student) prisoner's request to sing "Happy Birthday" to a fellow (student) inmate was, in Zimbardo's words, a "prisoner-initiated break in routine to share some positive feelings among themselves" that was "turned into another occasion of learned dominance and submission" (76).

What is so chilling about Zimbardo's account are his descriptions of how *his* ethical discernment was affected by playing the role of prison superintendent. He admits that he was unable to recognize ethical issues while the experiment was in progress. Not until a colleague directly confronted him about how the study caused (student) guards to humiliate and harass (student) prisoners did he begin to recognize that there was something "evil" going on.

Zimbardo made another important finding during post-experiment interviews. He discovered that one student was able to resist some of the unethical routines of prison communication. Before the experiment began, this student had taken time to articulate to himself his value commitments and promised himself that he would follow them. Because this student was mindful of his value commitments, he could more easily use them to guide his decision making and actions during the study (120–5).

To further explore this study and his recommendations for promoting ethical action, you can visit a website Zimbardo created about the Stanford Prison Experiment at www.prisonexp.org.

A common ethical problem in communication is whether to tell the truth. While lying may produce an immediate personal benefit, as noted in Chapter 2, many cultures have prohibitions against lying or presumptions for truth telling (Jenson, "Bridging the Millennia"). Despite cultural presumptions for honesty, it takes little effort to discover examples of widespread dishonesty. Yet, telling a lie, even a white lie, can damage the trust needed to maintain relationships between friends, family members, coworkers, or a speaker and an audience. Your immediate self-interest might be to lie, but being honest is what you should do, because of the potential impacts of that lie on others.

An **ethical dilemma** is a conflict between two competing beneficial outcomes. In the chapter's opening case is an ethical dilemma between being honest to a friend and not hurting your friend's feelings. Both are beneficial outcomes, but Ben cannot achieve both benefits simultaneously. In addition, if Ben is honest with Titus, he may damage his relationship with his cousin Carl, who told him about Krystal in confidence. What makes ethical dilemmas so difficult is that by choosing one benefit, you, at minimum, deny the other benefit to someone else in a way that risks inadvertently causing someone harm. If Ben chooses to tell Titus the truth, he risks losing a friend, especially if Titus is seeking only positive information about Krystal. If Ben tells Titus a white lie and Titus finds out, he risks losing Titus's trust and possibly the friendship. If you were in Ben's situation, your decision to tell a white lie to preserve a relationship or tell the truth and risk damaging that relationship would depend on your deliberation about the facts and your personal ethical standard. Choosing how to respond to an ethical dilemma is a matter of ethical discernment and judgment.

Everyday Communication Ethics

❖ *Think of a recent ethical issue with a friend or family member. Was it an ethical problem, ethical dilemma, or ethical tragedy?*

An **ethical tragedy** is a special type of dilemma where the conflict is between two harmful outcomes. The tragedy is that any action you choose will create significant harm for someone, despite your best intentions and careful deliberation. These are the most difficult ethical issues we face, where we cannot avoid making a decision, but all our choices are harmful. Ethical tragedies remind us that a pure ethical decision, a decision that causes no one harm or creates no injustice, is rare and, perhaps, humanly impossible. The challenge an ethical tragedy poses is acting to minimize harm as best you can. Telling your friend what you think of a romantic interest in some situations could be an ethical tragedy. For example, you could face a choice whether to tell a good friend, let us call her Mara, that her husband is cheating on her. You value not hurting your friend and you want to keep the relationship. If you tell Mara the truth, she may be more likely to believe her husband's denials than you, so you could be risking your friendship. Depending on what happens between Mara and her husband, she may need you as a friend in the future. Not telling her allows her to look foolish to others and when she does find out, she could become angry with you for not telling her and allowing her to save face. If Mara and her husband have children or important decisions to make, such as a career change or move to a different city, the significance of the potential harm increases. It appears that consequences of anything you would do, including doing nothing, are harmful in some way, and potentially could end some relationship. As Mara's friend, you have a responsibility to discern an ethically fitting response to this interpersonal ethical tragedy.

Recognizing that you face an ethical issue and deciding whether it is an ethical problem, ethical dilemma, or ethical tragedy is the first step in deciding how to communicate ethically in a difficult or complex situation. The next step in ethical reasoning is discerning what you know and need to discover about your situation before you make your decision.

Step Two—Get the Facts about the Situation

Once you recognize that an ethical issue exists, you need to discover relevant facts about that situation. How well you identify and understand the facts of your specific situation affects the quality of your ethical discernment, deliberation, and decision making. Of course, complete or perfect information is impossible. If you wait until you have all the possible facts, you will never make a decision. Although ethical decision making often is hard because we do not have all the facts we need or want, it is surprising how many facts are available once you start thinking about an ethical issue.

Everyday Communication Ethics

❖ *Think of a recent problem with a friend. Identify what you know, what you need to discover and can find out, and what you need to discover but cannot find out.*

After listing relevant facts, identify all individuals or parties who could be affected by your decision. Once you recognize a stakeholder, your moral emotions are engaged, confirming or disconfirming the initial direction of your ethical reasoning. Recognizing stakeholders sometimes is a challenge, because stakeholders are not always clearly identifiable in the facts of a situation. Too often, we limit our ethical reasoning to easily recognizable stakeholders, instead of searching for unrecognized or unseen stakeholders who also have an interest in a situation. Our understanding of an ethical issue may change, sometimes dramatically, when previously unseen stakeholders trigger our moral emotions. Newly engaged moral emotions may prompt understanding that the legitimate interests of previously unseen stakeholders are as important, and sometimes more important than legitimate interests of named stakeholders.

Routines, conventions, and communication patterns may obscure or hide the existence of some stakeholders. How a bureaucratic report presents facts or how the narrative structure of a story outlines an event can make it difficult to recognize ethically important stakeholders. A practice to help you identify unseen stakeholders is rhetorical listening. **Rhetorical listening** is an attentiveness to how the routines, patterns, forms, and structure of communication acts and how episodes make the existence of some stakeholders recognizable, while obscuring or hiding the existence of other ethically important stakeholders (Tompkins). The form and structure of the communication messages you receive make the existence or presence of some stakeholders clear, so your recognition of them engages your moral emotions and you imagine their interests as you consider the facts of a situation. The form of messages that identify stakeholders, however, may also obscure the presence of other stakeholders. If you do not know that these stakeholders exist, your moral emotions will not be engaged and you cannot imagine their viewpoints, so you cannot "hear" their interests to survive and thrive as you deliberate. Rhetorical listening is a practice of moral imagination that promotes recognition of unseen stakeholders as persons who may have legitimate interests in your decisions.

When you practice rhetorical listening, you pay attention to how the form, pattern, and structure of a communication act or an episode influences your perception and understanding of a situation and its stakeholders. The structure of an agenda for a meeting, procedures for conflict resolution or mediation, the narrative structure of a story, the structure or conventions of a business report or news article, patterns of arrangement in a speech or essay, cultural conventions of speaking and writing, as well as symbolic forms such as metaphor influence our perceptions and what we find meaningful or believe to be true. Listening rhetorically encourages us to be aware of how symbolic forms, patterns, and structure influence how we understand a situation and discern the presence of stakeholders.

As a student of communication, your understanding of communication as a transactional process that creates relational connections and meaning can help you identify unseen stakeholders. To practice rhetorical listening, you imagine recognized stakeholders as communicators in relationships that link them to unseen others. Because the impact of a decision or action travels along relational networks created in the communication process, these newly recognized others might be stakeholders whose interests would be significantly affected by any decision made or action taken. By practicing rhetorical listening, a decision maker's recognition of persons who may be impacted by her decision shifts focus from abstract others (people who could be affected) to concrete others (e.g., a recognized stakeholder's partner or children). This shift from understanding consequences as abstractions to discerning human faces of unseen stakeholders can trigger moral emotions in a new way, prompting new insights about ethical issues in a situation.

Table 3.1 Stakeholders

Stakeholders	*Nature of Stakeholders' Interests*
Individuals	
Groups	
Organizations	
Unseen Stakeholders	

Everyday Communication Ethics

❖   *Use rhetorical listening to identify seen and unseen stakeholders in an ethical issue at work.*

The case of a divorce involving young children can illustrate how rhetorical listening can influence discernment and understanding of ethical issues in a divorce. Whether a divorce is an ethical problem, dilemma, or tragedy would depend on the facts of a specific divorce. Typically, the legal documents or story of a divorce name the married couple and their dependent children, because they are parties in the legal reporting process or key characters in the "typical" divorce story. There are, however, unnamed stakeholders whose presence is hidden by the conventional forms of legal communication or narrative structure of a divorce story. These hidden or obscured stakeholders are connected to the divorcing couple and their children by the relational bonds of communication. These communication bonds signal the presence of possible stakeholders with a potentially significant interest in the divorce. The bonds of communication may link grandparents, an aunt or uncle, godparents, friends, or teachers to the divorcing couple and their children. Depending on the facts of a divorce, the interests of each stakeholder will vary, with some having a greater interest than others. By imagining relational connections in the facts of a situation, a decision maker's recognition of previously unseen stakeholders would trigger empathy or sympathy that helps her understand the legitimate interests of these now seen stakeholders. Sometimes this reshapes her understanding of ethical issues. In a difficult divorce, recognizing the existence of unseen stakeholders, their interests, and their viewpoints can help a decision maker discern which ethical issues have more significance than others. Identifying grandparents as significant stakeholders in a difficult divorce, for example, could prompt a decision maker to imagine and then recognize that the issues involve extended family rather than only parents and children. Recognition of an unseen stakeholder may engage a decision maker's moral emotions and moral imagination, prompting reexamination of ethical issues in ways that create a new focus for ethical reasoning and deliberation.

Rhetorically listening to the facts of a situation can help you explore what you know, what you do not know but can find out, and what you do not know and cannot find out.

Step Three—Think about Alternative Ethical Responses

After considering the facts of a situation, the next step in ethical reasoning is to think about different possible communication responses and their outcomes. *What is the best possible outcome in this situation and what possible communication responses could help you achieve that outcome?* In thinking about this question, take care not to limit yourself to either/or thinking. **Either/or thinking** limits ethical deliberation to polar opposites—what is right or wrong, good or bad, and ethical or unethical. With either/or thinking, we also limit the stakeholders to two parties, one of whom has the most important interest and the other who does not. In fact, either/or thinking about stakeholders can encourage us to see one stakeholder as having a legitimate interest in the outcome of a decision, while the other stakeholder has none. Stakeholders who do not easily fit into the two recognized categories are unseen.

Textbox 3.2

**Rhetorical Listening and the Tuskegee
Syphilis Study**

The Tuskegee Syphilis Study (TSS) is a medical research study of the long-term effects of untreated syphilis on 399 African-American men that lasted approximately 40 years. Researchers withheld penicillin, the cure for syphilis, from men in the study without their permission. Researchers also told these men that they had "bad blood," instead of explaining their disease and the consequences of withholding treatment. Public outcry against TSS forced its end in 1972, after a whistleblower brought public attention to the study. The TSS, however, was not a secret to the medical community. Martha Solomon ("Dehumanization") wanted to understand why, for almost 40 years, there was no similar outcry to end the study from the medical community. Her analysis of 13 published medical reports explains how the rhetorical forms and conventions of the reports that focused on the discovery of scientific knowledge also hindered the readers' recognition of the humanity of TSS participants, promoting ethical nearsightedness.

Besides discouraging readers from empathizing with TSS participants as men and imagining their viewpoints, the rhetorical form and structure of the scientific reports hid existence of important stakeholders. Medical historian Thomas Benedek points out the most glaring absence in the medical reports—the effect of untreated syphilis on the family. If the readers or other decision makers had rhetorically listened to their communication about this research, they could have imagined TSS participants as persons communicating and relationally connected previously unseen stakeholders who had vital interests in the conduct of the TSS—wives, girlfriends, children, brothers, sisters, parents, aunts, and uncles of TSS participants. Recognizing the existence of these and other stakeholders is critical for discerning the significance and extent of the harm caused by the TSS.

Discerning an ethically fitting response sometimes requires using your moral imagination to develop creative alternatives that address the ethical issues you discover (see Johnson). One of the contributions of rhetorical listening is that it discourages either/or thinking by helping identify unseen others and stimulating your imagination to understand their points of view. When your understanding of ethical issues is limited to considering the viewpoints of two stakeholders whose interests are presented as an either/or conflict, you may have difficulty recognizing ethically fitting alternative responses. Brainstorming alternatives, reframing the ethical problem by imagining the viewpoints of different stakeholders you identified with rhetorical listening, and thinking about the facts of a situation using ethical principles or theories, are strategies for generating alternative responses that are not apparent when you first recognize an ethical issue and examine the facts of a situation.

Everyday Communication Ethics

❖ *Think of a situation where either/or thinking kept you from seeing an alternative solution.*

The example presented earlier of parents who are getting divorced can illustrate how either/or thinking affects ethical deliberation. Either/or thinking limits consideration of the stakeholders to the divorcing couple and any children. Notice how the interests of three stakeholders are collapsed into two parties, the parents and the children. Alternatively, either/or thinking may limit the stakeholders to the husband and wife, ignoring the interests of the children. Some individuals have begun to argue that grandparents who want to continue their relationships with their grandchildren also have an interest in a divorce. Decisions based only upon the interests of the divorcing parents or children, the clearly identifiable stakeholders in stories or legal reports of divorce, obscures the interest of grandparents and their grandchildren. In a difficult divorce where there are questions about potential harm or conflicting needs and rights, recognizing the interest of a grandparent, aunt, or uncle could offer an ethically fitting alternative solution that was not apparent in either/or thinking about the divorce. Sensitive and responsive listening—rhetorical, appreciative, comprehensive, empathic, and evaluative—can help decision makers discern ethical issues and imagine alternative communication responses that could be ethically fitting to the interests of key stakeholders. In the divorce example, whether the interest of grandparents would receive priority depends on an ethically sensitive assessment of the interests of the key stakeholders using the facts of the situation. Serious consideration of such an alternative would be evaluated in the next step in ethical reasoning.

Step Four—Evaluate Alternatives from Different Points of View

Ethical reasoning involves making a judgment about what is the most ethically fitting or best ethical communication response in a situation, so you can make a decision and act. Your moral emotions and personal ethical commitments will influence your judgment about what is the most ethically fitting response. This is an important stage of ethical reasoning, where decision makers evaluate and consider the ethical quality of different communication responses. A significant challenge to making a judgment about what is the most ethically fitting response is distinguishing between arguments that ethically justify an action and arguments that rationalize. **Rationalizations** are arguments that solely use personal self-interest or poorly examined social convention to support a decision. An **ethical justification**, in contrast, is responsive to what is good, right, or virtuous for stakeholders, which makes it ethically sound. Rationalizations discourage ethically responsive decision making. Scholars studying ethics for millennia have grappled with the problem of distinguishing between arguments that rationalize and those that justify what is ethical. Two approaches for distinguishing between ethical justification and rationalization are using everyday practices of ethics or ethical theories to evaluate your thinking. Below is a brief synopsis of everyday practices of ethics and ideas from ethical theories. In later chapters, you will read about concepts and theories that further explore these practices and ideas.

The Everyday Practice of Ethics. Some ethicists have recognized that everyday decision making about how to act ethically has an important role in ethical reasoning, especially when decision makers communicate their ethical decisions and reasoning to others who do not share their ethical values (see Sidgwick). Leaders from various spiritual traditions have taught their followers practices of daily living that provide ways to consider and communicate about the interests of others. Listed below are four concepts and related questions for evaluating ethical alternatives that are useful for distinguishing between rationalization and ethical justification in the everyday practice of ethics.

- **The Golden Rule**. You may be familiar with expression of the Golden Rule as "Do unto others as you would have them do unto you." Many cultures and religions have some version of this rule. Different forms of the Golden Rule are listed in Chapter 10. The Golden Rule asks you to think about how you would think or feel, if you were in this situation and the roles were reversed. *Would you consider the chosen communication response fair, honest, or caring, if you experienced the expected consequences of this alternative?* The Golden Rule formalizes the practice of using your moral imagination to consider the consequences of a response from another's point of view.

- **The Platinum Rule.** "Do unto others as they wish to have done to themselves." This rule is advocated by those who criticize the Golden Rule for being egocentric or ethnocentric. *As a decision maker, have you presumed to know what others want or think, without asking or listening to them? Have you taken into consideration differences between yourself and the stakeholders, such as age, culture, ethnicity, gender, race, etc., in your deliberations?* A limitation of the Golden Rule is that it does not necessarily recognize that you may not share ethical commitments or values with others, or may have significantly different experiences. An important part of treating others with dignity is recognizing and respecting how they are different from you, as well as how they are similar. The Platinum Rule is helpful in encouraging us to examine egocentric or ethnocentric tendencies in our ethical reasoning and decision making.

- **Generalizability.** This principle can help you distinguish between what is momentary or limited to an individual and what is more enduring or broadly applicable. *Can you generalize from the value or principle you are using to justify your preferred alternative and apply it to other, similar ethical situations?* This principle also helps assure consistency in your ethical reasoning, as well as helping avoid arbitrary or capricious decision making. If you cannot use your value or principle in other similar situations, you may unknowingly be using a different ethical value or principle or rationalizing exceptions, especially for yourself, family, or friends. Probe your justification further if you cannot generalize, applying this principle to other similar situations.

- **Tests of Publicity.** As you deliberate about the ethical benefits and limitations of different alternatives, you are beginning to create arguments that support your communication response to the ethical issue and the stakeholders of a specific situation. You should be able to present to others the reasons for any decision you make, so others can examine the decision and the quality of your reasoning. Tests of publicity challenge you to convince others that your chosen alternative is an ethically fitting response, and not a rationalization. Sissela Bok (94–8) has identified three tests of publicity that differ in difficulty. *Relying on your own conscience* is the first and usually least difficult test of publicity, because it relies only on your personal ethical standard and your mindfulness of the human tendency to rationalize. It is an important first step in developing and testing your justification. *Asking friends or colleagues* usually presents a greater challenge, for it requires that your ethical justification meet ethical standards acceptable to others, in contrast to relying solely upon your personal ethical standard. Yet, friends and colleagues are members of the groups to which you belong and with whom you share experiences, ideas, and values. While friends or colleagues may be less quick to agree with you than your conscience, similarity in values and experiences could predispose them to agree with you. Substituting poorly examined social convention for ethical justification is a risk of practicing this test of publicity. The most difficult test of publicity is *asking persons of all allegiances*. We cannot handpick these persons, as we can friends or close colleagues. Persons of all allegiances include those who could be affected by your decision or have previously experienced consequences from a similar decision. If your ethical justification is convincing to persons of all allegiances, you have greater confidence that you have avoided rationalization and ethically justified your chosen communication response.

Ethical Theories. Philosophers and ethicists have used some of these everyday practices of ethics as a starting point in developing concepts and theories to help us deliberate about alternatives for acting in an ethically fitting manner in difficult situations. One benefit of using different ethical theories to evaluate alternatives is that the care and rigor encouraged by ethical theories helps us recognize unseen ethical issues, unseen responsibilities, alternative ethical points of view, creative ethical solutions, as well as rationalizations. Below is a short list of questions based on some of the ethical theories that you will read about in later chapters.

- Which alternative will produce the most good or happiness and do the least harm?
- Which alternative allows all the stakeholders to get what they need and treats them fairly? If any stakeholders are left out, why are they?
- Which alternative respects the rights and dignity of all stakeholders? If any stakeholders are left out, why are they?
- Are any stakeholders treated as a means to achieving the desired outcome?
- Which alternative promotes the care and welfare of the stakeholders to survive and thrive?
- Which alternative promotes the common good, helping all stakeholders to participate fully in the benefits of society, the community, or the family? If any stakeholders are left out, why are they?

By answering such questions, you begin to clarify which issues and values you consider most important for acting ethically in a situation. This narrows your list of alternatives, moving you closer to choosing an ethically fitting communication response.

At this moment, you may be asking yourself "Why is the process of ethical reasoning so complicated? Isn't it just a matter of right or wrong? Aren't moral emotions enough to tell me what is the right thing to do?" In many situations, what is right or wrong to communicate is clear. In fact, sometimes there is no ethical issue involved when you make a decision about whether to speak, listen, or take a turn in a discussion. In such situations, the ethical question is simply an ethical problem of having the courage to communicate ethically. There are, however, some situations in which the answers about how to communicate ethically are difficult to discern, even to the point that they seem to disappear. In these situations, the process of ethical reasoning can help you discern and deliberate about what is good or right to say or how to respond with honesty, care, justice, or honor. You can use ethical reasoning to think about and evaluate alternative communication responses, to help you decide which alternative best ethically fits the difficult situation you face.

Ethical reasoning is not a checklist or formula for identifying an **ethically pure** communication act in which no one is harmed and everyone benefits. While this may be a worthy ideal, the desire for ethical purity may produce ethically questionable behavior in two different ways. First, when a person has a sense of certainty that what she says or how she communicates is ethically pure, she may also view negative consequences as deserved or irrelevant. When a decision maker repeatedly views people who are harmed by a decision as deserving what they get or that harmful consequences are unimportant, a decision maker may not recognize that her action has some flaws. If these flaws are noteworthy, she may not recognize that she is causing ethically significant harm. Second, the desire for an ethically pure solution to a difficult problem may produce indecision, even paralysis. When someone recognizes that it is difficult or impossible to avoid all harmful or unjust consequences of communicating, the desire for a "pure" ethical outcome where no one is harmed may motivate a decision maker to avoid making any decision. When this happens, a decision maker can rationalize that by doing nothing at least she will not make things worse and, so, she is not responsible for consequences of her inaction.

A desire for a pure ethical decision can limit ethical reasoning to either/or thinking. When we see our choices only as ethical or unethical, pure or impure, it is difficult to imagine creative alternatives for responding to ethical issues. Either/or thinking can limit our moral imagination and our capacity to act. Vernon Jenson encourages us to think about the ethicality of action by considering the different ethical points of tension in a situation. You can judge the **ethicality** of a communication act or episode by identifying how it addresses points of ethical tension in a situation. Different communication actions can have different ethical qualities because they address different ethical tension points. Some communication acts have more ethical qualities than do others, because they address more ethical tension points that are significant in a situation. The concept of ethicality helps us recognize that while our choices for communicating may not be ethically pure, some alternatives are more ethically fitting, good, right, or virtuous for stakeholders than others, because the ethicality of some choices is greater or more fitting in that situation than other choices.

The example of a difficult divorce used throughout this chapter can illustrate the concept of ethicality. The process of ending a committed relationship, especially one with young children, involves some degree of hurt and harm for everyone involved. While a divorce can create benefits and be good for stakeholders, few people go through a divorce unscathed, especially young children. While making an ethically pure decision in a divorce involving young children may not be possible, it is possible to choose a course of action that is ethically better or worse for the divorcing couple and children. Deciding which course of action is ethically better or worse involves evaluating their ethicality in promoting the interests of the children and each parent to survive and thrive. By using ethical values, principles, or theories to identify the ethical qualities or dimensions of different actions, a decision maker has a basis for judging which action would be the most ethically fitting choice for the divorcing couple and their children.

Everyday Communication Ethics

❖ *When has your decision making been limited by the either/or thinking of ethical purity?*

Sometimes when we face an ethical problem, our choices are clear—to act ethically or unethically. In these situations, either/or thinking may clarify what we should do and, perhaps, motivate us to make the ethical choice. When we find ourselves in more complex or ambiguous situations, especially when more than one stakeholder has a legitimate interest, such as ethical dilemmas or tragedies, the ethically fitting communication response may not be so obvious. In these situations, either/or thinking can limit our ability to discern an ethically fitting communication response. In complex or ambiguous situations, either/or thinking makes it difficult to imagine and recognize unseen stakeholders and to identify and consider alternative ethical responses. Considering the ethicality of alternatives promotes a mindful attitude of ethically responsive discernment and decision making.

Step Five—Act, Then Reflect on Your Decision

Ethical reasoning does not end when you choose your communication response. After you have communicated, it is important to think about your decision and its consequences. As you reflect on the impact of your decision on others, consider what you learned about communicating ethically in this type of situation. You may identify an ethical practice of communication that you can use in the future. Spend some time identifying what are the short- and long-term consequences of your decisions. Consider how your decision influences what you or others consider good, right, or virtuous communication.

Ethical Decision Points of Human Communication

Situations in which you reason about how to communicate ethically will vary a great deal. There are, however, three recurring **ethical decision points of human communication** where communicators use ethical reasoning. In difficult communication situations, ethical reasoning may require reconsidering the ethical issues and interests of key stakeholders at each ethical decision point.

Decision point one—"Should I speak or. . . ?" Asking yourself if you should speak raises a question about how to participate ethically in the communication process. If you consider communication a linear process, this question asks whether you should speak or perhaps give feedback. If you consider communication an ongoing process of communication transactions which create meanings and relational connections that constitute your world, you ask how your communication would engage others in a continuous process of communication. You would consider different possible communication responses besides speaking—listening comprehensively, listening empathically, listening critically, turn taking, dialogue, debate, or even silence. A decision to listen or wait your turn to speak may not only be ethically responsive to stakeholders, it may also give you a chance to better understand the facts of a situation or the interests of different stakeholders.

Everyday Communication Ethics

❖ *Think of your most recent difficult communication situation. How would your decision to speak, listen, wait for a turn, remain silent, or do something else impact different stakeholders?*

Decision point two—"If I speak, what should I say?" Asking yourself "What should I say?" raises questions about the quality of your understanding of the facts and circumstances of an ethical situation. If you decide to speak, you must discern what to say. Active listening, perception checking, asking questions by conducting an audience analysis, conducting a survey, or investigative and traditional research are different ways to thoughtfully assess the quality of your understanding of the ethical issues and different viewpoints relevant to a situation. Identifying what you do not know, what you do not understand, and what you cannot know are important in discerning what is ethical to say. Listening is important in identifying what you do not know or understand. In discerning your decision about what to say, it is important to use your moral imagination, to consider your thoughts and judgments alongside your understanding of the thoughts and judgments of others.

Everyday Communication Ethics

❖　*In this difficult communication situation, did you listen thoughtfully to discover what you did not know?*

Decision point three—"When I communicate, *how* should I communicate?" Deciding how to speak, listen, or even take turns can too easily become a matter of technique, even in communication ethics. Scholars and practitioners can generate checklists and protocols of language strategies and listening techniques to aid in communicating more authentically, more honestly, more dialogically, with more care, or with more justice. While rules and checklists can help make our communication actions consistent, it is also possible for a skilled communicator to use such techniques to harm others, even unintentionally. Communicating ethically, like communicating competently, involves more than consistently applying rules. In a survey of definitions and theories of communication competence, Steven Wilson and Christina Sabee discuss how competent communication involves a communicator discerning when to adjust, adapt, flexibly apply, or break a communication rule to communicate appropriately or effectively in a specific situation. Communication competence involves *judgment* about what would be appropriate or effective in a specific situation. Communicating ethically involves judgment about what is ethically fitting (good, right, or virtuous) to communicate in a specific situation. Ethical communication is responsive to people, facts, and circumstances, as well as to ethical issues. What makes ethical decision making difficult is that any number of the factors of a situation can be in tension or conflict with one another. Ethical reasoning is a method for systematically thinking about and considering these factors to discern if, what, and how you may communicate ethically.

Everyday Communication Ethics

❖　*In this difficult communication situation, how could you communicate your decision ethically?*

Communicating Your Ethical Reasoning to Others

Ethical reasoning is an art, not a science. There is no formula or checklist to guarantee that your decisions are the most ethical possible. If following a checklist guaranteed an ethical outcome, there would be no ethically difficult situations. Ethical issues would disappear. Ethical reasoning is a process you use alongside your moral emotions, personal ethical standard, and experience to help you discern how to communicate in ethically difficult situations. Besides aiding your decision making, ethical reasoning provides a basis for explaining your decisions to others. Communicating the reasons for your decision is one way to practice communication ethics. Whenever we explain or justify our ethical decisions to others, our communication influences the ethical quality of our relationships and communities.

When you explain an ethical decision to others, you help construct what is meaningful about ethics in your relationships with others. There are **four ways your explanation contributes to the practice of communication ethics**. First, explaining an ethical decision affirms your relational connection to others. The process of ethical reasoning helps a communicator move beyond individual self-interest to acknowledge and be responsive to what is good, right, or virtuous for others. Ethical issues exist because communication affects and involves others. When you explain to others the reasons for your ethical decision, you communicate that these relationships are important. You engage others in a conversation where they can ask questions, agree, disagree, discuss, appreciate, evaluate, or debate. You affirm your relationship to them as communicative and ethical beings.

Second, explaining an ethical decision respects others because it assumes reasonable people can disagree. Because justifications for ethical communication practices are not always clear or obvious, engaging in conversation about ethical issues is important. When others critically evaluate your explanation, they may identify communication responses that you did not consider or encourage you to more careful discernment and deliberation. Your understanding of ethical issues deepens as you discuss your decisions with others who may disagree with you.

Third, conversation about your decisions creates an opportunity for recognizing areas of ethical agreement, as well as areas of disagreement. The study of communication shows that there can be many ways to achieve a communication goal. In applying this idea to ethical reasoning, there could be more than one way to ethically justify the same communication response. You and another person could choose the same communication response to an ethical problem but provide different justifications for that choice. Focusing conversation on the facts of a situation, you may find you have more agreement with others than you first thought, although your ethical commitments or reasoning may vary in important ways.

Fourth, conversation about ethical decisions can develop an appreciation of the different values and principles others use in their ethical discernment and deliberation. Although you may not agree with a decision, you have a new understanding of the thought and care others devote to this process. Public communication of ethical justifications encourages examination and evaluation of ethical reasoning that promotes the ethical dimension of community life. This broadens and deepens a community's resources for the practice of ethical communication.

Conclusion

Moral emotions provide direction for ethical reasoning by helping us initially discern the existence of an ethical issue. When we are mindful of how our emotions influence how we discern ethical issues, we can become more mindful of how we reason and apply our personal ethical commitments. Mindful ethical reasoning about communication helps decision makers become more conscious of themselves as communicative and ethical beings, creating awareness of the importance of ethical practices of communication for everyone involved in the communication process. You can improve the ethical quality of your communication practices by rhetorically listening for stakeholders who have an interest in an ethical issue, identifying alternatives for action, and evaluating the ethical quality of those alternatives. Ethical reasoning helps you gain a greater understanding of how your communication matters ethically.

Vocabulary

Either/or thinking 60
Ethical decision points of human communication 67
Ethical dilemma 55
Ethical discernment 52
Ethical issue 53
Ethical justification 62
Ethical problem 54
Ethical reasoning 52
Ethical tragedy 56
Ethicality 65–66
Ethically pure 65
Five steps in ethical reasoning 52
Four ways explanation contributes to communication ethics practice 69–70
Generalizability 63
Golden Rule 62
Platinum Rule 63
Rationalization 62
Rhetorical listening 57
Stakeholders 53
Tests of publicity 63–64

Cases for Discussion

Directions: Use steps 1 and 2 of ethical reasoning to identify ethical issues, key stakeholders, and their interests. Identify unseen stakeholders with rhetorical listening and ethical decision points of communication.

1. Raising Children

Maggie listened as her daughter, Jayne, talked about a girl who asked to sit with Jayne and her friends at lunch. Maggie knew that Jayne and her ten-year-old friends were popular. "I haven't heard about Alyssa," said Maggie. "Oh," replied Jayne, "she's new. She talks different. It's hard to understand her sometimes. We're not mean to her. We're nice! We just want her to leave us alone. We tried not talking to her, but she keeps following us around!"

Maggie remembered being the new girl in school. Her parents moved a lot. She knows making new friends is not easy. There is a difference between not being mean and being kind. What type of person does Maggie want Jayne to become?

What should Maggie do?

2. Life in a Fraternity

Putting away the checkbook, Carl wondered if being fraternity treasurer was worth the trouble. Checks were missing, so he could not balance the fraternity's checking account and identify how much money the fraternity had to spend. The student housing manager, Kevin, had ordered a replacement refrigerator without executive board approval.

Last summer, Carl studied the financial records and attended executive board meetings and concluded that Kevin was part of the problem. At the June meeting, Kevin proposed a $500 new member recruiting campaign. Carl asked for more information, including an itemized budget and list of proposed activities. His request persuaded other board members to postpone voting until Kevin provided this information. That night the fraternity president, Jason, stopped by Carl's room. Jason mentioned that although he agreed with the board's decision, he thought Carl had been too hard on Kevin. "Kevin was taking initiative. I want to encourage members, not discourage them. Besides, a personality conflict between board members interferes with good relationships among members." Carl was surprised by Jason's statement. Carl just wanted the fraternity to spend their money wisely and have enough to pay for their activities all year.

After reviewing the fraternity's financial and other records, Carl thought Kevin had one of the two fraternity checkbooks, because he had written checks. However, there was no record in the executive board minutes authorizing those purchases and no record of who had the second checkbook.

Yesterday one of the fraternity's two commercial refrigerators stopped working, just before school started. This morning Kevin told Carl that he had ordered a replacement without executive board approval. It would be delivered next Tuesday. Carl did a quick search online. He was no expert, but it looked like the wrong refrigerator.

What should Carl do?

3. Medical Student

This case is based on the Tuskegee Syphilis Study, discussed as an example in this chapter. Imagine yourself as the student who is attending medical school in the late 1960s and must decide how to respond to articles published in medical journals.

In 1932, the US Public Health Service (PHS) contracted to conduct a longitudinal study of syphilis comparing 339 black men with syphilis to a control group of 201 black men free of the disease. Before this time, there was no continuous longitudinal research on syphilis among blacks. Study participants, who were largely uneducated, received free medical attention, although those in the experimental group received no penicillin for their syphilis once penicillin was discovered to cure the disease. Consequences of untreated syphilis include blindness, deep skin lesions, insanity, heart disease, and early death.

You are in your third year of medical school. You have read one article on the study in a major medical journal. The report indicates that as many as 100 men in the experimental group have died from syphilis-related causes. You are appalled that such a study is being conducted on human beings, especially because penicillin cures syphilis. Further research reveals that there have been ten other reports of this research published in major medical journals.

You want to do something to draw attention to this horrifying research, but are concerned about how this could affect your status as a medical student. What should you do?

Note

1 Recent research in moral psychology suggests that some ethical judgments are intuitive, relying on moral emotions and unconscious psychological processes (see Hauser, et al.). While it is important to acknowledge the role of intuition in making ethical

judgments, a communication ethics approach to ethics focuses on the communicative qualities of ethical practice. This includes communication that explains or justifies ethical decisions to others. Justifications are important communication acts that promote ethical practices in groups, organizations, and communities.

References

Benedek, Thomas. "The 'Tuskegee Study' of Syphilis: Analysis of Moral vs. Methodological Aspects." *Tuskegee Truths: Rethinking the Tuskegee Syphilis Study*. Ed. S. M. Reverby. Chapel Hill, NC: North Carolina UP, 2000. 489–94.

Bok, Sissela. *Lying: Moral Choice in Public and Private Life*. 1978. New York: Vintage Press, 1989.

Hauser, Marc, Fiery Cushman, Lianna Young, R. Kang Xing Jin, and John Mikhail. "A Dissociation Between Moral Judgments and Justifications." *Mind and Language* 22.1 (2007): 1–21.

Jenson, J. Vernon. "Bridging the Millennia: Truth and Trust in Human Communication." *World Communication* 30.2 (2001): 68–92.

Jenson, J. Vernon. "Ethical Tension Points in Whistleblowing." *Journal of Business Ethics* (May 1987): 321–8.

Johnson, Mark. *Moral Imagination: Implications of Cognitive Science for Ethics*. Chicago, IL: Chicago UP, 1993.

Nussbaum, Martha C. *Upheavals of Thought: The Intelligence of Emotions*. Cambridge: Cambridge UP, 2001.

Sidgwick, Henry. *Practical Ethics: A Collection of Addresses and Essays*. 1898. New York: Oxford UP, 1998.

Solomon, Martha. "The Rhetoric of Dehumanization: An Analysis of Medical Reports of the Tuskegee Syphilis Project." *Western Journal of Speech Communication* 49.3 (1985): 233–47.

Tompkins, S. Paula. "Rhetorical Listening and Moral Sensitivity." *The International Journal of Listening* 23.1 (2009): 60–79.

Wilson, Steven. R. and Christina M. Sabee. "Explicating Communication Competence as a Theoretical Term." *Handbook of Communication and Social Interaction Skills*. Eds. John O. Green and Brant R. Burleson. Mahwah, NJ: LEA, 2003. 3–50.

Zimbardo, Philip. *The Lucifer Effect: Understanding How Good People Turn Evil*. New York: Random, 2007.

4

SIX ETHICAL VALUES OF HUMAN COMMUNICATION

Gayt interrupted Khou's thoughts, "Finished for another three months."
Startled, Khou looked up, "Excuse me?" Gayt replied, "We won't have
another section meeting until next quarter." "Yeah, right," replied Khou,
lost in thought. His supervisor, Caitlin McGuire, just made a presenta-
tion proposing a new customer service system, a proposal Khou had
written with his coworker Amisa.

At the section meeting last quarter, the vice-president for marketing
presented data on customer service complaints and negative service
ratings. Good customer service creates a competitive edge. The next
day, Supervisor McGuire assigned Khou and Amisa the designing of
a new system for processing customer complaints, explaining that
taking initiative would benefit everyone in the department. They took
on the challenge, doing further research, including interviewing dis-
satisfied customers. They presented their findings and a proposal for
a new customer service system to Supervisor McGuire last week.
Although she liked their proposal, nothing more was said . . . until
today. Supervisor McGuire made the same proposal Khou and Amisa
made last week, down to the presentation slides, without giving them
credit. The vice-president of marketing seemed impressed. As Khou
headed for the door, Amisa walked up beside him, "Well, what do you
think?"

Values help us distinguish between what is good or bad, right or wrong.
We use values to evaluate experiences, ideas, and actions. In the opening case, your judgment about the ethical acceptability of the supervisor's
actions applies your ethical values. Emotions help us initially identify what

is important and motivate us to act (Nussbaum). However, there are situations where moral emotions alone are insufficient to identify the best ethical course of action. If Khou or Amisa angrily accuse their supervisor of stealing their work, negative consequences could harm them and others.

For over two millennia, discussions about the tension between good and harmful consequences of acting solely on our emotions have produced ideas and theories that help us think and reason about our actions. Some discussions have identified values that help us distinguish between what is good or bad, right or wrong when we evaluate choices. Sometimes we express values as statements of principle, such as the value of truth expressed as "never tell a lie." This chapter discusses six ethical values important in communication—truth, justice, freedom, care, integrity, and honor. Each value highlights ethical issues in the content and relational dimensions of communication. Truth and the related value of truthfulness involves the content and relational dimensions, specifically how the truth of communication messages influences trust in relationships. Justice involves relational issues of fairness, whether each person in a relationship or a community receives what he or she deserves. Justice develops from the moral emotion of the equality bias that encourages us to compare ourselves with others to identify what is fair. Freedom concerns both the content and relational dimensions. Relationally, freedom highlights how communicators are separate and independent, promoting the content of individual expression and action. Care focuses on the relational connections between communicators that create responsibilities for meeting the needs of others. Care develops from the moral emotions of empathy and sympathy. Integrity highlights the content and relational dimensions of communication acts, that your words and actions are consistent and ethically good. Such consistency creates reliability in relationships. Finally, honor highlights the relational dimension of communication in its focus on the right to respect, both for yourself and others. Honor develops in complex ways from the moral emotion of disgust.

You may be asking, "Why six values? Could one or two be enough?" Using only one or two values to examine a communication situation, we can risk oversimplifying the communication process and its ethical issues and, so, are more likely to make misjudgments. Considering each value when thinking about a communication situation provides a richer explanation of potential benefits and harms, aiding you in identifying resources for your decision making. The following sections present introductory discussions of these six ethical values of communication.

Truth and Truthfulness

Communication ethicist Vernon Jenson ("Millennia") argues that truth and trust exist in almost every culture and throughout history. Mass media scholar

Dietmar Mieth argues for truthfulness as a universal norm. Philosopher Donald Davidson argues that truth is indefinable, yet central and fundamental to dealing with life's practical concerns. This chapter's discussion focuses on the Western notion of truth and truthfulness. Chapter 7 will present ideas and concepts that some call "post-truth" in discussing postmodern "justified truth."

Truth concerns the content dimension of communication. This includes practical consideration of whether the content of communication is as accurate as possible and reliable. When we **trust** someone's communication, we rely on the accuracy and reliability of ideas and information presented when making decisions. In this chapter's opening case, when Supervisor McGuire represents Khou's and Amisa's work as her own, she does not accurately represent their contribution to the proposed customer service system. When our understanding of a situation is not accurate, we are more likely to make mistakes. The vice-president of marketing could involve Supervisor McGuire in future meetings, presuming that she, and not Khou and Amisa, had the best understanding of the company's customer service problems. When the stakes for our decisions are high, we depend on accurate and reliable information to avoid harming others or ourselves. As listeners, we rely on the truthfulness of others to discover what is accurate or reliable. We soon learn whose communication we can trust and whose we cannot. As speakers, we want others to take us seriously and, so, we speak truthfully. The communication of a liar is undependable and not worthy of trust.

Three Western philosophers—Plato, Immanuel Kant, and Sissela Bok—help us explore issues of truth and trust in communication. For Plato, ethical communication is face-to-face, a give-and-take between individuals who love the truth. Ethical communication searches for the heart of a matter, a truth that can be trusted (*Phaedrus*). Truth-filled communication between equals is possible only for an elite few who can recognize and understand the truth (*Republic* Book VII). **Plato's concept of the truth** is enduring and universal but difficult to recognize or discover. Most people mistake their perceptions for truth, deceiving themselves with falsehoods and lies. Without the truth, communication is trivial and meaningless, and should be disregarded. Plato's concept of truth is based on the idea that truth may be bigger than facts and certainly is different from our perceptions. He charges early teachers of communication, called Sophists, with teaching rhetorical techniques that flatter listeners by telling them that they understand the truth, when all they understand are appearances and falsehoods (*Gorgias*). When people discover they have been deceived into believing appearance rather than truth, they lose trust in communication, because without truthfulness communication is trivial. When people lose trust in the truthfulness of communication, they can become cynical.

Philosophers have debated about truth for centuries. Whether you agree with Plato, his ideas help us distinguish between **two approaches for**

understanding truth. Either we search for universal and enduring truth through reasoning or other mental processes, or we rely on our experiences and observations. Because people have different experiences, there can be many different truths. While debates about what is truth and how to search for it are centuries old and will continue in the future, there is a common point of agreement—there may be more to truth than what we already know or understand. There is always another question to be asked or an answer to be reexamined for its accuracy, completeness, or reliability. There is always something more to discover, learn, or examine. Human understanding of truth is *always* incomplete. One explanation for incomplete understanding of truth is that the finite and limited human mind has difficulty simultaneously understanding the breadth and depth of truth on a universal scale. Another explanation is that the truth of experience is so varied that it is humanly impossible to understand all experience. The common point is that a person can never be certain that she knows the complete truth, so she must be open to listening to and examining different points of view. Someone committed to the truth must be curious, to motivate her continuing search for truth. Certainty undermines our capability to recognize truth.

Immanuel Kant and Sissela Bok present two more ways to think about truth and communication. One of Kant's important contributions to communication ethics is his discussion about *why* it is important to communicate the truth. Telling the truth should be a universal law or duty because it is a fundamental practice for respecting human dignity. This is part of his discussion of the categorical imperative, a key idea in Kant's theory of ethics. He expresses the categorical imperative in three different statements. Each expression has influenced ethics in different ways. The second expression makes an important contribution to understanding truth in communication. **Kant's second expression of the categorical imperative** is, "Act in such a way that you always treat humanity, whether in your own person in the person of any other, never simply as a means, but always at the same time as an end" (*Groundwork* 96). In other words, we should recognize the humanity or human dignity of persons, by treating their interest to survive and thrive as an ethical goal or end, rather than treating other persons solely as a means to achieve a personal or social goal. Kant claims that respecting human dignity is *the* most important ethical end or goal. Communicating the truth respects the dignity of others as decision makers. Communicating the truth illustrates the ethical obligation we each have not to abuse others by treating them as objects. Lying is unethical because lies treat others as a means to achieve the liar's goal. It is irrational to make decisions knowing you have incorrect information. Lies trick listeners into believing they have the truth, denying their nature as rational decision makers. Telling the truth is a practical and fundamental way to respect human dignity, while telling lies always treats people as objects to be used.

Point to Ponder

❖ *How important is truth or truthful communication for you? For your relationships? For the communities where you live or work?*

Sissela Bok respects the truth, but claims that questions of what the truth is are beside the point. She makes a simple observation—that it is not possible to know the whole truth (6–7). She avoids the debate between those believing the truth is universal and enduring and those believing in different truths based on different experiences. She focuses on a different question: Do you *intend* to tell the truth, as you understand it? Whatever you believe the truth to be, do you communicate it honestly? This is **truthfulness**. For Bok, human communication is based upon a presumption that communicators are honest (30–1), called the **principle of veracity**.

The importance of veracity becomes evident when we think about what happens when we lie. Bok offers a broad definition of a **lie**, "any intentionally deceptive message that is stated" (13). Lies do not need to be false to deceive. A lie technically may be true, as when a liar accurately tells only part of the story, leaving out the facts that put her in a bad light. Technically accurate communication can deceive by omission or deflection of the truth. Children learn this at a young age. Brian knows he is not supposed to eat a snack before dinner. When his mother asks him if he took a cookie from the cookie jar, he says "No," because his sister gave him the cookie. While Brian was technically accurate, according to Bok's definition he told a lie, deceiving his mother by omission. Adults tell lies of omission as easily as children.

Lies are unethical because of what they do relationally to the deceived. Bok echoes Kant in her argument that lies are a form of violence, a communicative assault on another person (18–22). The **perspective of the deceived** reveals this relational violence. Lies give the liar power by communicating falsehoods that the deceived uses in making decisions. Liars gain power by misinforming, hiding alternatives, and reducing the confidence of the deceived in her decision making. Each of us has been a victim of lies, some malicious, some trivial or benign. Even trivial lies can leave us feeling manipulated or coerced. We wonder why the liar decided not to trust or respect us enough to be honest. When we are deceived, we become wary and less trusting of others.

One danger of lying is that we become unable to recognize truthful communication, because we have lost trust in others. This happens gradually. When we have been hurt or harmed by a lie, we protect ourselves by being skeptical about the truthfulness of others. When skepticism becomes a habit, it can develop into a cynical attitude that everyone lies. A **cynic** always doubts that others are truthful and, so, has difficulty recognizing honest communication. Cynicism damages the trust needed to maintain the communication process. When we tell what we consider a trivial lie, we can harm the trust needed for good communication. Teaching provides an example of how cynicism and mistrust can grow out of repeatedly hearing what some people consider a trivial or benign lie. Students have many reasons for their absences from class. When faculty members require explanation for absences, some students lie. After listening to many deceptive or questionable student excuses for absences, some faculty become skeptical about the truthfulness of any student excuse for an absence. An old joke among faculty is that the grandparents of some students die as many as ten times before graduation. To warn new faculty of the cynicism this skepticism can create, one professor told a story about a first-year student visiting his office after an unexplained absence of two weeks. There was no phone call to explain the absence, and email did not yet exist. When the student appeared the faculty member asked cynically, "Did your grandfather die?" With tears brimming in her eyes, she responded, "No, my father did." When we communicate lies we consider trivial or benign, such as lying about an absence from school or work, we promote cynicism in others and help construct a more cynical world. Victims of lies can lose trust in the veracity of communication, and protect themselves with cynicism. When we proactively protect ourselves from liars with cynicism, we can hurt or harm truthful communicators.

Lies also harm the liar. Once a person lies, the next lie becomes easier, as does the next, and so on (Bok 24–8). Lies may continue until the liar is unable to keep track of her lies. Her communication becomes so unreliable that she no longer recognizes what is accurate in her own communication. She may believe her own lies. In the chapter's opening case, if the supervisor continues to represent Khou's and Amisa's work as her own, she could deceive herself into believing that she is a good supervisor. Just because liars deceive themselves does not mean that others do not recognize a lie as false. Khou and Amisa recognize their supervisor is deceiving others. Yet, repeated lies can harm those who recognize a lie as a falsehood, because lies affect everyone involved in the communication process. Lying promotes lying, to protect ourselves from others who lie, damaging our ability to recognize when someone is being honest. An individual communication practice of lying can cocreate a shared practice of lying in a friendship, family, workplace, or community, creating social worlds of lying, deception, and cynicism.

Point to Ponder

❖ *What would your life be like if all your friends told lies rather than the truth? What would your life be like if all your friends told the truth and never lied?*

At this point, you may be wondering about white lies you have told. Is it ever ethical to lie? To answer, it helps to ask another question, "Is it always good to tell the truth?" Kant would answer yes, because honesty is a duty. Ethical duties are universal laws of ethics, although individuals may choose not to follow them. Deciding to tell a helpful lie does not change the fact that an **altruistic lie** is still a lie. Kant's example to illustrate this idea is whether a person should lie to a murderer searching for his intended victim (*Philosophy* 346–50). The example uses **Kant's first expression of the categorical imperative**— "Act only according to the maxim ['honesty is the best policy'] by which you can at the same time will that it should become a universal law" (*Groundwork* 88). I have a duty to apply a principle, "honesty is the best policy," if I believe its universal application respects human dignity and prevents abuse of others. Telling the truth, for Kant, is a universal law of ethics. You have a duty to tell the truth to all persons and in *all* situations, even to an inquiring murderer. Truth telling maintains the trust needed for human community to exist; lies damage this trust. Altruistic lies present an ethical dilemma between telling the truth and preventing harm to an innocent person. Using the categorical imperative, Kant resolves this dilemma with the universal duty to communicate the truth that is greater than any other responsibility (*Groundwork* 346–9).

Whether you agree with Kant's solution to the ethical dilemma of telling an altruistic lie, there are other situations where you might ask if it is ever ethical to lie, such as when a lie's potential harm is insignificant. When someone says, "Hello, how are you?" and you reply, "I'm fine," but you have a migraine headache, you have told a white lie. **White lies** are lies we consider trivial or unimportant. While Bok is unwilling to claim that there are no good reasons to lie, she warns that all lies desensitize us to the importance of truthfulness. Telling a white lie makes it easier to lie again. Any lie signals that others do not deserve honest communication. A decision to lie must justify that the good of the lie is greater than our responsibility to be honest (Bok 30–1). To ethically justify a lie, we must weigh the potential good of the lie against its potential to harm others and promote distrust. Because the principle of veracity is a foundation of trust in our relationships and communities, Bok urges us to test the quality of our reasons for lying by using the three tests of publicity—asking your conscience if this lie is ethically justified, asking friends or colleagues, or asking persons of all allegiances (94–103).

Many consider truth and truthfulness foundational for practicing communication ethics. What place does truth or truthfulness have in your personal ethical standard, if they are not there already?

Justice

The ethical value of justice concerns the relational dimension of communication, specifically fairness among communicators. **Justice** focuses on what is fair or deserving among persons, developing from the moral emotion of the equality bias. The chapter's opening case raises an issue of justice—is it fair for Khou's and Amisa's supervisor to represent their work as her own? Ethical issues of justice can be more complicated than ethical issues of truthfulness, because people have different understandings of what is just or fair. If you asked for advice from your friends about how to act toward a former significant other after a difficult breakup, you may receive very different answers based upon different types of justice. Below you will read about six types of justice—corrective, retributive, procedural, distributive, restorative, and harmonic.

Corrective justice is the most basic form of justice (Barry and Matravers 141). Wrongful action, such as stealing or lying, deserves punishment that corrects the harm created by a wrongful act. Corrective justice "rights" a wrong by punishing the wrongdoer. In the chapter's opening case, if upper management gave Supervisor McGuire a warning that she should recognize the work of her subordinates when making proposals, upper management would use corrective justice to punish cheating. The symbol of a balancing set of scales represents corrective justice. The scales represent the search for proportion in practicing corrective justice, weighing the severity of a punishment against the wrongness of an act. This weighing is a form of discernment that helps insure fairness, that the punishment "fits" or is an appropriate corrective to the wrongful action. Practicing corrective justice requires that a correction or punishment is not too severe or too lenient.

One issue in practicing corrective justice is who makes the decision about punishment. A variation of corrective justice that addresses this issue is **retributive justice**. In retributive justice the victim of a wrongful act, or the victim's family and friends, are sometimes considered the individuals best able to decide what is a "deserving" punishment. They best understand the impact of the wrong and what is needed to restore relational balance. This personal quality of retributive justice, and the negative emotions accompanying it, can create tit-for-tat conflict spirals. An act of retributive justice can result in the wrongdoer's equally strong feelings that she is now unfairly wronged. She then seeks retributive justice to restore her sense of relational balance, like neighbors feuding over loud music. Sometimes retributive justice spirals out of control, creating a cycle of violence that threatens others and sometimes the stability of the community. The challenge of corrective justice is discerning the fairest form of punishment for a wrong that also manages the destructive potential of retributive justice. To accomplish this, corrective justice may involve procedural justice.

Point to Ponder

❖ *What does it mean to be a fair communicator?*

Procedural justice involves processes for deciding what is fair or deserving. With retributive justice, the parties rely on their personal sense of fairness to guide efforts to restore relational balance. Because retributive justice can be so personal, parties often lose sight of how their actions affect others or whether the punishment is in proportion to the harm created by the wrongful act.

Procedural justice provides an alternative to the personal search for justice by creating a more impartial process for deciding what is fair or deserving. Procedural justice could be as simple as drawing a name out of a hat or as complex as a legal trial by a jury of one's peers. Procedural justice may use a third party who is uninvolved with the disagreement to administer the procedure. An uninvolved third party is more neutral in weighing the legitimate interests of everyone involved, because decisions made do not have consequences for her. Procedural justice focuses more on the system or process for decision making than a decision's content. If the procedures are just (unbiased by self-interest of family or friends), the results produced by following the procedures are considered just. Sometimes a procedure raises questions about whether it gives individuals what they deserve. Addressing this issue of justice often involves the fourth type of justice, distributive justice.

Textbox 4.1

Fairness: In the Eye of the Beholder

The equality bias creates an emotional baseline for fairness as to what each of us deserves to receive. Discerning what is fair requires comparing what we receive with what others receive. Research of the relationship between behavior and individual perception of what others deserve provides insight into how retributive justice develops (Shergill et al.). Two participants were paired using a mechanical device that each participant used to deliver pressure to the fingers of their partner. Each participant was instructed to use the mechanical device to administer the same amount of pressure on their partner's fingers that they perceived they had received through the mechanical device from their partner. Impartial measurement of the pressure showed that participants typically responded with almost 40% more force than the amount of pressure they actually received from their partner. This means that every time a participant felt pressure on her fingers, she touched back harder but perceived she was using equal force. She perceived herself as responding fairly, but actually was responding unfairly.

Distributive justice concerns how benefits and burdens (or harms) of community life are handed out among community members (Fleischacker; Kolm). Education is a benefit of community life. While funding education is a burden, lack of education or poorly funded education is a harm for a community and its members. Distributive justice involves identifying and fairly distributing benefits, burdens, and harms within a community using relevant criteria.

If your criteria are fair and you use the proper procedure, the result is presumed to be fair. Disagreement about the fairness of distributive justice often focuses on criteria. Different communities using different criteria have different practices of distributive justice. Typical criteria include merit (e.g., individual accomplishment, character, family lineage, or position), equality (e.g., equality of condition, opportunity, or outcome), or special needs and abilities (e.g., physical, emotional, health, or special circumstance). The same community may use different criteria for distributing the same benefit in different situations. Distributing the benefit of education in US society illustrates using different criteria. US social community applies the criterion of equality to distribute the benefit of education to children below the age of 18, using the system of public K-12 education. Distributing the benefit of post-secondary education uses the criterion of merit. Prospective students apply to colleges and universities, providing evidence of their merit through grades, graduation from high school or an equivalent achievement, test scores, essays, and references. Special needs and abilities criteria are used for students who can demonstrate that they require customized educational resources to learn. Decision makers decide which criteria achieve the fairest possible distribution of benefits or burdens within their community. Sometimes distributive justice is called social justice to emphasize its focus on the community rather than on specific individuals.

Textbox 4.2

Retributive or Procedural Justice?

The Oresteia is a trilogy of plays by the ancient Greek playwright Aeschylus. It vividly presents the destructive potential of retributive justice for individuals and a community. The plays are set after the Trojan War in which the Greeks destroyed the city of Troy to rescue Helen, the kidnapped wife of Menelaus. The victorious king of the Greeks, Agamemnon, comes home from the war to his wife, Clytemnestra, and his family. Clytemnestra, however, murders Agamemnon immediately after his arrival to satisfy the call for retributive justice. Agamemnon had sacrificed their daughter, Iphigenia, to the gods in preparation for the war. The gods had demanded her sacrifice before they would allow the winds to blow the Greek ships to Troy. To lure his daughter, Agamemnon told her that she would marry the warrior Achilles. Dressed in her bridal clothes, she was sacrificed. With good winds, the army sailed to Troy and war.

Retributive justice demanded that King Agamemnon die in payment for Iphigenia's death. Clytemnestra's murder of Agamemnon is an act of retributive justice. However, as soon as she kills Agamemnon, his death demands retributive justice. Clytemnestra must now die. This responsibility belongs to their son, Orestes, who must now kill his mother. The destructive cycle of retributive justice would continue until the entire ruling family is dead, leaving the community leaderless. Only intervention of the gods prevents this, by introducing procedural justice in a trial by jury. In the first trial for murder, Orestes is freed by a hung jury of the men of Athens. The goddess Athena presides as judge, with the god Apollo defending Orestes. The plays show procedural justice, in the form of a jury trial, as flawed but ethically superior to retributive justice. Without procedural justice, people can destroy themselves and their community in a spiral of violence created by retributive justice.

Distributive and procedural justice are often practiced together. Communities need procedures for fairly distributing benefits, burdens, or harms. You can evaluate procedures for fairness using questions such as: "Is the procedure impartial or is it susceptible to special interests? Are there unrecognized or irrelevant criteria that decision makers use in making their decisions? Does the procedure exclude or overlook relevant criteria for distribution of a benefit or burden within the community?"

Restorative justice is the fifth form of justice. Interest in restorative justice grew out of dissatisfaction with practices of corrective and procedural justice in criminal justice systems. **Restorative justice** attempts to meet the needs of victims while helping wrongdoers understand the harm their actions caused (Johnstone 10–35). Restorative justice has two aims. The first aim is holding offenders accountable for their actions by helping them recognize the harms they have caused. After recognizing how their actions have affected their victims, who may include individuals, groups, or the entire community, offenders are encouraged or required to repair these harms by making reparations. The second aim is to empower victims and wrongdoers in a way that has potential to reconcile relationships and rebuild communities. This sometimes involves apology or forgiveness. In restorative justice, the goal of repairing relationships and rebuilding community is as important as, and sometimes more important than, the goal of punishing a wrong. A well-known effort to practice restorative justice is the South Africa Truth and Reconciliation Commission (see Tutu).

Some critics of restorative justice argue that it is idealistic and impractical. Other critics argue that restorative justice is unjust, because it allows wrongdoers a way to avoid the punishment they deserve, circumventing corrective justice. Proponents of restorative justice argue that although it is a difficult form of justice to practice, it has the potential to end or prevent cycles of violence by facilitating the healing and rebuilding of relationships and communities damaged by conflict and violence (see Doxtader "A Reply" and "Reconciliation").

Harmonic justice is the sixth type of justice. It offers a different understanding of what is fair or deserving than traditional forms of justice as corrective, retributive, distributive, procedural, or restorative. **Harmonic justice** is a localized, interpersonal practice of fairness where you focus your attention on the legitimate interests of your interpersonal partner to survive and thrive (Tompkins). Traditional justice is based on the moral emotion of the equality bias, requiring relational or social comparison to discern what is fair or deserving, so that everyone receives the same or equivalent benefits or outcomes (Bloom). The greater the number of persons involved in the comparison, the more complicated the issues of traditional justice become in comparing the legitimate interests of each person to survive and thrive. When you practice harmonic justice, you focus your attention on your communication partner, instead of comparing her to yourself or others. This prompts you to offer a deserving or harmonic response to her legitimate interests. In harmonic justice, there is no point for comparison, because your attention is not divided by comparing what is fair for her, yourself, or someone else.

Point to Ponder

❖   *What does it mean to deserve communication?*

Turn taking can highlight differences between traditional and harmonic justice. Turn taking can be a practice of corrective justice—"It's my turn!"— when interrupting someone who speaks too long or ignoring others waiting to speak. Retributive justice occurs when a formerly ignored speaker takes extra time, to assure that her speaking time equals or is greater than other speakers. These turn taking practices of corrective and retributive justice use relational comparison. Time limits or talking sticks are practices of distributive and procedural justice for treating speakers fairly by using a single standard for comparing speaking time. Restorative justice in turn taking begins when ignored or silenced victims speak and are heard by their victimizers. For harmonic justice, turn taking is beside the point. Traditional justice involves consideration of where "I" fit in—"When is it my turn?" Harmonic justice considers what is deserving or in harmony with the legitimate interests of a conversational partner to survive and thrive. You do not consider or compare to anyone else. What is deserving might be your listening, sitting quietly, or doing some activity together in silence. Acknowledgment is a practice of harmonic justice (Hyde; Tompkins).

There are several answers to questions about what is just, fair, or deserving. A challenge of practicing justice is identifying whether a question of fairness is an issue of corrective, retributive, procedural, distributive, restorative, or harmonic justice, or some combination of these types. Clarifying ethical issues of justice is important for discerning how to communicate ethically. The chapter's opening case involves issues of corrective, procedural, restorative, and harmonic justice. Supervisor McGuire commits a wrongful act of cheating that harms the trust between her and her subordinates. Correcting this wrong by punishing Supervisor McGuire would help restore relational balance among employees, rebuilding trust. If there were no procedures about misrepresenting others' work as your own in the employee handbook, punishment by upper management could be seen as retribution, rather than deserving or proportionate corrective justice. Restorative justice is possible, if Supervisor McGuire speaks with Khou and Amisa about the impact of her actions on them, other subordinates, and the company. Harmonic justice could be practiced in several ways. Both Khou and Amisa deserve to have their concerns acknowledged by coworkers, upper management, as well as Supervisor McGuire. Even Supervisor McGuire deserves harmonic justice, in listening to her explain her actions. Harmonic justice does not require believing someone, only that your response be fitting and deserving. In fact, practicing harmonic justice alongside other forms of justice helps assure that corrective or procedural justice are applied properly, so concerns of everyone involved are heard.

Understanding different types of justice develops your moral imagination, creating resources for ethical reasoning. Thinking about how retributive justice is different from corrective, procedural, distributive, restorative, or harmonic justice, and how they could be combined, can help you imagine alternative practices of justice. Consider the disclosure of confidential information. Corrective justice focuses on the undeserved harm of breaking a confidence. Distributive justice focuses on the undeserved benefit or harm of giving or receiving confidential information. Procedural justice focuses on the fairness of how such a disclosure was given or received. Restorative justice focuses on repairing the harm and then on rebuilding relationships damaged by disclosing confidential information. Harmonic justice focuses on affirming and understanding the concerns and feelings of everyone involved. Thinking about the different types of justice helps you imagine different ways to practice communication justice, providing you with more resources for discerning what would be the most ethically fitting communication response.

Justice encourages thinking about how your communication promotes or diminishes fairness in your relationships and communities where you live and work. The different types of justice, in contrast to the moral emotion of the equality bias, asks you to consider what is fair for others, not simply what is fair for yourself. Chapter 9 will explore issues of communication justice for communities.

Consider how you could include justice in your personal ethical standard, if it is not there already. Think about which types of justice are most important for your practice of communication ethics.

Freedom

Freedom is a well-recognized ethical value, especially in Western societies. **Freedom** is absence of coercion and constraint. In the chapter's opening case, Supervisor McGuire might claim that she was exercising her freedom to use Khou's and Amisa's presentation at the section meeting. Freedom focuses more on individuals than on relationships. Closer examination of freedom, however, shows its practice is more complicated, and Supervisor McGuire's claim that she is exercising her freedom becomes less convincing. Sociologist Orlando Patterson encourages us to think of **freedom as a musical chord** of three notes (1–5). In our practice of freedom, one or two notes of the chord can be heard more clearly than other notes. The three notes of freedom are personal freedom, sovereignal freedom, and civic freedom.

Personal freedom is freedom from being coerced or restrained. This is the most common understanding of freedom, to do what you wish, insofar as you do not harm others. Isaiah Berlin distinguishes between two forms of personal freedom—**positive freedom** to act that realizes human potential (16–9) and **negative freedom** from constraint that protects a person from harm by others (7–16). Although positive and negative freedom appear to be two sides of the same coin, there are differences. When you realize your human potential by exercising positive freedom you not only create something, you become the best you can be. Negative freedom protects persons by establishing limits on the action of others. Berlin was concerned that government might require us to exercise positive freedom, interfering with our lives. Negative freedom prevents others, particularly government, from interfering with our lives. The Bill of Rights to the US Constitution practices negative freedom in protecting the personal freedom of US citizens from the authority of government; however, it does not promote their human potential (positive freedom) beyond limiting government interference. Personal freedom has two limitations. First, when you exercise your personal freedom you are accountable for the positive and negative consequences of your actions. Second, your personal freedom to act ends when it interferes with the personal freedom of others. When there is no accountability for consequences or interference with the personal freedom of others, sovereignal freedom, the second note in the chord of freedom, is practiced.

Points to Ponder

❖ *What rights are most important in protecting opportunities? Is communication one of those rights?*

The second note in the chord of freedom is **sovereignal freedom**, the power to do what you want to do as far as you possibly can. Patterson notes that sovereignal freedom is found in practice, rather than in theory. He states, "Human beings have always sought . . . the power to restrict the freedom of others . . . to do as they please with others beneath them" (4). While philosophers and political theorists have condemned this type of freedom as unethical, it is an all too common practice. The clearest example of sovereignal freedom is slavery. A master can exercise power over the slave to the point of torture or death. Patterson argues that the experience of slavery, for both the enslaved and the slaveholder, is a key element in developing the concept of freedom in Western culture (47–63). **Benjamin Constant**, a French 19th century political theorist, argued that the ancient Western republics of Rome and Athens relied upon slaves to work, so citizens were free to participate in community life. Political freedoms to speak and vote depended upon slaves to create resources needed for the community to survive and thrive, such as growing food or construction. Without slaves maintaining the infrastructure of the community, citizens would not have the time and resources to exercise their personal or civic freedoms. Constant argued that modern freedom does not require slavery to support it because the modern economic system of commerce, which today we call business, provides sufficient resources to maintain communities, allowing community members time to exercise their personal and civic freedoms (314–5). Constant also warned that without careful attention, unlimited exercise of personal freedom promoted by business had potential to undermine civic freedom required for communities to thrive (324–8).

Constant's analysis, that our exercise of individual liberties requires resources, challenges us to think carefully about resources we use when practicing personal or civic freedom. Combining Constant's analysis with Patterson's concept of sovereignal freedom prompts questions about what resources our freedom depends upon, how those resources are created, how we acquire those resources, and what happens when these resources are depleted.

Everyday Communication Ethics

❖ *What resources are necessary to practice freedom in your communication?*

The third chord of freedom is civic freedom. **Civic freedom** is the capacity of adult community members to participate in the life and governance of their community. While civic and personal freedoms often coexist, civic freedom involves *both* rights and responsibilities. As a citizen, your rights make it possible to participate freely in the life of the community. Rights are created by meeting civic responsibilities that maintain the community through active involvement in the public life of the community. Fulfilling civic responsibilities such as volunteering and voting maintain the community, making rights possible. Oftentimes, practices of civic life require setting aside personal self-interest for the good of the community, for example volunteering to lead an organization that meets an important community need, organizing candidate debates, providing free community meals to people in need, or being a coach for the local children's sport team.

Communication is important to civic freedom. Freedom to speak makes it possible for individual citizens to participate in discussions and debates on important community issues. Yet, to sustain community life citizens also need to listen to each other, as they exercise their freedom to speak. Without careful listening, it is difficult for communities to make good decisions. Tension between the rights and responsibilities of civic freedom is a continuous theme of democratic public life (see Ashley; Foner). If you study the history of social movements in the UK or US, such as ending the British transatlantic slave trade, the US abolitionist movement, British and American labor movements, the British and American 19th and 20th century feminist movements, the US civil rights movement, as well as British and American LGBTQ movements, you will see struggles over how a society defines civic rights and responsibilities, and struggles over who gets to practice them. Chapter 9 will explore further the tension between the rights and responsibilities of community members.

Points to Ponder

❖ *What are responsibilities of communication? Do any of these responsibilities create resources for practicing the freedom to communicate?*

Freedom is a fundamental value in Western societies. This is evident in the importance of freedom of speech. How might you include freedom in your personal ethical standard, if it is not there already?

Care

Care highlights the relational dimension of communication. Carol Gilligan argued for care as an ethical value in her research on moral development. Care focuses on the responsibilities we have for others in our interpersonal relationships. Agnieszka Jaworski argues that the capacity to care for another person is an alternative to reason in identifying the key characteristic of human nature. In the chapter's opening case, Supervisor McGuire might claim that she is caring for her department, including Khou and Amisa. A question to ask is whether Supervisor McGuire's care is ethical care. Not all practices of care are ethical. **Care** involves understanding and meeting the needs of people in our interpersonal relationships. It requires both a person to give care, the **caregiver**, and someone who receives care, the **cared-for**. Nel Noddings argues that practicing care requires caring for real people, not abstractions or ideas. This is the difference between donating money to a cause that you think is important and doing something to meet the needs of real people. If you donate money for the homeless or war refugees, you are not practicing care, because you are caring in the abstract. Noddings would say that you *care about* the homeless or war refugees, but you do not *care for* them. Her point that care involves specific and local interpersonal relationships is important in understanding how to practice care.

Care focuses on the needs of the cared-for. It acknowledges and incorporates emotions that develop out of the caregiver's interest in and relational involvement with the cared-for (Timmons 224–32). One danger of practicing care is when caregivers think they understand the needs of the cared-for, but do not. This can be unintentional, when caregivers fail to recognize that practices of care in one relationship may be uncaring in another relationship. Caregivers must listen to the cared-for, because caregivers do not entirely know or understand what the cared-for needs. Without careful listening, acts of care may become uncaring and, sometimes, harm the cared-for.

Everyday Communication Ethics

❖ *How important is it that practice of your personal ethical commitments directly involves people you know or could meet?*

The distinction between caring and the ethical value of care is an important one. According to Julia Wood, **caring** is a culturally understood practice of selflessness typically limited to women (33–61). Caring can come at great personal cost to caregivers, who nurture others while often neglecting their own needs. Society does not value the work of caregivers, classifying them as subordinate to others in society, especially those they care for. Jobs that nurture or care for others, such as teaching, nursing, housekeeping, and janitorial work, are not seen as professional or are considered lower status professions. People working in service (caring) jobs most often are women, minorities, immigrants, or the poor. The **ethical value of care** addresses the needs of both the caregiver and the cared-for (162–9). Ethical care does not require caregivers to repeatedly sacrifice their needs for the cared-for.

Care is a recently recognized value that philosophers and ethicists have only begun to examine as an ethical value. Natural caring is essential to human survival and thriving. Chapter 7 will further discuss the ethic of care.

How might you include care in your personal ethical standard, if it is not already there?

Integrity

If you looked up integrity in the dictionary, you would find phrases like "uncompromising adherence to moral principles," "soundness of moral character," or "honesty." Integrity concerns the ethical quality of what an individual communicator says and does, affecting both the content and relational dimensions of communication. While honesty is important, it is not enough for integrity. **Integrity** is an ethical practice based upon a public commitment and consistent practice of an ethical value or principle. In the opening case of the chapter, Supervisor McGuire's representing Khou's and Amisa's work as her own raises questions of integrity. When you practice integrity, you feel personal responsibility to put your ethical commitments into practice, even when your life would be easier setting these commitments aside (Forrest 441).

Stephen Carter's definition of integrity outlines its practice—discern what is right, act on that discernment, and then publicly explain why you acted as you did (10–2). This definition begins with discerning what is good, right, or virtuous, not consistency. Individuals consistent about their racism do not have integrity, because they have not discerned what is ethically right. The third step is publicly stating why you acted as you did. Integrity is a public matter, not a private one. Carter identifies two reasons why it is important for integrity to be public (36–9 and 52–65). First, when we publicly state reasons for our actions, we encourage public discussion and debate about what is ethical. This cocreates ethical qualities of the communities where we live. Second, communicating our reasons provides others opportunity to disagree with us. We need others to question, even challenge our discernment and reasoning about what is ethically good, to test whether our reasons are rationalizations or sound ethical justifications. Despite our best efforts, our discernment or reasoning may be flawed. A racist may be consistent and publicly honest about her racism, but she has not discerned what is ethically good, right, or virtuous. Silence about the reasons for her racism sidesteps opportunities to test her discernment and reasoning. Consistency alone lacks integrity.

In the chapter's opening case, Supervisor McGuire lacks integrity for two reasons—she did not discern what was ethically right and was not publicly honest. Without public communication to her subordinates of her decision and reasoning, she could not sufficiently test the ethical quality of her discernment and reasoning. Carter recognizes that there are some situations where publicly stating your reasons for acting would prevent integrity (174–6). Examples include hiding slaves traveling on the Underground Railroad before the US Civil War or Jews from the Nazis during World War II. Some instances of blowing the whistle about an organization's corrupt or illegal practices cannot be defended publicly, because public disclosure would harm the whistleblower and possibly prevent ending the corrupt or illegal actions. Most of the time, however, public truthfulness is needed to test, preserve, and promote integrity.

Your practice of integrity draws upon your sense of identity, your understanding of who you are as a communicator and an ethical actor (Diamond 864). Your personal ethical standard expresses your ethical identity. If you are not ethically consistent in practicing your personal ethical standard, you are not being true to yourself. You would lack personal integrity. One working definition of integrity is doing what is right when no one is looking.

Point to Ponder

❖ *What role does personal accountability play in practicing ethics?*

One challenge of practicing integrity in communication ethics is discerning when to be steadfast and consistent and when to compromise. **Compromise** is a decision to make an exception in your practice of an ethical value or a principle to achieve a different goal or objective. When we choose to compromise our personal ethical standard, we feel that we lack integrity, because we are inconsistent. "Like fire, compromise is both necessary and dangerous to human life. Were we never to accept political compromise on matters of ethical conviction, we would cut ourselves off from large numbers of our fellow humans; were we always to accept it, we would become alienated from ourselves" (Benjamin 3). When considering compromise, we face a decision about what is most important—our ethical values and principles or our relationships to others and our community. This is a significant issue, because practicing communication ethics involves deliberation and decision making about both the content and relational impacts of our decisions and actions. Answering two questions may help in discerning if you can preserve your integrity in a compromise. First, "Am I being steadfast and uncompromising to promote what is ethically good, right, or virtuous or am I being steadfast and uncompromising to make it easier to ignore those who disagree?" The former is acting with integrity, while the latter signals that you may be promoting your personal integrity for its own sake, which is a rationalization of self-interest. Not allowing disagreement makes critical thinking difficult, even preventing it, by reducing opportunity for someone to point out a limitation or weakness of your intended decision. The second question to ask yourself is, "Will this compromise help me move toward my goal of practicing this ethical principle or value, or will it move me away from my goal?" Compromise that moves you toward an ethical goal can preserve integrity by laying a foundation for further practice of your ethical standard in the future. While compromise is not consistently pure, it can be ethically good if it moves you toward rather than away from practice of your personal ethical commitments.

Facing an ethical dilemma or tragedy can compromise your personal integrity. Whatever you decide, your integrity suffers. Lying to hide escaping slaves or Jews are examples of an integrity compromising dilemma. People living in those times chose between being honest or saving people from slavery or death. Whatever they decided would diminish their integrity in some way. Yet, avoiding these situations demonstrates a lack of integrity. The ethical reasoning process outlined in Chapter 3 can help you make decisions about how to compromise with integrity. Identifying ethical issues, seen and unseen stakeholders, and understanding their interests can clarify the ethical issues you face, including issues of integrity. Ethical reasoning can help you recognize when you have become more concerned with promoting your personal integrity than considering what is ethically good or right for others.

People often use integrity to evaluate whether the actions of others are ethical. How would including integrity in your personal ethical standard influence your everyday practice of ethics, if it is not already there?

Honor

The final ethical value discussed in this chapter is honor. **Honor** is the right to be respected. Acts of respect communicate honor, whether respect recognizes human dignity, a place within a social hierarchy, or personal accomplishments. Moral or human rights and honor are interrelated, because respecting the dignity of each person is a basis of human or moral rights (Appiah). For some, acts of respect honor the divine or sacred as it appears in other people or creation. This concept of honor is found in many religious traditions, including the Abrahamic religions of Judaism, Christianity, and Islam, and Eastern religions of Jainism, Hinduism, Buddhism, and Confucianism.

Some do not consider honor an ethical value. Kant considered it important but not ethical, because it varies by culture. Honor does not meet the test of the categorical imperative. Honor is a complicated ethical value. Some punishments for violations of honor codes are considered disrespectful, questionable, or even unethical by some people inside and outside a culture (Stewart). Social psychologist Jonathan Haidt argues that honor is the value that distinguishes **WEIRD** (Western, educated, industrialized, rich, and democratic) cultures from **non-WEIRD** cultures. Western societies' focus on individualism and freedom has an equalizing effect that downplays what people from honor cultures consider acts of respect. Thus, members of non-WEIRD cultures may consider WEIRD cultures *dis*respectful. Haidt's explanation of honor is a descriptive approach to ethics that sidesteps judgments about whether some actions motivated by honor, such as physical violence to enforce honor codes are unethical. Judging the ethicality of an action is prescriptive ethics. Kwame Anthony Appiah explores the ethical and unethical nature of honor practices by examining how **honor codes** influence behavior and evaluations of who is or is not honorable. Appiah concludes that honor is important ethically because it motivates ethical action. Arguments about honor and appeals to cultural identity based upon honor can be important in persuading and motivating people to end unethical practices. Yet, honor can also motivate unethical action, when honor codes sanction coercion and violent punishments that deny human dignity. This dual nature of honor is apparent in the moral emotion on which honor is based, disgust.

Point to Ponder

❖   *Is there a practice of respect that every person deserves?*

Chapter 2 described three moral emotions important to ethics and human survival—empathy, the emotional bias to equality, and disgust. Of these three, only disgust does *not* have a biological basis. Babies must learn disgust (Bloom). Disgust keeps us away from sources of disease such as human waste, blood, infection, rotting carcasses, and the like. Each of us was taught to avoid or limit physical contact with things that we intuitively feel are disgusting, revolting, or repugnant to keep ourselves clean and relatively germ-free. Disgust lays a foundation for vertical social hierarchy that distinguishes between what is disgusting or impure from what is untainted or pure. Contact with persons associated with impurity, for example those whose jobs require contact with human waste or rotting carcasses, must be limited to maintain the purity of persons higher in the social hierarchy. Over time, people associated with what is impure are seen as evil and those associated with purity are sacred, even divine (Haidt 121–4).

    Where a person is located within a social hierarchy classifies their honor identity and accompanying honor code of behavior. There is pride in following an honor code and being respected for maintaining an honor identity, while not following the code is dishonorable and shameful (Appiah; Stewart). Acts of sacrilege that violate social hierarchy are disgusting and must be punished, because they taint what is pure with impurity. Such acts violate honor identity, creating a personal affront to persons of honor, who have a duty to restore honor by performing rituals or punishing violators. Rules regarding honor codes and identity can be complex and vary by culture. Many honor codes identify honesty and keeping promises as a basis for honoring the dignity of each person. Practices of honor that respect human dignity can be resources for changing an unethical honor identity and honor code.

    Discussions of honor often describe differences in honor codes and their honor identities, rather than examine how honor functions as an ethical practice of respect. Most simply, you are entitled to respect or honor when you have an identity that is consistent with an honor code. You have no right to respect if you lose your honor (Appiah; Stewart). Different identities have different honor codes, for example military honor codes, professional honor codes, athletic honor codes, as well as cultural honor codes. Your **external honor** is how others view your reputation, good name, prestige, or respect. This is "realistic" honor because you must deal with the reality of others' perceptions. Public recognition of honor is important in motivating individuals to keep the respect of others. **Internal honor** is a factual assessment of character that focuses on how a person acts in keeping the honor code. Sometimes a person is especially worthy of honor and receives the **esteem** of others, because she does more than the honor code requires. Concepts of external honor, internal honor, and esteem, however, have nothing to do with ethics, for they also apply to the competitive honor of being "the best." Being the best at something may be honorable, but it is not necessarily ethical. What makes honor ethical is whether the honor code promotes respect for human dignity. Honor codes that lack this ethical good are not ethical. Competitive honor would not be ethical if it focuses on winning by any means instead of telling the truth, not cheating, keeping promises, humility, and respecting your opponent or adversary. Similarly, professional honor is not necessarily ethical, if it focuses only on competence in professional skills. In addition, if competitiveness becomes part of a professional honor code, ethical practices may be de-emphasized, as competitiveness sets aside respect for human dignity to achieve the competitive honor of being "the best."

Everyday Communication Ethics

❖ *What could you do to be worthy of honor? Worthy of esteem? What are you willing to do?*

Honor is significant in ethics because honor makes integrity public (Appiah). This fits Stephen Carter's definition of integrity—discerning what is right, acting upon this discernment, and explaining publicly why you did what you did. Honor motivates us to go beyond what is right, and insist we publicly do good and condemn what is wrong. Doing *public good* establishes our right to be respected by honorable people. In identifying ideals to aspire to, honor motivates ethical action by inspiring us to live a life *worthy* of respect. Honor encourages communication that maintains a culture of respect for people who are honorable, and esteem for those who go beyond the honor code's ideals. Motivation to go beyond an honor code's ideals was an important motivation for ending dueling, the transatlantic slave trade, and foot binding in China (Appiah). Honor motivates us to make a better world by bringing integrity into public view. There are three questions to ask about whether an action is ethically honorable and worthy of respect. First, does it respect human dignity? Second, is it part of a group's or culture's honor code? This question focuses on the public nature of honor as a practice of integrity. Third, is it explained so it can be examined by others who also follow the honor code to determine its worthiness of respect? This question highlights how an honor code contributes to the social construction of ethics within a group, community, or culture.

At first, honor appears to have little to do with the chapter's opening case, beyond the dishonor of Supervisor McGuire presenting Khou's and Amisa's work as her own. Supervisor McGuire also dishonored her profession as a manager, and perhaps dishonored her company's mission, values, and its code of conduct if it has one. It is reasonable to assume that Supervisor McGuire was expected to follow standards of professional management that include honesty in communicating with subordinates.

Honor is a complex and controversial value. Although some question whether it is ethical, honor can be an important motivation for ethical action. How would practice of your ethical commitments change if honor were part of your personal ethical standard, if it is not already there?

Your Personal Ethical Standard

You may decide that one ethical value is so essential that you make this value your personal ethical standard. Your discernment and deliberations become clearly focused. In testing your ethical reasoning for rationalization, you can more clearly discern how to practice ethical communication. A challenge using one ethical value for your ethical communication is consistency.

Alternatively, you may decide that two or more ethical values are important for your practice of ethical communication. Your discernment, deliberation, and decision making can then address a broader range of ethical issues, such as truthfulness and justice. You use more than one value to guide or test your reasoning for rationalization. Your discernment and decision making can be responsive to more stakeholders. Some practices of truthful communication, for example, can be very harsh, uncaring, and possibly unfair. Communication practices of procedural justice often restrict personal freedom or may be uncaring. Reasoning with more than one value offers decision makers more resources for being ethically responsive to stakeholders. Finally, reasoning with more than one ethical value helps you better understand the ethical reasoning of others.

When a decision maker faces an ethical dilemma or tragedy with conflicting ethical values, a personal ethical standard with more than one ethical value may appear to create more confusion than clarity. Recall the earlier discussion of altruistic lies, specifically Kant's application of the categorical imperative to the dilemma of honesty and the inquiring murderer. Kant's categorical imperative easily resolves this dilemma between honesty and not harming an innocent person, because honesty is an ethical duty and preventing harm is not. While Kant's arguments are logical, many do not agree that we have a duty to tell an inquiring murder the whereabouts of her innocent victim. Using other values, they judge the decision protecting an innocent victim more important.

The concept of ethicality (Jenson "Tensions") can help in discerning and reasoning about how to communicate in complex or ambiguous situations. **Ethicality** is the idea that there are different ethical dimensions or qualities of an act, in contrast to seeing an act as ethical or unethical. The six ethical values of communication discussed in this chapter focus on different ethical dimensions of communication. When a single value organizes your personal ethical standard, your discernment and reasoning focuses on how to practice that value. When your personal ethical standard contains more than one value, you begin to discern and evaluate ethical qualities of communication alternatives. Because communication alternatives in ambiguous or complex situations are ethically flawed in some way, thinking about the ethicality of alternatives helps in searching for what Ron Arnett calls the ethically good, in contrast to the ethically pure alternative (92–113).

Textbox 4.3

Communication Ethics in Popular Film—
American Gangster and Ethicality

The film *American Gangster*, directed by Ridley Scott, illustrates the importance and some challenges of evaluating the ethicality of action. Based on a true story, the film portrays Frank Lucas, an importer of heroin in Harlem, New York, and Richie Roberts, a police officer who heads a federal government joint narcotics task force. The film depicts tensions between the ethical values of honesty, justice, and care. Lucas is an ethically attractive character, because he cares for his wife and extended family, financially supporting them. In contrast, Roberts is an ethically unattractive character, because he does not care for his wife or daughter, admitting before a judge at his divorce hearing that it would be better for his daughter not to live around him. Lucas's care for his family, however, involves deception, violence, and distribution and sale of heroin. While Roberts does not personally care for his family, he is honest and committed to justice as fairness, in the forms of procedural and corrective justice for the community. Although neither man is ethically pure, the film makes a case for judging one man as ethically good and the other ethically bad. Using more than one value to evaluate the ethicality of Lucas's and Robert's actions, a viewer can recognize and think about both the ethical and unethical dimensions of these characters' actions, and make a judgment about whose actions are ethically good.

Conclusion

Truth, justice, freedom, care, integrity, and honor are values that can guide our personal practice of communication ethics. These values deserve thoughtful consideration for inclusion in your personal ethical standard. Each value provides resources for discerning and deliberating about the ethical dimensions of issues and problems you face as a communicator, and for evaluating the ethical dimensions of your communication choices. They also encourage your moral imagination in thinking about different ethical alternatives and viewpoints. Whether or not you decide to include any of these values in your personal ethical standard, your careful consideration of each value can help you imagine how to practice truth, justice, freedom, care, integrity, and honor as an ethical communicator.

Vocabulary

Altruistic lie 80
Benjamin Constant 88
Care 90
Cared-for 90
Caregiver 90
Caring 90
Civic freedom 88
Compromise 92
Corrective justice 81
Cynic 78
Distributive justice 82
Esteem 95
Ethical value of care 90
Ethicality 97
External honor 95
Freedom 87
Freedom as a musical chord 87
Harmonic justice 85
Honor 93
Honor codes 94
Integrity 91
Internal honor 95
Justice 80
Kant's first expression of the categorical imperative 80
Kant's second expression of the categorical imperative 77
Lie 78
Negative freedom 87
Non-WEIRD culture 93
Personal freedom 87

Cases for Discussion

Directions: Use the process of ethical reasoning outlined in Chapter 3 to identify an ethically responsive communication decision at the three recurring decision points of communication. Identify which ethical values you use in your ethical reasoning.

1. Friends and Acquaintances

"Oh, no! Here he comes again," thinks Rita. She smiles anyway, as David waves. He pays the cashier and picks up his lunch. As he brings his tray over to the table to take the empty seat at Rita's table for two, she thinks, "He's going to ask me if I've seen this week's movie at the Student Union. I've seen it. I'd like to see it again, but not with David! He's sweet in a weird, geeky way, but after a while he's just irritating. There's only so much David I can take at one time." Rita remembers the last time she talked with her roommate Sharon about David. "Sharon asked why I keep talking to him. I know it encourages him, but I'm one of the few people who talks with him outside of class."

David sets his food down and the table. "Hey Rita, did you see what's showing at the Union this weekend? Are you thinking about going?"

What should Rita do?

2. Asking About Grades

Sara is struggling in Professor Martinez's statistics class. The psychology major requires students pass statistics with a C. So far, Sara has earned a D. She is waiting for Professor Martinez to arrive for an appointment to discuss her grade. This is the second appointment about her grade.

As she walks down the hallway, Professor Martinez sees Sara. Statistics is the second course Sara has taken from Professor Martinez. Sara earned a B in introduction to psychology. In statistics, Sara is consistently working at a D/D- level, with an occasional C- on daily work. Professor Martinez thinks, "To earn a C, Sara needs to show substantial and consistent improvement in her work. It's possible, but in my experience, students like Sara rarely succeed raising their grades."

Professor Martinez invites Sara in. Sara tells her how much she enjoys psychology classes and that she's finally found her place at the university. She wants to work in the field of psychology when she graduates. "It's important that I get a C in statistics. I'll do what I need to do to earn a C."

What should Professor Martinez say? How should she say it?

3. A Family Member in Trouble

Tim and his family knew something was wrong for more than a year. Two years ago, Mark was excited about getting out on his own. For some reason, college had not worked out for him. He dropped out and moved home to live with Tim and Mark's parents. Mark had changed. He did not talk much. If anyone asked how things were going, his answers were short and unrevealing—"Fine," "OK," or "Nothing much."

When Mark did talk, it usually was about work. However, his jobs rarely lasted more than a couple of months. There were weeks he did not work and disappeared with friends that the family did not know. Now this—Mark's boss, Karl, had accused Mark of stealing. Karl, an old friend of Tim and Mark's father, had contacted the family and said that Mark was fired because he was stealing money.

Tim confronted Mark. At first, Mark denied stealing from Karl, saying Karl made a mistake and Mark was innocent. Tim pressed Mark to tell the truth, saying that Karl had nothing to gain from lying to the family. If Karl was lying, the family friendship would be over. After a long pause, Mark admitted stealing the money, saying he needed money to pay for his drug habit. He knew it was wrong, but had to find money quickly to pay off a debt. Mark explained that before college he only occasionally used drugs. Eventually he was using so much that he stopped attending classes and starting failing classes. That was when he moved back home. Mark said, "I know it was wrong to steal from Karl. It bothered me. So . . . I decided to stop using drugs. I haven't used any for the last three days. I'm in recovery. I'm a different person."

What and how should Tim respond? What should Tim and Mark's family do?

4. Colorblindness?

Steven knelt beside the unconscious woman in the middle of the store. His instincts as an emergency medical responder took over. "Her pulse is rapid and breathing shallow," he thought. Steven asked the growing circle around the woman that someone call an ambulance. "Does anyone know who she is? Did anyone see what happened?" No one did. Steven said, "I am a certified emergency responder. I will stay with her until the ambulance arrives." People began to drift away, until the woman opened her eyes with a gasp, looking straight at Steven. Just then the ambulance personnel arrived. As Steven moved away from the woman, a man in the crowd said loudly, "She was surprised to wake up looking at the face of a black man."

What should Steven do? What should bystanders do?

References

Aeschylus. *The Oresteia*. Trans. Alan Shapiro and Peter Burian. New York: Oxford UP, 2003.

American Gangster. Dir. Ridley Scott. Prod. Ridley Scott and Brian Grazer. Universal City, CA: Universal Studios Home Entertainment, 2007.

Appiah, Kwame Anthony. *The Honor Code: How Moral Revolutions Happen,* New York: Norton, 2010.

Arnett, Ronald C. *Dialogic Confession: Bonhoeffer's Rhetoric of Responsibility*. Carbondale, IL: Southern Illinois UP, 2005.

Ashley, Mike. *Taking Liberties: The Struggle for Britain's Freedoms and Rights*. London: The British Library, 2008.

Barry, Brian and Matt Matravers. "Justice." *Routledge Encyclopedia of Philosophy,* Vol. 5. Ed. Edward Craif. New York: Routledge, 1998. 141–7.

Benjamin, Martin. *Splitting the Difference: Compromise and Integrity in Ethics and Politics*. Lawrence, KS: U of Kansas P, 1990.

Berlin, Isaiah. *Two Concepts of Liberty*. Oxford: Clarendon Press, 1958.

Bloom, Paul. *Just Babies: The Origins of Good and Evil*. New York: Crown Publishers, 2013.

Bok, Sissela. *Lying: Moral Choice in Public and Private Life*. 1978. New York: Vintage Books, 1989.

Carter, Stephen L. *Integrity*. New York: HarperCollins, 1996.

Constant, Benjamin. "The Liberty of the Ancients Compared with that of the Moderns." *Constant: Political Writings*. Ed. and trans. Biancamaria Fontanta. 1816. New York: Cambridge UP, 1988. 307–28.

Davidson, Donald. "The Folly of Trying to Define Truth." *The Journal of Philosophy* 93.6 (1996): 263–78.

Diamond, Cora. "Integrity." *Encyclopedia of Ethics*. Vol. 2. Eds. L.C. Becker and C.B. Becker. New York: Routledge, 2001. 863–6.

Doxtader, Erik. "The Potential of Reconciliation's Beginning: A Reply." *Rhetoric and Public Affairs* 7.3 (2004): 378–90.

Doxtader, Erik. "Reconciliation—A Rhetorical Conception." *Quarterly Journal of Speech* 89.4 (2003): 267–92.

Fleischacker, Samuel. *A Short History of Distributive Justice.* Cambridge, MA: Harvard UP, 2004.

Foner, Eric. *The Story of American Freedom.* New York: Norton, 1998.

Forrest, Barbara. "Integrity." *Ethics.* Vol. 2. Ed. J.K. Roth. Englewood Cliffs, NJ: Salem Press, 1994. 441–2.

Gilligan, Carol. *In a Different Voice: Psychological Theory and Women's Development.* Cambridge, MA: Harvard UP, 1982.

Haidt, Jonathan. *The Righteous Mind: Why Good People Are Divided by Politics and Religion.* New York: Vintage Books, 2012.

Hyde, Michael J. *The Life-Giving Gift of Acknowledgement.* West Lafayette, IN: Purdue UP, 2006.

Jaworski, Angieszka. "Caring and Full Moral Standing." *Ethics* 117.3 (2007): 460–97.

Jenson, J. Vernon. "Bridging the Millennia: Truth and Trust in Human Communication." *World Communication* 30.2 (2001): 68–92.

Jenson, J. Vernon. "Ethical Tensions in Whistleblowing." *Journal of Business Ethics* (May 1987): 321–8.

Johnstone, Gerry. *Restorative Justice: Ideas, Values, Debates.* Portland, OR: Willan Publishing, 2002.

Kant, Immanuel. *Groundwork for the Metaphysic of Morals.* 1797. Trans. H.J. Paton. New York: Harper, 1964.

Kant, Immanuel. *The Philosophy of Immanuel Kant.* Ed. C. J. Friedrich. Trans. L. W. Beck. 1785. Chicago, IL: U of Chicago P, 1949.

Kolm, Serge-Christophe. "Distributive Justice." *A Companion to Contemporary Political Philosophy.* Eds. Robert E. Goodin and Philip Petit. Cambridge, MA: Blackwell, 1993. 438–61.

Mieth, Dietmar. "The Basic Norm of Truthfulness: Its Ethical Justification and Universality." *Communication Ethics and Universal Values.* Eds. Clifford Christians and Michael Traber. Thousand Oaks, CA: Sage, 1997. 87–104.

Noddings, Nel. *Caring: A Feminine Approach to Ethics and Moral Education.* Berkeley, CA: U of California P, 1984.

Nussbaum, Martha C. *Upheavals of Thought: The Intelligence of Emotions.* Cambridge: Cambridge UP, 2001.

Patterson, Orlando. *Freedom: Vol. 1, Freedom in the Making of Western Culture.* New York: Basic Books, 1991.

Plato. "Gorgias." Trans. W.D. Woodhead. *Plato: The Collected Dialogues.* 229–307.

Plato. "Phaedrus." Trans. R. Hackforth. *Plato: The Collected Dialogues.* 475–525.

Plato. *Plato: The Collected Dialogues, Including the Letters.* Eds. Edith Hamilton and Huntington Cairns. Bollingen Series LXXI. Princeton, NJ: Princeton UP, 1961.

Plato. "Republic." Trans. Paul Shorey. *Plato: The Collected Dialogues.* 575–844.

Shergill, Sukhwinder, Paula Bays, Chris Frith, and Daniel Wolpert. "Two Eyes for an Eye: The Neuroscience of Force Escalation." 301.5630 *Science* 11 July 2003: 187.

Stewart, Frank Henderson. *Honor.* Chicago, IL: U of Chicago P, 1994.

Timmons, Mark. *Moral Theory: An Introduction.* New York: Rowman & Littlefield, 2002.

Tompkins, Paula S. "Acknowledgment, Justice, and Communication Ethics." *Review of Communication* 15 (2015): 240–57.

Tutu, Desmond. *No Future Without Forgiveness.* New York: Random, 1999.

Wood, Julia. *Who Cares? Women, Care and Culture.* Carbondale, IL: U of Southern Illinois P, 1994.

5

APPLYING VALUES AND PRINCIPLES IN ETHICAL REASONING

Clarice took a deep breath. She just finished talking with Joycelyn, a council member of Kid's Klub. Kid's Klub is an organization for boys and girls ages 8 to 18. Its goal is to build confidence, strong character, and leadership through service and social activities. It is not associated with any organized religion, but is loosely religious. Clarice is surprised that Joycelyn, the youngest council member, had confided that she is pregnant and decided to keep the baby. Joycelyn is so private. Clarice knows that Kid's Klub is important to Joycelyn. She was a member growing up, and adult leaders helped her through tough times. The kids really like Joycelyn. Council members are expected to be role models. Other council members are parents or grandparents. Some will be upset that a council member is unmarried and pregnant. It does not help that the father is another council member. Joycelyn asked Clarice to keep this confidential until she and the father sort this out. Clarice said she needs to think this through and would get back to her.

Do you apply the values and principles without exception when you communicate, or do you consider the specific circumstances of a situation in your decisions? In the chapter's opening case, Clarice faces a decision about keeping a disclosure confidential. The decision whether to say something about Joycelyn's pregnancy or to remain silent involves ethical reasoning about the first decision point of communication discussed— "Should I speak or . . . ?" If you were in a similar situation, would you speak honestly or remain silent? Are there situations where the truth is so important you would break a confidence? Perhaps you believe honesty is always the best policy, so you have a responsibility to disclose a confidence, or are there some circumstances where the right thing to do is to leave some things unsaid (Bok *Secrets*)? These are questions about how to apply ethical values and principles. Do you apply ethical values and principles absolutely and consistently? Alternatively, do you look for factors in a situation to provide clues about how to respond? Deciding whether to break or keep a confidence involves applying the principles and values of your personal ethical standard. When deciding how to practice your ethical standard, you justify your decisions using ethical reasoning. Justifying an ethical decision involves carefully considering values and principles in your ethical reasoning and rigorously examining your reasoning for rationalization of self-interest or of poorly examined social convention. This chapter will discuss three approaches for applying the values and principles of your personal ethical standard in ethical reasoning—absolutism, relativism, and casuistry.

Absolutism as an Ethical Imperative

Applying values and principles absolutely means applying your values and principles consistently, whatever the circumstances. Applying your ethical commitments is an obligation, even when it is difficult. If honesty is the best policy, it is *always* the best policy. **Absolutism** involves consistently applying values and principles because it is the right thing to do, not because it makes people feel good or happy. Potential negative consequences do not justify modifying how you apply ethical values, principles, or rules, if you are committed to applying them absolutely. In the chapter's opening case, Clarice faces an ethical dilemma of interpersonal trust: keep Joycelyn's disclosure confidential or be honest and disclose Joycelyn's situation to the parents of Kid's Klub members. These parents are stakeholders with an interest in the actions of council members as role models for their children. If Clarice considers honesty universally good whatever the situation, she has an ethical obligation to communicate honestly.

Immanuel Kant's categorical imperative provides guidelines for applying an ethical principle absolutely in its first two expressions. **Kant's first expression of the categorical imperative** states "Act only according to that maxim by which you can at the same time will that it should become a universal law" (88), meaning that your ethical actions should be consistent in applying an ethical principle universally, without exceptions. Because ethical principles identified by the categorical imperative are universal laws of ethics, the duty to follow them does not vary with a situation. The categorical imperative is not a law of nature, like the law of gravity. It concerns human beings who can reason about whether they will fulfill their obligation or duty to act ethically for its own sake. The categorical imperative does not guarantee ethical action, only that people *should* act according to their ethical duty. If you do not fulfill this duty, you act unethically.

If you use this first expression of the categorical imperative in ethical reasoning, you would ask yourself, "What would happen if everyone acted this way?" Imagine you are looking for a used car. As you meet the salesperson, you are thinking about negotiating the price. Maybe you consider a strategy of lying about what you are willing to pay for a car by making a false promise to the sales person. If you make a **false promise**, you do *not* intend to keep that promise. Using the categorical imperative you ask yourself, "What would life be like if everyone lied about their ability to pay when they made an agreement?" In your reasoning, you think about what it would be like to live in a world where everyone makes false promises. While lying to the salesperson would be personally beneficial to you, if everyone made a false promise when negotiating an agreement, would anyone be able to trust what others say when they make agreements? Reasoning with the categorical imperative, you conclude that making false promises damages our ability to make good decisions when negotiating, because we cannot rely on what others promise. If everyone makes false promises, no one would trust what anyone says. Such mistrust would make social life, even family life, difficult if not impossible. Reasoning with the categorical imperative, you conclude that we must *not* make false promises when making agreements even when we gain a short-term benefit—all people have a duty or obligation not to make false promises.

Reasoning with the categorical imperative, you understand that ethical action is about what you ought to do because it is good for its own sake, not about what you prefer or like to do. The categorical imperative values consistency over personal emotion or feeling. Even when a duty is unpleasant or difficult, you have an ethical obligation to "never give a false promise." The categorical imperative discourages us from rationalizing special permission for ourselves to act in ways that we would not allow others to act in. If we expect others to keep their promises to us, we do not have special permission to make promises we have no intention of keeping. The discussion in Chapter 4 of the ethical value of truth pointed out the negative consequences of deceiving others, because others deceive us. Not only does the deception of making false promises undermine the trust needed for relationships and society to exist, making one false promise makes it easier to make another false promise. When making false promises becomes a habit, we lose our ability to recognize when promises are real or false (Bok, *Lying*).

Point to Ponder

❖ *Is there a relationship between absolutism and integrity? Between absolutism and honor?*

Kant's second expression of his categorical imperative is "Act so that you treat humanity, whether in your own person or in that of another, always as an end and never as a means only" (96). This is different from

Kant's first expression. In the second expression, he claims that when you act ethically, you do not solely treat people as objects, as instruments or means to achieve goals. For Kant, the universal or absolute nature of ethical practice affirms intrinsic human worth or dignity, which is based upon the capacity to make decisions by reasoning about choices. Treating others as a means for achieving a personal or institutional goal *without their permission* denies their dignity as reasoning agents. When we do not recognize a person's intrinsic worth or dignity, it is easier to use her as a means for meeting our personal or institutional goals. People become objects, rather than our equals. For Kant, persons capable of reasoning have a right to make their own decisions, including the right to choose to be treated as a means to an end, as when volunteering to sacrifice personal well-being for the good of a relationship, group, or community. According to the second version of the categorical imperative, lying or breaking a promise denies human dignity, because it is irrational to make decisions based on false promises. Informed decision making is impossible. Intentionally making a false promise undermines the interpersonal and social trust needed for human survival and thriving. Kant's categorical imperative argues against abusing people by using them as objects for achieving personal or social goals.

Textbox 5.1

**Communication Ethics in Popular Film:
Promises in *The Lord of the Rings***

Keeping a promise is an ethical good in and of itself, while a false promise is ethically wrong. The communication act of making a promise creates an ethical obligation to keep that promise.

Peter Jackson's films of the fantasy adventure *The Lord of the Rings* illustrates the ethical challenges and importance of keeping promises, although the promises made are between wizards, elves, dwarves, hobbits, and humans living in the imaginary land of Middle Earth. The story begins when the hobbit Bilbo Baggins keeps his promise to the wizard Gandalf to leave his nephew Frodo a dangerous weapon, the One Ring of Power. Fear of the Ring divides leaders of Middle Earth, until Frodo makes the promise to bring the Ring to its point of creation and destroy it, to prevent its maker from acquiring the Ring and using it as a weapon to conquer Middle Earth. Yet Frodo is unable to keep this promise, unless he trusts the promises of others—the wizard Gandalf, the ranger called Strider, the former ring-bearer Gollum, and many others. As the Ring and its maker attempt to thwart Frodo's quest to destroy it, characters keep and break many promises.

The films show how promises matter, whether in making a promise, making a false promise, keeping an ancient promise, or breaking a promise between friends. Promises matter to promise makers and unseen others. Words that relationally bind characters to one another in a promise, whether it is a new promise or an ancient one, also connect them to unseen others whose communication relationally connects them to the promise makers. Promises involved in the quest to destroy the One Ring of Power reveal unacknowledged and unseen bonds of relational connection throughout Middle Earth. Promises relationally bind promise makers to individuals who live with the consequences of a promise, whether that promise is kept or broken.

When using the categorical imperative in ethical reasoning, you ask what is good by its very nature, no matter what the situation and your personal feelings about the situation. This assumes that careful and rigorous use of reason helps you act in a way that is good for its own sake, because the categorical imperative identifies a universal good that does not rely upon personal feelings or happiness. In the chapter's opening case, Clarice did *not* promise to keep Joycelyn's secret from the parents of Kid's Klub members. Withholding information about Joycelyn's pregnancy would be dishonest, because it withholds information important in their decision making about their children's involvement in Kid's Klub. If Clarice considers telling the truth a universal duty, she must communicate this information to parents, as part of her reasoning about the first ethical decision point of communication, "Do I speak or . . .?" The categorical imperative discourages Clarice from rationalizing that she has special permission not to communicate the truth, when she expects honest communication from others. If Clarice decides she must disclose Joycelyn's pregnancy, she now faces the second and third ethical decision points of communication—what information about Joycelyn's situation is ethical to disclose and how to communicate this disclosure ethically.

You may consider the categorical imperative a good approach for applying the values and principles of your personal ethical standard. It is one way to practice integrity, to be consistent in practicing your ethical commitments and explaining your actions to others. You might wonder, however, about special circumstances where applying an ethical principle such as "never tell a lie" or "always keep your promise" would harm others. If you have thought about these issues, you may want to consider one of the next two approaches to applying ethical values and principles—relativism or casuistry.

Many Faces of Relativism

Relativism assumes that how a person applies values, principles, or rules can vary. There are three types of relativism—individualist, situationist, and conventional (Jaska and Pritchard 18–21). With **individualist relativism**, application of an ethical value depends on the individual's ethical commitments. Because ethical standards are personal, no one has a right to judge another person's ethics. In a highly individualist society such as the US, many people use this form of relativism in their decision making. Using individualist relativism for the chapter's opening case, Clarice would recognize Joycelyn's ethical commitments as the most relevant in deciding how to communicate and, so, would keep Joycelyn's disclosure confidential. In fact, you could use individualist relativism to conclude that what Joycelyn does is none of Clarice's business.

With **situationist relativism**, the principles, values, or rules a decision maker applies depend upon the facts and circumstances of a situation. Each situation is so unique that a decision maker must let the facts of a situation determine which ones to apply. People making decisions using situationist relativism believe that it is difficult, even impossible, to generalize from one situation to the next, because each situation presents a unique set of facts and circumstances. A decision maker approaches each situation with as few preconceptions as possible, letting the facts of the situation point to the most relevant value or principle to apply. In practicing situationist relativism, Clarice would consider the individual adults and children, their relationships, and the special circumstances of Kid's Klub to arrive at a decision about what she considers ethically good without using experience or universal principles to determine her decision. What she decides to do would depend on what she considers the unique or most distinctive and important factors in this situation.

Clarice could use the third form of relativism, conventional relativism, to guide her deliberation about whether to keep Joycelyn's disclosure confidential or tell the parents. **Conventional relativism** recognizes that when persons are members of different groups, organizations, or cultures, they often use different values, principles, or rules in decision making. With greater awareness of cultural differences, conventional relativism has become prominent in discussions of ethics. For example, Archbishop Desmond Tutu's book about the South African Truth and Reconciliation Commission, *No Future Without Forgiveness*, has increased Western awareness of differences between African and Western cultural approaches to violent conflict. According to Tutu (30–2), the South African Truth and Reconciliation Commission practiced the African value of **ubuntu**, illustrated by the Zulu maxim "A person becomes a person through other people." This maxim is understood as a quality of a person's character or as an ethic emphasizing human interconnection (Gade). "To acknowledge others as human beings worthy of respect, one should simultaneously have to acknowledge oneself as a person who should exercise respect" (Waghid and Smeyers 14). The more collectivist African cultural value of ubuntu differs from Western individualism characteristic of US and European cultures, leading to different practices of justice. Returning to the chapter's opening case, if Clarice uses conventional relativism to deliberate about keeping Joycelyn's disclosure confidential, she would use ethical principles and values shared by the parents of the Kid's Klub organization.

Everyday Communication Ethics

❖ *What type of relativism do you see practiced most often?*

Tolerance is essential to practicing relativism. **Tolerance** is the practice of suspending judgment about people who are different from you. If you apply ethical values relatively, you are unwilling to judge the actions of others as unethical, if they are acting according to their ethical commitments that differ from your own. Whatever form of relativism Clarice might use in deciding whether to keep the disclosure confidential, she must suspend her personal judgments about Joycelyn's choices. Practicing tolerance also involves interacting or living with people whose ideas or behaviors make you uncomfortable, because they are different. You may even initially think these ideas or behaviors are wrong. When we practice tolerance, we push ourselves outside our comfort zones.

Tolerance helps us manage the tendency to make quick judgments about what is ethical or unethical, before we understand the facts and circumstances of a situation. Too often, we act quickly with confidence about the "rightness" of our actions or the "wrongness" of others, without understanding the facts. We do not listen competently to the viewpoints of others, especially if their viewpoints differ from our own. When we make ethical judgments so quickly that we have not carefully examined the facts and circumstances of a situation or considered the viewpoints of others, it is easy to make an error or mistake rationalization for ethical justification.

I have participated several times in community forums on Islam, where observant Muslims explain their faith and religious practices to people who live in a predominantly white, Christian community. A growing number of Muslim families, especially from the traditional culture of Somalia, stimulated community interest and concern about Islam. The topic of women and young girls wearing hijabs or headscarves have been discussed repeatedly, including high school teachers concerned about the ability of Muslim girls to participate in athletics and Muslim mothers concerned about the immodesty of athletic clothing (especially swimming suits). Others saw hijabs or headscarves as political statements or signs of cultural separatism, while others did not understand why women and girls would wear hot and confining dress from the Middle Ages. On each occasion, Muslim women shared what wearing a headscarf meant to her, while other Muslim women shared why they did not wear one. These differences represent diversity in the Muslim community, which mainstream American culture often sees as monolithic. Wearing a headscarf can make a Muslim woman a target for derogatory comments, harassment, or abuse. At one community forum, a Muslim woman explained how her headscarf was part of her identity as a Muslim feminist, which surprised many members of both the Muslim and Christian communities. Over the years, these discussions gave participants opportunities to listen and better understand each other. At a recent forum, local community members could submit questions online that Muslim community members answered at the public forum. In each public forum, some community members began to recognize how fears, assumptions about respecting girls and women, and misunderstandings of women who violated social conventions of dress, influenced their judgments. These face-to-face presentations and discussions provided opportunities to practice ethically responsive tolerance. It is more difficult to be intolerant of a person when you communicate face-to-face with her, as you listen to her and she listens to you.

Practicing tolerance has ethical challenges. Practicing tolerance with integrity requires practicing it consistently. To be consistent, you may become absolute in your tolerance, repeatedly suspending your ethical judgment and, perhaps, demanding others to practice tolerance as you do. You may have wondered if there is a limit to tolerance. If so, you have experienced the ethical dilemma of tolerance. An **ethical dilemma of tolerance** exists when you see someone's actions creating harm for another, and you *repeatedly* do not communicate your ethical concerns, nor do you do anything to respond to the harm, because it would be intolerant. Barry Brummett argues that the ethical dilemma of tolerance can be a significant challenge for practicing ethical communication. Communication theory has shown that language and symbols do not neutrally transmit information, but communicate a point of view or value orientation. Values are embedded in language and symbols. Because speaking communicates a value orientation and implies a value judgment, to practice tolerance consistently communicators should listen to understand rather than speak (288–90). Listening to understand *is fundamental* to practicing tolerance. Some critics of relativism argue that commitment to be consistently tolerant would lead a communicator to be consistently silent in the face of unethical practices such as slavery or torture, if slavery or torture were accepted cultural practices.

Rather than the give and take of communication among people with different points of view, an absolutist practice of tolerance can encourage a communication practice of **almost perpetual listening** where communicators listen to understand while not communicating their thoughts, concerns, or ethical judgments. How almost perpetual listening would create an ethical dilemma of tolerance varies for different forms of relativism.

For an individual relativist, almost perpetual listening would involve never communicating a judgment about the violent behavior of another person, for example, if violent behavior were consistent with that person's individual values. A situationist relativist would practice almost perpetual listening by repeatedly avoiding the communication of a judgment because she does not yet understand what is unique about a situation and, so, would repeatedly defer getting involved. Conventional relativists would practice almost perpetual listening whenever they are not members of a group, organization, or culture whose actions have raised ethical concerns. When conventional relativists are outsiders, they have no right to speak about their ethical concerns or judgments. Conventional relativists would withhold their ethical concerns and judgments on such important issues as the practices of war (e.g., torture of prisoners), the consequences of economic policies (e.g., international debt and debt forgiveness), educational practices (e.g., whether girls should be educated), or health practices (e.g., contraception, female or male circumcision, immunization, or treatment of diseases). Issues like these are part of larger problems of war, global environmental change, disease, and poverty that transcend cultural boundaries and require intercultural problem solving (see Bok, *Common Values*). Intercultural problem solving poses significant challenges for the practice of communication ethics. Chapter 10 will explore further some of these challenges.

Point to Ponder

❖ *Is there a relationship between practice of relativism and freedom? Between practices of relativism and care?*

Jonathan Sacks offers a different criticism of tolerance. Tolerance, he argues, is an ethical application of the political virtue of toleration. **Toleration** developed in the 17th and 18th centuries in response to that era's religious wars between Catholics and Protestants in Europe. One of these wars, known as the Thirty Years War, killed the equivalent of over 1% of the world's population ("Population Control"). The Thirty Years War demonstrated that the perpetual violence required to enforce governmental sanctioned belief threatened to destroy both Christianity and governments in Europe, unless Catholics and Protestants learned to politically tolerate the beliefs each considered wrong. Political reality is that majorities eventually lose power and become minorities who would be persecuted, a political reality experienced several times by Catholics and Protestants in England in the 16th through 18th centuries (Davies 343–552). Political toleration developed as that era's philosophers and political theorists concluded that faith or belief cannot be coerced, but must be freely chosen. Arguments and memories of the Thirty Years War arguably shaped the First Amendment to the US Constitution that prevents the US government from establishing an official religion. This created a legal basis for practices of political toleration needed for religious freedom. Toleration is a political virtue that protects everyone's freedom to believe, especially when political fortunes change and a majority becomes a minority. Sacks argues that the ethical value of tolerance in relativism changes toleration from *political acceptance* of belief, that others with whom I disagree with have a right to their beliefs even if I believe these beliefs are wrong, into *ethical acceptance* of beliefs, that beliefs of others with whom I disagree are now ethically correct or good. Political toleration treats disagreement as politically acceptable. Ethical tolerance treats disagreement as ethically unacceptable because tolerance requires ethical acceptance. Ethical tolerance requires that a communicator practicing ethical relativism keep her ethical disagreement to herself.

Casuistry: Balancing Values and Principles with Responsiveness

Both absolutist and relativist approaches to applying ethical values and principles have limitations in the practice of communication ethics. While absolutism encourages consistency, thus promoting integrity, absolutist reasoning also may produce ethical harm, when decision makers are not responsive to key stakeholders or the facts and circumstances of a situation. Recall Chapter 4's discussion of truth, Kant's argument that you must tell the truth to a murderer inquiring into your knowledge of her intended victim. Relativist approaches are more responsive, emphasizing tolerance and listening to people with different ideas and from different cultures. However, consistent practice of tolerance can promote powerlessness, even withdrawal from human interaction by encouraging silence in the face of significant ethical harm or atrocities. Casuistry offers a third approach for applying ethical values, principles, or rules. **Casuistry** is a method for balancing commitment to ethical values and principles with responsiveness to the persons, facts, and circumstances of a situation.

As Aristotle noted in the *Nicomachean Ethics*, there is a broad outline of what is usually good in ethics, but what is good can vary with the circumstances of a situation (64–5). The aim of casuistry is for a decision maker to first consider what is presumably ethically good, right, or virtuous and then consider facts and circumstances of a specific situation in deciding what is ethically fitting or responsive. Using casuistry to apply an ethical value or principle is similar to the practice of competent communication.

Competent communication involves applying principles, rules, or theories of communication in a way that is responsive to the people and circumstances of specific communication situations (Wilson and Sabee). Competent communicators recognize that sometimes we need to make exceptions in applying communication rules, principles, or theories to discern a fitting communication response. Casuistry is a process of reasoning that balances consistency in applying ethical values and principles with ethical responsiveness to the interests of key stakeholders to survive and thrive and the facts and circumstances of a situation. Casuistry sometimes results in making an exception to an ethical value, principle, or rule. Making an exception in casuistry does not diminish the importance or presumption of a value, principle, or rule, such as honesty is the best policy. What casuistry does, is provide a systematic method for recognizing and responding to ethical harm that sometimes is caused by a rigorously consistent practice of an ethical value, principle, or rule, such as being honest with an inquiring murderer.

To discern an ethically fitting course of action, casuistic reasoning uses a paradigm case that illustrates applying an ethical principle to the facts and circumstances of a situation (Duval 31; Jonsen and Toulmin 251–2; Toulmin 167–74). Casuists begin with careful examination of the facts and circumstances of a situation and identifying key stakeholders and their interests. In casuistry, sometimes a decision maker would be consistent in applying an ethical value or principle, such as following a paradigm case of telling the truth. Other times a decision maker would make an exception, because of facts or circumstances of a situation. Casuistry offers a way to navigate between absolutism and relativism, by searching for a point of proportion between consistency and tolerance that is ethically fitting to the facts and circumstances of a situation. The goal of casuistry is discerning the most ethically fitting or good way to act in a specific situation by using ethical reasoning to decide whether or how to make exceptions to the practice of an ethical value, principle, or rule.

Careful examination of the facts and circumstances of a situation helps a decision maker identify ethical values, principles, or rules that are relevant in deciding how to communicate ethically in that situation. A decision maker using casuistry then would identify a paradigm case for applying a relevant ethical principle. A **paradigm case** illustrates in a story or narrative a clear application of an ethical value, principle, or rule. "Honesty is the best policy," "Keep a confidence secret," or "Take turns when speaking" are examples of ethical principles expressed as maxims. "Honesty is the best policy" applies the value of truthfulness. "Keep a confidence secret" applies the value of privacy, while "Take turns when speaking" applies procedural justice. A casuist may draw upon her experience or a story learned as a child for the paradigm case to apply an ethical principle or value. A paradigm case for the maxim "Keep a confidence secret," could be based on an experience from childhood or a family story about someone who faced the choice of whether to disclose a secret. A paradigm case could also be a story from history, literature, or even current events that clearly illustrates the good or harm of keeping or disclosing a secret. In casuistry, decision makers use paradigm cases that clearly illustrate how to apply an ethical principle or rule as a guide for thinking about and evaluating communication choices. Using the relevant paradigm case, a decision maker would compare the facts of a situation to the facts of the paradigm case to identify how the situation's facts and circumstances are similar to or different from those of the paradigm case. The goal is to identify ethically significant similarities and differences. When there are ethically significant differences, a decision maker has more reason to make an exception.

In the chapter's opening case, the principle of "keeping secret communication told in confidence" applies to Clarice's ethical issue, whether to disclose or keep secret Joycelyn's pregnancy. In a paradigm case of keeping a confidence, the recipient of confidential self-disclosure would not reveal private information unless the discloser gives permission. Real-life situations, however, may not neatly fit paradigm cases. Joycelyn is a volunteer working in a loosely religious organization for 8- to 18-year-old children. Using casuistry, Clarice would decide how to act by first identifying the legitimate interests of all the stakeholders, along with the other facts and circumstances of this situation. She then would consider those interests, facts, and circumstances with the accumulation of arguments for making an exception to the ethical principle of keeping a confidence secret. It might include an argument that children need adult role models as part of their moral development or that parents should have a role in identifying acceptable role models for their children. In casuistry, a decision maker evaluates the different arguments for making an exception for applying an ethical principle in two ways. First, how well does the argument identify and incorporate factual differences from the paradigm case and, second, how well does the argument justify an action that is ethically responsive to the legitimate interests of key stakeholders to survive and thrive?

Everyday Communication Ethics

❖ *What stories would you tell to explain to others the values of your personal ethical standard?*

The concepts of presumption and burden of proof are critical to the practice of casuistry. The principle or rule of a paradigm case is presumed to apply in any situation that presents the same ethical issue. A **presumption** is a belief, value, principle, or rule that is accepted without argument. In casuistry, a decision maker *begins* with presumption that an ethical value, principle, or rule should be applied. It is applied unless there is an ethically justifiable argument based upon the facts and circumstances of the situation that the principle or rule should be modified or discarded. Reasoning with presumption contributes to the integrity of casuistry. Modifications or exceptions to the application of an ethical value, principle, or rule must be ethically justified by an argument that has two qualities. First, the argument must be based upon facts and circumstances identified in the first two steps of ethical reasoning that identifies ethical issues and facts, including legitimate interests of seen and unseen stakeholders. Second, the argument must meet a burden of proof. A **burden of proof** is a test of reasoning that an argument must meet before a decision maker is justified in modifying or making an exception to presumption. Meeting a burden of proof does not change the presumption that the ethical value, principle, or rule should be practiced. Rather, it provides a method for compromising with integrity in a specific situation. Modifying or making an exception to presumption is possible but not automatic or easy. Discussion of Bok's principle of veracity and white lies in Chapter 4 (*Lying*) is an example of granting exceptions using burden of proof.

When decision makers use presumption and burden of proof in their deliberations, they create a justification for themselves and to present to others for examination about what is good, right, or virtuous in a specific situation. Using presumption and burden of proof in casuistry helps distinguish ethical justifications about what is good, right, or virtuous from rationalizations based upon self-interest or poorly examined convention. In the chapter's opening case, if Clarice considers presumption and burden of proof in her ethical reasoning about whether to remain silent and keep Joycelyn's confidence secret or to speak and disclose her secret to the parents involved in Kid's Klub, she would be developing an ethical justification for her decision. The quality of the justification depends upon how well it meets the burden of proof for different audiences or publics. **Bok's three tests of publicity** are burdens of proof for ethical justification in casuistry: that the decision maker convinces her conscience; that the decision maker convinces her friends and colleagues; and the most difficult test of all, that the decision maker convinces people with all viewpoints and allegiances, including persons who are more likely to disagree with her (*Lying,* 94–103). An argument to make an exception to presumption should pass at least one of these tests of publicity. The strongest ethical justifications meet the most difficult burden of proof of convincing people of all viewpoints and allegiances. In the case of Clarice and Joycelyn, if Clarice decides that she should talk to the parents of Kid's Klub members about Joycelyn's pregnancy and her role in the organization, justifying her decision to *both* Joycelyn and to the parents would meet a stronger burden of proof than justifying her decision only to her conscience.

Everyday Communication Ethics

❖   *Use one of Bok's three tests of publicity to examine a reason you gave to make an exception to your personal ethical standard.*

Turn taking is a communication practice of justice that illustrates how you may use presumption and burden of proof in ethical decision making about communication. In a democratic society, a paradigm case of turn taking presumes a rule that everyone present should have a turn speaking her mind. Your paradigm case for turn taking may be an experience from school, work, or a club, or your paradigm case might be a story of a historical event. Perhaps your paradigm case allows each participant to speak as long as she wishes before a decision is made. Whatever your paradigm case is, it would clearly illustrate how this rule practices distributive justice of the opportunity to speak. Now, imagine you are organizing a meeting on a controversial topic. You expect a large attendance, which could justify modification of the turn taking rule illustrated in your paradigm case, for example using a time limit for each speaker. If there is evidence that most of the people present at a meeting will share the same viewpoint, you might argue for an exception to a presumption of equal turn taking that would allow expression of different viewpoints. You might argue that the facts of this situation indicate that the presumed practice of "everyone getting an opportunity to speak" should be modified to taking turns between voices expressing different views. Your argument would need to convince others that modifying the ethical presumption of turn taking is justified in this circumstance to assure that a minority viewpoint is not drowned out. If your argument is convincing to people with different viewpoints, including those who may not get a chance to speak, you have a strong ethical justification for making this exception. If your reasons are not convincing that granting this exception is fair, it indicates that you need to reexamine your proposal and justifications for a fair distribution of the opportunity to speak.

Casuistry is a method that provides an opportunity to compromise with integrity the presumption for consistently applying an ethical value, principle, or rule. It encourages consistent practice of your personal ethical commitments while also allowing for ethical responsiveness to the key stakeholders and facts and circumstances of a specific situation. Sometimes the facts of a situation are clearly comparable to a paradigm case, allowing for consistent application of a value, principle, or rule. Some situations, however, can vary in significant ways, calling into question the ethical responsiveness of a one-size-fits-all principle or rule.

Casuistry may also help with decision making in situations where more than one ethical value, principle, or rule can be applied. Here, you can use casuistry to consider, weigh, or prioritize your ethical responsibilities and commitments by focusing on the facts of the situation, rather than focusing solely on the tension or conflict between ethical principles or values. Casuistry encourages you to think about what is ethically at stake by focusing your decision making on what is ethically responsive to the interests of key stakeholders and the facts and circumstances of a specific situation, rather than the ethical certainty of universally and abstractly applying ethical values, principles, or rules. Jonsen and Toulmin's experience with casuistic reasoning on a commission of biomedical ethicists led them to conclude that when the commissioners applied their ethical principles to problems with certainty, the process of ethical decision making among the commissioners fell apart. When their reasoning focused on what was ethically at stake in a situation by careful examination of its facts and circumstances, they could agree upon a course of action as a commission (16–9). Reasoning with casuistry enabled this group to make a decision, while reasoning with certainty stalled or stopped decision making.

Casuistic reasoning offers a way to honor your personal ethical commitments, while also being ethically responsive to the stakeholders, facts, and circumstances of situations you face. Some may find the responsiveness of casuistry to stakeholders, facts, and circumstances too inconsistent to fulfill ethical responsibilities with integrity, whether those responsibilities are to tell the truth, keep confidences secret, practice tolerance, or some other ethical principle of communication. Others may find it too rigid to be ethically responsive to the interests of others.

Conclusion

Ethical reasoning is important for making decisions about how to communicate ethically. An important element in ethical reasoning is discerning how to apply values, principles, or rules of your personal ethical standard. This chapter has presented three different approaches to applying values, principles, or rules—absolutism, relativism, and casuistry. Each approach helps you examine your ethical reasoning for rationalizations in different ways. Absolutism characteristic of the categorical imperative encourages you to recognize when you are tempted to apply ethical principles to others, but to make exceptions for yourself by rationalizing your self-interest or the interests of those you care for, while ignoring the legitimate interests of others. The different forms of relativism encourage tolerance and, so, discourage you from assuming you have the ethical answer without careful examination of the facts and circumstances of a situation. Relativism discourages certainty, challenging you to suspend your ethical judgment to listen to others and encouraging use of your moral imagination. With casuistry, decision makers make judgments about what is ethically fitting to a specific situation by responsively considering and weighing the legitimate interests of key stakeholders and the facts and circumstances of a situation while also honoring presumption of an ethical principle or rule. This is accomplished by requiring that situational exceptions to presumption be justified with reasoning that meets a burden of proof. Casuistry encourages the exercise of your moral imagination to responsively consider the interests of stakeholders to survive and thrive and the facts and circumstances of a situation, in order to apply with integrity relevant ethical principles and values. Absolutism, relativism, and casuistry are three approaches to ethical reasoning, each of which offers a coherent and rigorous approach for applying the ethical principles and values of your personal ethical standard for communication.

Vocabulary

Cases for Discussion

Directions Use ethical reasoning to identify key ethical issues, facts of each case, seen and unseen stakeholders and their interests, and the three recurring questions of communication ethics. Identify which ethical values are relevant for each case. Explain whether absolutism, some form of relativism or casuistry is most ethically relevant to applying ethical values and principles you would use.

1. Time and Timeliness—Three Cases for Comparison

Time is precious in our fast-paced world. Practices of time create nonverbal messages about what is important. How we use time is often seen as a practice of respect or disrespect. Below are three different cases about the practice of "timeliness" in relationships. After examining each of these cases using the process of ethical reasoning, identify similarities and differences among the three cases in your approach to ethical reasoning. Did you use absolutism, some form of relativism, or casuistry? Identify strengths and limitations of your use of absolutism, relativism, or casuistry.

Case One—The Game Mikayla checked her watch for the third time. Carolyn had not shown up. The team was short one player. If Carolyn did not arrive before the referee inspects the equipment, the team would forfeit the game. Mikayla did not know why she was surprised. Carolyn rarely arrived early for anything. The other day Susan, another team member, joked that Carolyn would be late for her own funeral. The referee called for the two teams to line up to inspect their uniforms and equipment. As Mikayla walked out to meet with the referee to forfeit the game, up walked Carolyn, in uniform carrying her shoes.

What and how should Mikayla communicate?

Case Two—Brothers Chris tapped the steering wheel in time to the music. He had been waiting ten minutes for his brother, Burt. Burt did not own a car and needed a ride to a doctor's appointment that was required for his new job. Chris had offered Burt a ride, with the warning that Burt needed to be on time so Chris would not be late for work. If Burt did not show up soon, Chris would have to drive off without Burt or be late for work. Chris's supervisor did not tolerate people showing up late for shifts.

What and how should Chris communicate when he sees Burt?

Case Three—The Meeting Karen looked around the table. Everyone was there, except Ari. "If Ari is late, at least he shows up at the meeting," Karen thought wryly. Ari always had an explanation for being late. Whenever he is late, Suellen, the team leader, just nods her head and continues the meeting. Today's is a last-minute meeting about the Morrison project. Last Tuesday's agenda was to decide the project's final timeline. Ari showed up for the last half of that meeting, after everyone else had agreed to the timeline. Looking over the timeline, Ari told Suellen that he could not possibly meet these deadlines. Today's meeting is to create a new timeline, and was supposed to start 15 minutes ago. Ari just now walked in, apologizing and saying that he had been on the phone talking to another client. Suellen nods and says, "Now that everyone's here, let's look at a realistic timeline for the Morrison project."

What and how should Karen communicate? What are the ethical issues and tension points for Karen remaining silent? For speaking up?

2. Dating

Every fall Stephanie's extended family gathered at the family farm for a weekend of picking apples. Her grandparents started this tradition. The farm now belonged to Uncle Jordan. He never married and had children. Jordan is Stephanie's favorite uncle. When she was little, she followed him around the farm. He answered her questions and when she was big enough, showed her how machinery and equipment worked.

The rest of the family is outside, either playing or watching the annual family touch football game. Stephanie's boyfriend of two years, Amir, is playing football. Stephanie stayed inside to talk to Uncle Jordan.

"Are you going to convert?" Stephanie blinked. "Excuse me?" Uncle Jordan repeated, "I said, are you going to convert?"

What should Stephanie say? How should she say it?

3. Life and Death

Michael has terminal cancer. He has spent the last 18 months in and out of the hospital with surgery and chemotherapy. The treatments never stopped the cancer for long. He knows that this may be his last stay in the hospital.

Michael's doctor, Dr. Carlson, is visiting on morning rounds. Dr. Carlson sees that Michael's body systems are slowly failing. He is having difficulty breathing. At this stage, Dr. Carlson has two medical options to offer. The more aggressive option is to put Michael on a ventilator to help him breathe. If Michael goes on the ventilator, he would probably die on the ventilator. The second option is to administer morphine. With morphine, Michael would slip into death with less pain, although there would be no help with his breathing. There is a slender, remote chance that either treatment could help Michael rally and live, at least for a short while.

What and how should Dr. Carlson communicate to Michael?

References

Aristotle. *The Ethics of Aristotle: The Nicomachean Ethics.* Trans. J.A.K. Thomson. New York: Penguin, 1976.

Bok, Sissela. *Common Values.* Columbia, MO: U of Missouri P, 1995.

Bok, Sissela. *Lying: Moral Choice in Public and Private Life.* New York: Vintage Books, 1989.

Bok, Sissela. *Secrets: On the Ethics of Concealment and Revelation.* New York: Vintage Books, 1989.

Brummett, Barry. "A Defense of Ethical Relativism as Rhetorically Grounded." *The Western Journal of Speech Communication* 45.4 (1981): 286–98.

Davies, Norma. *The Isles: A History.* New York: Oxford UP, 1999.

Duval, R. Shannon. *Encyclopedia of Ethics.* New York: Facts on File, 1999.

Gade, Christian B.N. "What is *Ubuntu*? Different Interpretations Among South Africans of African Descent." *South African Journal of Philosophy* 31.3 (2012): 484–93.

Jaska, James A. and Michael S. Pritchard. *Communication Ethics: Methods of Analysis.* 2nd ed. Belmont, CA: Wadsworth, 1994.

Jonsen, Albert R. and Stephen Toulmin. *The Abuse of Casuistry: A History of Moral Reasoning.* Berkeley, CA: U of California P, 1988.

Kant, Immanuel. *Groundwork of the Metaphysics of Morals.* 1797. Trans. H.J. Paton. New York: Harper, 1964.

"Population Control Marauder Style: Data Points." *The New York Times.* 5 November 2011. www.nytimes.com/2011/11/06/opinion/sunday/population-control-marauder-style.html. Date accessed: 14 September 2017.

Sacks, Jonathan. *The Home We Build Together: Recreating Society.* New York: Continuum, 2007.

The Lord of the Rings Trilogy: The Fellowship of the Ring (2001), *The Two Towers* (2002), and *The Return of the Ring* (2003). Dir. Peter Jackson. Prod. Barrie M. Osborne, et al. Los Angeles, CA: New Line Home Entertainment.

Toulmin, Stephen. *Return to Reason*. Cambridge, MA: Harvard UP, 2001.

Tutu, Desmond. *No Future Without Forgiveness*. New York: Random, 1999.

Waghid, Yusef and Paul Smeyers. "Reconsidering *Ubuntu*: On the Educational Potential of a Particular Ethics of Care." *Educational Philosophy and Theory* 44.S2 (2012): 6–20.

Wilson, Steven R. and Christina M. Sabee. "Explicating Communicative Competence as a Theoretical Term." *Handbook of Communication and Social Interaction Skills*. Eds. John O. Greene and Brant Burleson. Mahwah, NJ: LEA, 2003. 3–50.

Part II

APPLYING ETHICAL THEORIES TO HUMAN COMMUNICATION

6

TRADITIONAL APPROACHES TO
ETHICAL THEORY

Today is Jordan's and Leslie's second anniversary as a couple. The plan for the evening is dinner at their favorite restaurant, then a concert by their favorite band. Jordan, a few minutes early, knocks on the door of Leslie's apartment. What he sees when the door opens surprises him. Leslie's hair is cut very short and dyed a color that, frankly, looks unhealthy, at least to Jordan. "Hi, Jordan. You're early. I'm just about ready" says Leslie. "You look different," says Jordan. Leslie replies, "I wanted a new look. What do you think?" Jordan swallows.

A friend lying, a coworker stealing, a family member breaking a promise, or receiving a gift from a relative or close friend that you really do not like are situations where you rely on your ethical judgment about how to communicate. In this chapter, you will read about three traditional ethical theories that you could use to guide your discernment and decision making about communication—virtue ethics, moral rights, and utilitarianism. Each theory is a well-developed and recognized ethical theory of Western culture before the 20th century. Virtue ethics focuses on ethical character. It was well developed in ancient Greece and Rome, over 2,000 years ago. Its popularity has grown and receded many times over the centuries. Philosopher Alasdair MacIntyre has again brought virtue theory into prominence. This discussion of virtue ethics relies upon Aristotle, who lived in the fourth century BCE. Communication ethicists are interested in Aristotle's theory of virtue, because he is an early theorist of public or civic communication (Aristotle *Rhetoric*). The ethical theories of moral rights and utilitarianism are newer, growing out of work of philosophers beginning in the 17th century CE, the modern era of Western culture. Moral rights theory identifies universal rights that belong to every human being. Decision makers use utilitarianism to guide decision making about how to act for "the greatest good for the greatest number." Virtue ethics, moral rights, and utilitarianism have adherents who claim that their approach to ethics is superior to other approaches.

In this chapter, you will read a summary of the main ideas of each theory, a brief discussion of its application to communication, some major criticisms or limitations, and questions about its relevance to your ethical commitments and practice of communication ethics. Notice how each theory reinforces or challenges your understanding of one or more of the ethical values of communication—truth or truthfulness, justice, freedom, care, integrity, or honor. Studying different ethical theories stimulates your moral imagination to think about alternative responses you may use in your ethical reasoning. You may decide to incorporate one of these theories into your personal ethical standard. Even if you disagree with a theory, understanding its ideas and concepts contributes to your ability to think about and consider different ethical viewpoints and distinguish between ethical justifications and rationalization.

Virtue Ethics

Virtue refers to the quality of a person's character. **Virtue ethics** presume the foundation of ethical action is good personal character. People who have good character, such as kindness or courage, act ethically. We do not expect a person of good character to lie. Aristotle claims that personal goodness or virtue is the result of habit. Habits are based upon a person's disposition (emotions and personality) and their past actions. **Aristotle's concept of virtue** is a personality characteristic or habit of feeling and action with two qualities (*Nicomachean Ethics* 98–108). First, it is ethically good or excellent. Second, it exists as a mean or point of proportion on a continuum between two extremes of personality or feeling that are **vices**. One vice or extreme is a lack or deficiency of the emotion or personal quality. The other vice is an excess of that quality. The emotion of fear and disposition of confidence has a deficiency of cowardice and an extreme of rashness. The virtue or excellence of fear and confidence is courage. Not all habits are virtuous, only those that are ethically good. In fact, some emotions and dispositions are always wrong. There is no excellence or virtue for the emotions of malice or jealousy.

The table below presents examples of virtue according to Aristotle. Virtue exists as a mean or point of proportion between two vices. Once you know the mean for a virtue, you develop habits to practice the virtue. Virtue theory is distinctive because it focuses on what is good or not good in human emotion. In Chapter 2 you read how the moral emotions of empathy, the equality bias, and disgust influence moral development. In Chapter 4 you read about the emotional basis of justice in the equality bias, care in empathy, and honor in disgust. Philosopher Martha Nussbaum argues that emotions play an important role in ethical decision making, giving direction to our reasoning and helping us make judgments or appraisals of how objects, events, even people affect personal well-being. Relying on emotion alone sometimes makes decision makers overly optimistic that their actions are ethically good, because emotions can obscure negative consequences of an action. While emotion is important for recognizing ethical issues and motivating action, cognitive processes such as perspective-taking and reasoning balance emotion with critical evaluation. Reasoning with facts, a decision maker evaluates the relevance of her emotion, whether her emotion is serious or trivial regarding legitimate interests of others to survive or thrive, and whether her emotionally directed decision would be helpful or possibly make a situation worse. Aristotle's virtue theory recognizes that emotions alone can be unreliable guides for our thinking and action. Sometimes emotions promote human survival and thriving and sometimes they promote harm. When emotion is combined with cognitive processes, such as perspective-taking and reasoning with facts, decision makers are prompted to choose actions and develop habits that move from excess or deficiency towards excellence or virtue in emotion and action.

Aristotle's concept of virtue as excellence or the mean between excess and deficiency of character is often misinterpreted as a midpoint or middle ground between excess and deficiency. This reduces virtue to an ethical version of "splitting the difference" between extremes, as if virtue were a mathematical formula for computing an average. Aristotle notes in the *Nicomachean Ethics* that there may be exceptions to ethical practices of virtue in a specific situation (69–72). Stanley Cunningham points out that Aristotle uses the idea of the **mean as a metaphor for harmony or proportion** that varies with the person and the situation (7–8). For Aristotle, the mean must be proper to the person, because dispositions vary from person to person. What is courageous communication for a shy person would not be courageous for an extrovert. What is virtuous also may be different in different situations. Both a whistleblower and a reporter who refuses to reveal her sources for a news story could exhibit the virtue of courageous communication in different ways. Courageous communication for a whistleblower may require disclosing unethical or illegal conduct. For a reporter writing a story about illegal conduct, however, courageous communication may involve silence to protect a person revealing illegal conduct but is legitimately afraid of significant retaliation. In the chapter's opening case, an honest opinion

Table 6.1 Aristotle's Virtues

Disposition or Feeling	Excess	Mean	Deficiency
Fear and Confidence	Rashness	Courage	Cowardice
Shame	Shyness	Modesty	Shamelessness
Indignation	Envy	Righteousness	Malicious enjoyment
Self-expression	Boastfulness	Truthfulness	Understatement
Conversation	Buffoonery	Wittiness	Boorishness
Social Conduct	Obsequiousness	Friendliness	Cantankerousness

about how a new hair color looks would be virtuous, but a vice when asked for in front of other people at a party. Being consistently honest is not virtuous, because honesty may not be in harmony or proportion with the facts and circumstances of a situation. Honesty does not protect the intended victim of an inquiring murderer. Virtue is not absolute or about computing an average between excess and deficiency. It is a reason-based process of discernment that identifies an ethically good way to act in a specific situation. What is ethically good is in harmony with the facts and circumstances of that situation and the disposition of the communicator.

Points to Ponder

❖ *What dispositions, feelings, emotions, or personality characteristics are important for communication excellence? What are the excesses and deficiencies?*

Individuals and communities both have roles to play in practicing virtue. Although virtue is an individual excellence, it also is an ethical excellence recognized within a community. Different communities possess different virtues or standards of excellence. A community's stories illustrate virtues of a community (MacIntyre). Communities have an interest in developing specific virtues in their members which may become part of a practice of an honor code (Appiah; Stewart).

Developing individual virtue involves discerning the point of harmony between personal excesses and deficiencies that is closest to the community's standards of ethical excellence. Practicing honesty as a community-based or shared virtue challenges you to notice your tendency toward being untruthful and then to pull yourself toward the community's standard of honesty. Community members can help each other achieve or maintain their community's standard of virtue. One function of ethical persuasion is to help individuals locate a sense of proportion or harmony that identifies virtue within a community, and persuade audiences to act virtuously. Appiah provides examples of ethical persuasion based on virtues in honor codes that were successful in ending dueling in Western culture, the transatlantic slave trade, and foot binding in China.

Virtue theory provides a framework for talking about the relationship between character and ethics. Some critics argue the focus on character instead of action is a limitation of virtue ethics. Someone with a habit of honesty may lie in certain situations. In fact, the success of a lie depends upon others perceiving the liar as honest. A second criticism is that it presumes everyone understands and agrees upon the virtues of the community's standard of ethical excellence. Virtue theory does not tell us how to decide which virtues are most important. A communication ethics response to this criticism is that communication processes of debate, dialogue, discussion, and persuasion coconstruct, maintain, and sometimes change a community's standards of excellence. Appiah's analysis of how honor codes change points to the importance of argumentation and persuasion about virtue for a community. A third criticism is that virtue theory provides us with no guidance for making decisions in situations where two virtues are in conflict. How do we choose between the virtues of honesty and care in deciding whether to be honest with a friend or to accept an unwanted gift from a relative? Should a doctor tell the truth about recovery rates for a surgical procedure if it might cause someone to give up on therapy, reducing chances of recovery? While virtue theory alone does not help us resolve ethical dilemmas or tragedies, communication processes of debate, dialogue, discussion, and persuasion can help decision makers address such dilemmas. Finally, when the focus of virtue theory becomes personal integrity or honor, a decision maker's attention may turn away from the impact of her actions on others to herself. A focus on personal integrity or honor through the consistent practice of virtue may make it easy to overlook legitimate interests of unseen others or the community. Applying Appiah's analysis of how honor codes motivate actions, a decision maker may be more motivated by receiving respect of others in the honor community than by the virtues of the honor code. Such persons are not likely to go above and beyond the honor code by rigorously and responsively practicing the code's virtues.

Aristotle's theory of virtue encourages us to aim for ethical excellence, while also being responsive to how situations vary. What is ethically excellent in one situation might not be ethically excellent in another. What insights does Aristotle's theory of virtue as ethical excellence between excess and deficiency of feelings and personal dispositions contribute to your practice of communication ethics?

Moral Rights

In Western culture, the idea that everyone has rights is no surprise. Media crime dramas refer to the legal right to an attorney. American politicians often refer to the rights listed in the Declaration of Independence—"life, liberty, and the pursuit of happiness." The United Nations' Universal Declaration of Human Rights lists what some consider the most comprehensive list of rights. Organizations like Amnesty International issue reports on human rights violations around the world. When told by a bureaucrat that your request is denied, you may respond, "But it's my right!" Have you ever wondered if all rights are the same? There are legal rights guaranteed in law, civil rights based upon citizenship or membership in a community, and human or moral rights. While legal and civil rights are important, this discussion focuses on moral or human rights.

The ethical significance of **moral rights** is that they provide individuals significant protection from harm caused by government or other persons. Protection from harm is good, right, and virtuous for an individual, protecting fundamental interests of individuals that improve their lives. You may be familiar with the freedom to speak, a moral right recognized in the US Bill of Rights. In the chapter's opening case, Jordan might claim freedom of speech gives him the right to say what he thinks about Leslie's new look. After reading about moral rights, consider whether there are moral rights of communication other than freedom of speech or expression.

There are **two functions of moral rights**. The first function is to give us freedom of action. This includes such rights as freedom of speech, freedom of religion, or the freedom to move to another city to search for a job. By giving us freedom, moral rights protect our opportunities to make choices. The second function of moral rights is to protect fundamental interests of individuals as human beings, especially in how others treat them (Martin 325). For example, the moral right not to be killed or tortured protects the interest of a person to live until her natural or accidental death. By protecting fundamental ethical interests of human beings, moral rights help improve people's lives.

According to moral rights theory, people have moral rights because they are human, so **moral rights are universal** for all human beings. While moral rights are universal, they are not absolute (Feinberg; Martin). At first, this may seem confusing. While everyone has moral rights, exercising moral rights is not relevant in every situation. Understanding how food, clothing, and shelter are moral rights makes this clearer. Moral rights protect individual human interest against voluntary actions of a government that would deprive people of adequate food, for example by diverting domestic food supplies for sale on international markets to pay for government projects. In contrast, the loss of food, clothing, or shelter in a natural disaster, such as a flood, hurricane, or typhoon, does not violate anyone's moral rights. A flood is not voluntary; it is an act of nature which human decisions did not directly cause. Although a flood can deprive people of what they need to survive, it does not deprive people of their moral rights. Because natural forces are not voluntary, they are neither ethical nor unethical. Human action, however, is voluntary, because people can choose how they act. Human action may be ethical or unethical, because people make choices that impact the interests of others to survive and thrive. It is unethical to interfere with aid to victims of a natural disaster or interfere with reasonable efforts to prevent harm from future natural disasters. Such actions undermine moral rights of the victims to have basic resources to survive.

Point to Ponder

❖ *Are there limits to ethically practicing moral rights? Is it ethical to always exercise your moral rights?*

Moral rights are universal in a second way. They are not dependent on individual or government recognition, although societies differ as to which rights are recognized as most important. Western industrialized societies place high value on rights of freedom, while other societies may place high value on rights to food, clothing, and shelter. Such differences can be a source of intercultural misunderstanding, even conflict. Theorists claim that moral rights are universal because they are based on the fundamental quality of being human. Once you recognize a fundamental quality of being human, such as the capacity for reason or care of others, you have a basis for arguing for a moral right (Feinberg 85–91). One of the earliest legal articulations of the moral right of freedom is the UK's Magna Carta in 1215 (Vincent), which identifies areas of freedom for subjects that the king cannot violate. From this beginning, moral rights of freedom of speech and conscience, not to be enslaved, religious freedom, and civil rights developed in the UK (Ashley). These beginnings were brought by English colonists to North America. Human equality is a basis of the moral right of freedom articulated in the US Declaration of Independence and Bill of Rights to the US Constitution.

If you identify a moral right as part of your personal ethical standard, you have a **duty** or obligation to protect that right. If you do not meet this duty, you deny a person one of their fundamental rights as a human being. How can you meet these duties? Some duties require you *not* to act to protect a right, while other duties require action to protect and maintain a right. If you believe freedom of speech is a moral right, you have a duty to limit legal and other restrictions on resources for speaking. To protect the freedom to speak, you must refrain from actions that would censor or stop a speaker, even if you disagree with what she will say. Fulfilling this duty does not prevent you from speaking your mind, if you do not deny another person opportunity to speak. Is there an unpopular speaker whose right to speak you would need to protect? Protecting freedom requires action to maintain a freedom, including creation of community resources that maintain that freedom. For example, people need to be educated so they are prepared to speak and become confident speakers. They also need access to reliable and accurate information so they can knowledgeably contribute to public discussion; otherwise, they are unintentionally deceiving others and promoting cynicism. People also need access to spaces or technology to exercise their freedom in public conversation, debate, dialogue, and discussion. Maintaining the right to free speech or expression involves protecting and managing the resources needed for fair and just communication practices, especially when resources are limited.

There is no complete agreement on what are fundamental moral rights. The Universal Declaration of Human Rights lists rights in 30 articles, from "No one shall be subjected to torture or to cruel, inhuman, or degrading treatment or punishment," to parents having a "right to choose the kind of education that shall be given to their children." The US Declaration of Independence lists three rights—life, liberty, and the pursuit of happiness. In the UK, there is no clear consensus based on a constitutional document that identifies rights beyond Magna Carta. Because your understanding of what are fundamental moral rights will depend on what you see as the most significant quality of being human, your choice of the most important moral rights may differ from those prioritized by others.

Kant and Moral Rights

Kant's categorical imperative has significantly influenced understanding of moral rights in Western culture. Chapter 5 discussed the categorical imperative as an absolutist approach for applying ethical principles—"Act only on that maxim through which you can at the same time will that it should become a universal law" (88). The categorical imperative claims we have a duty to apply ethical principles consistently, without exceptions. Kant's second expression of the categorical imperative is less familiar but more relevant to the discussion of moral rights—"Act in such a way that you always treat humanity, whether in your own person or in the person of any other, never simply as a means, but always at the same time an end" (96). In the second expression, Kant is arguing against the abuse of objectification, treating a person without her permission as an instrument or means for achieving a goal. Treating people as subjects rather than objects recognizes their human dignity and promotes their survival and thriving.

For Kant, the basis for human dignity is the human capacity for reason and making choices. Communicators have a duty to tell the truth, as they understand it, to encourage development of this capacity. Applying Kant's second version of the categorical imperative to the chapter's opening case, Jordan would decide to be honest because he respects Leslie's human dignity. Leslie is not a means for Jordan to feel good about himself as he affirms Leslie, by saying he likes her new hairstyle. Dishonesty leads Leslie to draw inaccurate conclusions about Jordan and their relationship. It also could encourage Leslie to make arguably questionable or poor decisions in the future. When we use Kant to help us understand the nature of moral rights, we place a high value on the truthfulness of communication and freedom to make choices. We have two duties, to promote accurate and reliable communication for decision making and promote practices such as literacy so individuals can distinguish between deceptive and truthful communication.

Textbox 6.1

The Universal Declaration of Human Rights

On April 10, 1948, the United Nations General Assembly adopted The Universal Declaration of Human Rights. Below are articles that involve communication.

Article 1—All human beings are born free and equal in dignity and rights. They are endowed with reason and conscience and should act towards one another in a spirit of brotherhood.

Article 3—Everyone has the right to life, liberty and security of person.

Article 6—Everyone has the right to recognition everywhere as a person before the law.

Article 12—No one shall be subjected to arbitrary interference with his privacy, family, home or correspondence, nor to attacks upon his honour and reputation. Everyone has the right to the protection of the law against such interference or attacks.

Article 18—Everyone has the right to freedom of thought, conscience and religion; this right includes freedom to change his religion or belief, and freedom, either alone or in community with others and in public or private, to manifest his religion or belief in teaching, practice, worship and observance.

Article 19—Everyone has the right to freedom of opinion and expression; this right includes freedom to hold opinions without interference and to seek, receive and impart information and ideas through any media and regardless of frontiers.

Article 30—Nothing in this Declaration may be interpreted as implying for any State, group or person any right to engage in any activity or to perform any act aimed at the destruction of any of the rights and freedoms set forth herein.

From "Universal Declaration of Human Rights" United Nations General Assembly

© 10 December 1948. Reprinted with permission of the United Nations

Moral Rights of Communication

Freedom of speech is well recognized in Western industrialized countries in law and politics (see Tedford and Herbeck; Fraleigh and Tuman). The UN Universal Declaration of Human Rights recognizes freedom of expression in Article 19. Speaking or expression, however, is not all there is to communicating. The US Supreme Court has begun to recognize, in small ways, a right to hear, to learn, and to know (Bezanson). Are there other communication rights besides freedom of speech or expression, such as listening? A **moral right of listening** might require more than removing obstacles and restrictions on speaking. If a moral right of listening included a right to be listened to, it would involve a responsibility to listen, not only speak. We would have a duty to listen to understand, including listening to people with whom we disagree because we find their ideas objectionable.

Intercultural communication poses a different challenge. Different cultures have different understandings of what are moral rights. Cultural relativists argue that moral rights are not universal but reflect values of traditional Western philosophy (see Fagan). Global mass communication illustrates this challenge. Western mass media conglomerates use freedom of speech to justify use of Western mass media formats in non-Western cultures. This places more emphasis on the rights of conglomerates to communicate than the right of individual members of a local culture to communicate (Alleyne 388–9). You may be surprised by this claim, until you examine some of the practical obstacles to mass communication on a global scale. One obstacle is the cost and complexity of mass media technology. While satellite broadcasting and the internet have expanded opportunities to communicate, in practice the equipment and infrastructure needed is expensive for the average person around the world, except perhaps for mobile phone technology. Exercising freedom of speech is available to those with most access to media resources—media conglomerates, government, the wealthy, or other elites. Recall from the discussion of freedom in Chapter 4, that practicing freedom requires resources. Because global media conglomerates control significant resources, their practices of free speech may overwhelm local voices and cultural communication practices. Instead of freedom of speech, some mass media scholars argue for a **moral right to communicate** that recognizes the communication practices of local communities and cultures of less industrialized countries in Asia, Africa, and Latin America (Hammelink). A moral right to communicate would help maintain local communities and cultures by granting their local communication practices an ethical status. Proponents of the moral right to communicate argue that it is critical for the maintenance of local cultures.

Everyday Communication Ethics

❖ *How would you practice the freedom to communicate or a moral right to listening? What would be your duty to protect this moral right?*

The theory of moral rights is a thoughtful approach to communication ethics you might want to consider as part of your ethical commitments. It promotes thinking about whether there are fundamental rights of communication that belong to each person. You may have identified what you consider moral rights of communication, including some not mentioned in this discussion. Moral rights theory encourages you to consider the following questions about how you practice communication ethics. In thinking about these questions, consider how they challenge, expand, or support your personal ethical standard.

Utilitarianism

Cheating on tests and plagiarism have become commonplace today. Some people express surprise if a high school or college class has no one cheating.

Even parents can be involved. One father helped his son cheat by giving him a copy of the statewide high school graduation exam the father had access to at work (Lambert). Wells Fargo, a US bank, established work targets that were so high that employees had to open new bank accounts in the names of clients who did not ask for them (Corkery). Wells Fargo had policies that explicitly prohibited lying and cheating, but to keep their jobs, employees had to lie. German automobile corporation Volkswagen cheated on government tests for gas emissions and gas mileage for years (Ewing and Boudette), as did the Japanese corporation Takata in the production of faulty safety automobile airbags (Tabuchi). If you faced an opportunity to cheat, would you think about possible short-term consequences of cheating for yourself or consider long-term consequences of cheating for yourself and others? If you knew or suspected a classmate was cheating on a test, would you report it or remain silent? One way to decide the right thing to do is to think about the utility of cheating or not cheating. In ethics, the **utility** of an action is the beneficial consequences of that action for the greatest number of people. Arguably, if a greater number of people benefit from cheating than not cheating, cheating would have utility. In the chapter's opening case, Jordan might argue that lying about the new hairstyle benefits both Leslie and their relationship, making both feel good about themselves and their relationship. Utility is a central concept in utilitarianism. A utilitarian approach to your personal ethical standard would encourage you to think about the beneficial or harmful consequences of your communication on seen and unseen others, as well as yourself.

Point to Ponder

❖ *How does communication contribute to the happiness, in contrast to pleasure, of the greatest number of people?*

Utilitarianism guides us in making decisions based upon the amount of good our action would create for the greatest number of people. Utilitarianism focuses on action, rather than character or intentions. The goal of utilitarianism is to help the world become a better place (Chappell and Crisp 552). Utilitarians are not satisfied with doing enough to get by. They are committed to making the world a better place for the greatest number of people possible. If you included utilitarianism in your ethical commitments, you would focus on maximizing the benefits of your actions for others. As you read about the central concepts of utilitarianism, think about the potential of your communication practices to do good or harm others.

There are three aspects of utilitarianism—thinking about consequences, impartiality, and thinking about the welfare of others. First, utilitarianism asks us to think about the short- and long-term **consequences** of our actions on others. Utilitarianism helps us recognize that what and how we communicate matters. Would a communication act make a positive difference or would it cause harm? Are short-term consequences of our communication different from long-term consequences? Decisions about whether to speak or remain silent, which ideas we communicate, the verbal and nonverbal dimensions of a message, or to whom we listen, all have consequences for persons involved in the communication process. The important question for a utilitarian is whether you have thought about potential short- and long-term consequences of your communication.

The second aspect of utilitarianism is thinking about consequences of an action with impartiality. **Utilitarian impartiality** is different from being uninvolved or detached. It is extending the concern you have for yourself toward others (Chappell and Crisp 552–4). When a utilitarian evaluates the consequences of her actions, her individual interests are no more important than anyone else's interests. Utilitarian impartiality requires that you set aside individual self-interest for the good or happiness of others, whether it is your family, a group of friends, your workplace, community, nation, or even humanity. In the chapter's opening case, if Jordan practices utilitarian impartiality he would consider his feelings as no more important than Leslie's feelings. How might utilitarian impartiality work in practicing your ethical standard of communication? Using freedom of speech as an example, you could conclude that your right or opportunity to say what you think is no more important than anyone else's right to speak. Because of this, you may decide to defer your opportunity to speak to someone who has had less opportunity for or experience of speaking.

The third aspect of utilitarianism is thinking about the welfare of others, as many others as possible. The well-known utilitarian principle of the **greatest good for the greatest number** is based upon two important ideas—1) the good and 2) that the good should extend to as many people as possible. Jeremy Bentham, an early utilitarian thinker, argued that we could determine the good by calculating the amount of utility or pleasure in people's lives (1–7 and 29–31). Early critics pointed out that pleasure is not always ethically good. John Stuart Mill responded to these criticisms with the idea of **utility as an ethical good** (*Utilitarianism* 227–59). Mill claimed that ethical utility is not mere physical pleasure but the greatest happiness for as many people as possible. Utilitarian happiness is the pleasure of doing what is just, right, or beautiful so that as many people as possible are happy (207–14). Utilitarian happiness is more than feeling good as you do something for yourself or others. A utilitarian would promote freedom and education, because they are important for creating happiness for the greatest number of people. A utilitarian has a duty to promote the long-term happiness of others in contrast to working only for her own happiness, because her happiness is no more important than the happiness of others. A utilitarian approach to communication asks you to think about whether your communication would make others happy, not simply if it would make you happy. In fact, achieving happiness in the long term for the greatest number of people may involve frustration, even short-term unhappiness, as when you study for exams or write papers to earn a degree, because it will bring you and others future happiness.

Everyday Communication Ethics

❖ *How would communication change, if communicators practiced utilitarian impartiality? How would your communication change?*

The idea of "the greatest good for the greatest number" is well-recognized shorthand for utilitarianism. This idea also creates a limitation of utilitarian ethics, that the greater good minimizes the interests of the individual or minority for the happiness of the majority. There are three criticisms of the greater good, each involving justice. The first is that calculating utility is an unfeeling approach to ethics that devalues the individual, treating people more as numbers than human beings. Responsiveness to individual feelings is minimized, in favor of what can be calculated and what people share. This de-emphasizes moral emotions such as empathy or sympathy. Individuals and minorities are vulnerable to having their legitimate interests dismissed, in favor of a calculation of the greater good. This is the basis of the next criticism of utilitarianism.

Textbox 6.2

Communication Ethics in Popular Film
Utilitarianism in *X-Men*

Utilitarian thinking has become so commonplace that it appears in popular films. The science fiction series *X-Men* tells stories about humans who have evolved through genetic mutation. Mutant humans face discrimination by non-mutant humans. The films challenge viewers to distinguish between ethical justifications and rationalizations for the greater good. The two main characters in the film series, Xavier and Magneto, practice the utilitarian ideas of the greater good, consequences, and utilitarian impartiality.

Xavier—Leader of the X-Men

Xavier's mutant ability is to read and control minds. His vision of the greater good is humans and mutants coexisting. Xavier uses utilitarian principles in both his statements and actions. In *X-Men: The Last Stand* his actions practice utilitarian impartiality, that his happiness or good

---

is no more important than anyone else's happiness or good, when he sacrifices himself to save another mutant. Xavier's ethical practices are not purely ethical, however, for they cause harm. After his death, the X-Men learn that he was not completely truthful, even to the X-Men. Xavier sacrificed truth to achieve his vision of the greater good for mutants and humans.

Eric Lehnsherr or Magneto—Leader of the Brotherhood

Throughout the films, Magneto leads a group of mutants working against Xavier and the X-Men, arguing that the end or greater good of mutant survival justifies the means of destroying humanity. Magneto's experience as a survivor of a Nazi death camp shaped his vision of the greater good. He believes humans will hate and destroy whatever is different that they do not understand. Because mutants are superior to humans, they must protect themselves by destroying humans first. The greatest good is mutant survival. Since Xavier and Magneto are both old friends and opponents, their disagreement about what is the greater good and the means to achieve it appears throughout the film series.

The *X-Men* films shows some of the pitfalls of applying utilitarian principles. Decision makers using the language of utilitarianism are vulnerable to rationalizing their self-interest or poorly examined social conventions, especially when they do not apply the principle of utilitarian impartiality. The films also show that despite efforts to carefully and rigorously apply utilitarian principles, it may not be possible to make ethically pure decisions that create no harm.

A second criticism of utilitarianism is that the majority decision making for the greater good can become a means for rationalizing uncritical exercise of power at the expense of individuals or a minority. When we think critically about who makes decisions about the greater good, we begin to think about how power is exercised, whose interests are promoted, and whose interests are left out. These are questions of procedural and distributive justice. Because utilitarianism does not encourage us to ask questions about who exercises decision making power, it is easy to avoid examining how beneficial or harmful consequences of decisions are distributed among the majority and minority. John Stuart Mill addressed this weakness in his discussion of freedom of speech. He combined **utilitarianism and the moral right of freedom of speech**. *On Liberty* presents Mill's arguments for protecting the rights of individuals. He argued that protecting the right of the individual and especially the minority to speak helps protect the greater good of truth. Freedom of speech distributes more equitably the communication good of speaking. Mill does not claim that the majority must agree with the minority, but that there should be an opportunity to listen and think critically about the ideas and arguments the minority presents. It is important for you to consider whether Mill's solution of freedom of speech adequately addresses the role of power in utilitarianism.

Everyday Communication Ethics

❖ *What communication practices help insure that minority viewpoints are thoughtfully considered in decision making?*

The third criticism of utilitarianism is that it is impractical, because it obligates you to sacrifice your individual self-interest repeatedly for others. How many people would choose to practice utilitarian impartiality and sacrifice their self-interest to others on a regular basis? This question is important for a minority which does not share in the greater good. Is it fair if a minority is asked or required to sacrifice for the majority on a regular basis? An ethic based upon sacrifice can become dangerous, especially when questions of power are not considered. Using utilitarian terminology, powerful decision makers for the majority may rationalize the sacrifice of a minority which has limited or no involvement in decision making processes. When individuals or a minority lack access to information or are denied opportunities to speak and participate in decision making processes, there can be significant injustice.

Today, utilitarianism is a dominant voice in public conversations about ethics. You may have found some elements of utilitarianism familiar, even part of your personal ethical standard. Think about how you could use utilitarianism more rigorously by including evaluation of consequences and utilitarian impartiality in your ethical reasoning.

Conclusion

This chapter discusses three traditional theories of ethics—virtue ethics, moral rights, and utilitarianism. Communication virtue encourages thinking about habits that promote ethical communication practice in a community or culture, including honor codes. Aristotle's concept of virtue as a mean between the vices of excess and deficiency reminds us that our practice of virtue is dynamic, not static. Each one of us searches for harmony or balance between the excesses and deficiencies of our emotions and dispositions that is ethically responsive to situations, all within the context of a community's understanding of virtue. A moral rights approach to communication ethics encourages the identification of basic rights of communication belonging to every person that promote human survival and thriving. While freedom of speech is recognized as a moral right, communication scholars ask if there are other moral rights of communication, such as listening. A utilitarian approach to communication ethics is concerned with the greatest amount of happiness or good for the greatest number of people. It encourages you to think about how your personal communication practices would change if you considered your personal happiness no more important than anyone else's happiness.

Each of these theories presents ideas that may challenge your thinking about how to practice your ethical commitments. They encourage asking hard questions about whether your communication practices create more good and less harm. In different ways, each theory challenges examination of our thinking for rationalizations based solely on self-interest or poorly examined social convention. Even if you do not include one of these theories in your personal ethical standard, thinking about virtue, moral rights, and utilitarianism contributes to your moral imagination, expanding your resources for discernment and decision making about practicing communication ethics.

Vocabulary

Aristotle's concept of virtue 126
Consequences 135–136
Duty 131
Freedom of speech 133
Greatest good for the greatest number 136
Kant's categorical imperative 132
Mean as a metaphor for harmony or proportion 127
Moral right to communicate 134
Moral right of listening 133
Moral rights 129
Moral rights as universal 130
Two functions of moral rights 130
Utilitarian impartiality 136
Utilitarianism 135
Utilitarianism and the moral right of freedom of speech 138
Utility 135
Utility as an ethical good 136
Vices 126
Virtue 126
Virtue Ethics 126

Cases for Discussion

Directions: For each case use virtue theory, moral rights, or utilitarianism to guide your deliberation about how to communicate ethically at the relevant recurring decision points of communication. Identity the strengths and limitations of your decision.

Case 1: *Speaking or Keeping Silent—Closing a Restaurant*

Sales at the Boardroom BBQ had slowed for several months. Last year, this was the most profitable restaurant in the chain. Last week, management cut everyone's hours. Carina thought the restaurant would soon close.

Just before her shift, Carina always stops and says "Hi" to the restaurant manager, Jean. They have a good working relationship. Carina helps when Jean needs an extra hand, and Jean tries to schedule her extra hours when Carina needs cash. Jean sometimes uses Carina as a sounding board before presenting a new procedure or policy to the staff. Today, she lingered to ask a question, "Things have been really slow lately. Should I be looking for another job?"

"Funny you ask me," replied Jean. "Our last day of business will be this Saturday. Promise me you won't tell anyone. I don't want folks to stop showing up for work because we're closing! Besides, headquarters directed me to not tell anyone we're closing until our last day of business."

Carina told Jean that she would not tell anyone about the closing; after all, Jean had trusted her in the past with keeping things quiet. As she started his shift, Carina was having second thoughts.

What and how should Carina communicate with her coworkers? With Jean?

What and how should Jean communicate?

Case 2: *Speaking or Keeping Silent—Family-1*

"It's happening again," thought Isaac, with irritation, as he watched his dad kiss his date. Isaac's parents had divorced, after 20 years of marriage. The divorce was not a bad one, more like a formality. Isaac understood his parents had stayed together for the kids, for who knows how long. He could not remember his parents showing real affection for each other.

Isaac's dad starting dating within weeks of the separation. After the divorce, he would include his date whenever he saw Isaac, telling Isaac to bring a date along too. Each time, his dad would show his date affection—cuddling, hugging, and kissing. Isaac had not told his dad how this hurt him, seeing him show his date more affection than Isaac had seen his mother receive from his dad. The last thing Isaac wanted was to upset his father. But his dad's behavior was disrespectful—to him, his younger brother and sister, and his mom. "Dad is acting as if our years as a family mean nothing to him. It is getting harder to not say anything." Isaac did not want to push his dad away, but he wondered if he was going to snap at his dad, and the anger would come pouring out.

What should Isaac do?

Case 3: Speaking or Keeping Silent—The Team Project

After everyone left the room, Eddah, the project leader, asked David what was going on with Marcus.

Yesterday, the team presented the new PR campaign to Carlson management. While Carlson management liked the campaign, David knew the team had a close call because of Marcus. Marcus was responsible for making final changes to the presentation slides and sending the digital file to David. David was responsible for final editing and coordination of all materials. The day before the presentation, David still did not have the file. He stopped by Marcus's desk and asked when he would get it. Marcus replied that he had just sent it to David, and then asked if they could go out for a quick drink after work.

David and Marcus became friends as they worked together and found a shared love of basketball. Over drinks, Marcus said that he and his partner Pat were separating, after seven years together. Marcus asked David to promise to not tell anyone at work, because "it's personal, private." Marcus continued, "This is hard. I thought I would spend my life with Pat. It's not anyone's business at work. Thanks for understanding that. It means a lot to me."

Now Eddah wants to know if something is going on with Marcus. "The Carlson presentation went well, but Marcus was out of sync with the team, almost erratic at times. Normally, I wouldn't ask you if anything was going on, except that I'm considering recommending him for a project team with a new client that has potential to be our biggest account. He would have supervisory responsibilities. If he's not up to this challenge, I need to know."

What and how should David communicate?

Case 4. Speaking or Keeping Silent—Family-2

Tonny does not want to avoid his parents. It is just harder and harder to face them. Tonny grew up in a tight-knit, traditional Hmong family with two brothers, three sisters, and aunts and uncles. His parents had never learned to speak English, relying on their children to translate or act as intermediaries. Hmong children are expected to honor their parents and follow traditional roles. But like more Hmong his age, Tonny had never learned to speak Hmong well. Not speaking Hmong was only one way Tonny did not fit in well with his family. His parents do not understand what it is like being a university student. And then there is the fact that Tonny is gay. While he does not have a boyfriend, he knows that he will never fit into a traditional Hmong family. He loves his parents, and knows his parents love him. But they do not understand him, and he cannot speak Hmong well enough to explain his feelings and thoughts. What should Tonny do?

References

Alleyne, Mark D. "Global Media Ecology: Why There is No Global Media Ethical Standard." *The Handbook of Mass Media Ethics.* Eds. Lee Wilkins and Clifford G. Christians. New York: Routledge, 382–93.

Appiah, Kwame Anthony. *The Honor Code: How Moral Revolutions Happen,* New York: Norton, 2010.

Aristotle. *The Ethics of Aristotle: The Nicomachean Ethics.* 1955. Trans. J.A.K. Thomson and Hugh Tredennick. New York: Penguin Books, 1976.

Aristotle. *The Rhetoric and The Poetics of Aristotle.* Trans. W. Rhys Roberts and Ingram Bywater. New York: Modern Library, 1954.

Ashley, Mike. *Taking Liberties: The Struggle for Britain's Freedoms and Rights.* London: The British Library, 2008.

Bentham, Jeremy. *Introduction to the Principles of Morals and Legislation.* 1789. New York: Hagner, 1948.

Bezanson, Mary Elizabeth. "Kleindienst v. Mandel." *Free Speech on Trial: Communication Perspectives on Landmark Supreme Court Decisions.* Ed. Richard A. Parker. Tuscaloosa, AL: Alabama UP, 2003. 172–86.

Chappell, Tim and Roger Crisp. "Utilitarianism." *Routledge Encyclopedia of Philosophy.* Vol. 9. Ed. Edward Craig. New York: Routledge, 1998. 551–7.

Corkery, Michael. "Wells Fargo Fined $185 Million for Fraudulently Opening Accounts." *The New York Times.* 8 September 2016. www.nytimes.com/2016/09/09/business/dealbook/wells-fargo-fined-for-years-of-harm-to-customers.html?action=click&contentCollection=DealBook&module=RelatedCoverage&region=Marginalia&pgtype=article. Date accessed: 4 March 2018.

Cunningham, Stanley. "Getting It Right: Aristotle's 'Golden Mean' as Theory Deterioration." *Journal of Mass Media Ethics* 14.1 (1999): 5–15.

Ewing, Jack and Neal E. Boudette. "As VW Pleads Guilty in U.S. Over Diesel Scandal, Trouble Looms in Europe." *The New York Times.* 10 March 2017. www.nytimes.com/2017/03/10/business/volkswagen-europe-diesel-car-owners.html.Date accessed: 16 October 2017.

Fagan, Andrew. "Human Rights." *The Internet Encyclopedia of Philosophy.* 2004. www.iep.utm.edu/hum-rts/. Date accessed: 25 November 2017.

Feinberg, Joel. *Social Philosophy.* Englewood Cliffs, NJ: Prentice Hall, 1973.

Fraleigh, Douglas M. and Joseph S. Tuman. *Freedom of Speech in the Marketplace of Ideas.* New York: St. Martins, 1997.

Hammelink, Cees J. "Grounding the Human Right to Communicate." *Many Voices, One Vision: The Right to Communicate in Practice.* Ed. Philip Lee. London: World Association of Christian Communication, 2004. 21–32.

Kant, Immanuel. *Groundwork of the Metaphysics of Morals.* 1797. Trans. H.J. Paton. New York: Harper, 1964.

Lambert, Bruce. "L.I. School Official Helped Son Cheat on Test, Investigators Say." *The New York Times.* 28 June 2005. www.nytimes.com/2005/06/28/nyregion/li-school-official-helped-son-cheat-on-test-investigators-say.html. Date accessed: 25 November 2017.

MacIntyre, Alasdair. *After Virtue: A Study in Moral Theory.* 2nd ed. Notre Dame, IN: U of Notre Dame P, 1984.

Martin, Rex. "Rights." *Routledge Encyclopedia of Philosophy.* Vol. 8. Ed. Edward Craig. New York: Routledge, 1998. 325–31.

Mill, John Stuart. *On Liberty.* 1859. Ed. Alburey Castell. Northbrook, IL: AHM Publishing, 1947.

Mill, John Stuart. *Utilitarianism.* 1863. Buffalo, NY: Prometheus Books, 1987.

Nussbaum, Martha C. *Upheavals of Thought: The Intelligence of Emotions.* Cambridge: Cambridge UP, 2001.

Tabuchi, Hiroko. "A Cheaper Airbag, and Takata's Road to a Deadly Crisis." *The New York Times.* 26 August 2016. www.nytimes.com/2016/08/27/business/takata-airbag-recall-crisis.html. Date accessed: 16 October 2017.

Tedford, Thomas L. and Dale A. Herbeck. *Freedom of Speech in the United States.* 6th ed. State College, PA: Strata Publishing, 2009.

Stewart, Frank Henderson. *Honor.* Chicago, IL: U of Chicago P, 1994.

United Nations. *Universal Declaration of Human Rights.* www.un.org/Overview/rights.html. Date accessed: 6 June 2009.

Vincent, Nicholas. *Magna Carta: The Foundation of Freedom, 1215–2015.* London: Third Millennium Publishing, 2014.

X-Men. Dir. Bryan Singer. Prod. Lauren S. Donner, et al. 2000.

X-Men The Last Stand. Dir. Brett Ratner. Prod. Avi Arad, et al. 2006. Beverley Hills, CA: Twentieth Century Fox Home Entertainment.

7

CONTEMPORARY ALTERNATIVES TO MODERNIST ETHICAL THEORIES

President Wick read the resolution from the student senate again. "Be it resolved: that the university remove from campus the historical marker commemorating nineteenth-century newspaper editor Elizabeth Swisshelm because of her published racist statements against Native Americans. A university committed to diversity should not condone racism in any form." The resolution culminated two years of student protest and campus discussion. The students were correct. Elizabeth Swisshelm was a racist. She published her racist views of American Indians in her newspaper. However, she also was an abolitionist in a community divided about slavery before the US Civil War. The historical marker commemorates her abolitionist paper and her resistance to efforts to silence her. Pro-slavery supporters broke into her print shop and dumped her printing press into the river. The historical marker is on the site of her printing shop. If the president orders the marker's removal, the university will no longer honor a racist, and would erase public recognition of her work against slavery.

Deciding the right thing to say or do seems more complicated today than in the past. The more facts we learn, the more difficult it is to discern what would be ethically responsive communication. Ethical decision making appears to have become a process of identifying which harm is less ethically justifiable, rather than deciding what would be good, right, or virtuous. In situations like the Swisshelm historical marker, decision makers face the task of choosing from among flawed choices. Removing the marker raises issues of encouraging public forgetfulness and erasing public historical facts about the US Civil War. A decision to keep the historical marker, or to create a new one, presents complex issues of historical accuracy, fairness, and communicative power (see Gill). Discerning how to act in a way that causes no harm or reaching a decision that everyone agrees is ethically correct is elusive. Modernist theories of utilitarianism and moral rights create an impression that it is possible to make an ethically correct decision with which almost everyone can agree. The Swisshelm marker presents complex issues of power in the authoritativeness of a historical marker and of fairness regarding race and gender. Modernist ethical theories of moral rights and utilitarianism have been criticized for not adequately addressing issues such as these or acknowledging the strong emotions they evoke.

Twentieth century developments in ethics and philosophy offer alternatives to modernist ethical theories of utilitarianism and moral rights. This chapter introduces you to three alternative approaches to modernist communication ethics—postmodernism, dialogical ethics, and ethical care. Each approach offers different ways for discerning the ethicality of communication practices, without denying limitations of each practice. Practicing ethics becomes less black and white, and much greyer. Postmodernism, dialogical ethics, and ethical care encourage us to be honest about our limitations and offer different ways to examine rationalization in our reasoning. Each approach presumes that it is possible to discern and practice ethically good communication rather than ethically pure communication. To help you understand how each approach differs from modernist ethical theories, the next section presents a brief discussion of modernist thinking and some ways these assumptions were questioned as the 20th century progressed.

Modernist Thinking

We use modernist thinking, often without realizing it. Shopping for a digital device illustrates. When buying a digital device, we search for the most recent innovations for the lowest price possible. Last year's model is out of date, while this year's model is state of the art. This imaginary search illustrates a central quality of modernist thinking, belief in **progress**, that over time life will improve. **Modernist thinking** is characterized by belief in progress and the **certainty of knowledge**, that by consistently accumulating facts and knowledge established by careful observation and rational deliberation, our lives will progressively improve. Modernist ideas of progress, rationality, and certainty of knowledge influence our understanding of ethics—that if an ethical decision maker knows enough facts and thinks about an ethical issue, in time she can arrive at an ethical decision that everyone will agree with. Modernist ideas contribute to a sense that we can discern a decision so ethically correct that no one would question it. Once clear decisions are recognized we act decisively, with certainty. Recent research in moral psychology shows that we make daily judgments that are clear and decisive about what is ethical, using our moral emotions and intuition, not rationality (Haidt; Haidt and Joseph). In difficult or complex situations such as the Swisshelm monument case that begins this chapter, moral intuition can be insufficient in discerning ethical tension points and potential for harm. Relying on moral emotions and intuition alone makes it difficult to recognize limitations in our decisions or that others can make good arguments that our decision is unethical in some way. Yet, modernist assumptions of certain knowledge and progress imply that with careful ethical reasoning guided by rationality, we can achieve decisiveness and unquestioned certainty, if we try hard enough.

By the end of the 20th century, an increasing number of people questioned the modernist ideas of certain knowledge and progress. One reason for this questioning is the experience of communicating and living with people from cultures that do not embrace modernist ideas. Contact with people from different cultures, however, is not enough to cause the questioning of modernism that encouraged the development of the theories presented in this chapter.

A second motivation for questioning modernist assumptions comes from efforts to understand human violence in the 20th century. Some call the 20th century the bloodiest century in human history. While you might disagree with this claim, a survey of the century produces a long list of wars, genocides, police actions, coup d'états, and assassinations. Two wars covered so large a geographic area and involved so many nations that they were labeled world wars, World War I (1914–1918) and World War II (1939–1945). At the end of World War II, the US demonstrated that humanity possessed the ability to destroy itself and most life on the planet with weapons humans created. As the century progressed, we discovered that manufacture and use of these weapons, as well as other human inventions, were poisoning the water, land, and air, creating environmental crises that threaten human and other life. Some asked if life was really getting better, or were we just killing ourselves in the name of progress. Others began questioning the usefulness and appropriateness of ideas that produced these results, particularly the modernist ideas of progress, rationality, and the certainty of knowledge.

The Holocaust of World War II poses a special challenge for understanding violence in the 20th century. The culture that produced many of the greatest musical composers of Western culture—Bach, Beethoven, and Wagner—and key Western philosophers and ethicists—Kant, Hegel, and Heidegger—also produced the leaders who organized the extermination of Jews, gypsies, gays and lesbians, the mentally impaired, essentially anyone considered inferior or impure. Knowledge and expertise of persons in the arts, philosophy, ethics, medicine, and theology were insufficient to stop the Holocaust, although some individuals tried and, too often, died in the effort. Many educated people accepted arguments that rationalized this program of extermination as progress towards creation of a superior human race. Others sympathized with these rationalizations. The reputation of German philosopher Martin Heidegger, who some consider the most brilliant philosopher of the 20th century, is tainted by evidence of his Nazi sympathies (Caputo; Farais). Other critics argued that modernist thinking rationalized colonization of non-Western or nonindustrialized countries and the abuses of colonization. As the 20th century continued, some questioned the superiority of modernist thinking and culture, and the implicit evaluation that all non-modernist cultures were inferior. Others searched for ways of thinking that would not involve the violence that appeared to be an unspoken theme in modernist thought. Scholars began to examine the overt and covert ways violence is practiced in society, and the role of communication in supporting these practices. The chapter's opening case illustrates the complexity of addressing overt and covert violence in communication practices. The historical marker communicates Swisshelm's public stand against the violence of slavery before the US Civil War, but it also condones by omission the violence of her racist public communication about American Indians. The historical marker commemorates a woman who was an abolitionist and businesswoman at a time when women were expected to remain in the privacy and shelter of the home. Removing the marker would end the tacit public acceptance of her racism, but it would also erase public recognition of her courage as a woman before the Civil War speaking out against slavery, and as a victim of violent suppression of freedom of the press.

Textbox 7.1

Violence and the Emergence of Modernity

An era of violence and war also preceded the emergence of modernity and the European Enlightenment. Stephen Toulmin identifies two violent events as marking the emergence of modernist thought: the assassination of King Henry IV of France in 1610 and the 30 years of religious war between Catholics and Protestants (1618–1648). King Henry was a model of humanist toleration in the increasingly violent rivalry between Catholics and Protestants. His death was seen by many as a failure of humanism. The Thirty Years War is one of the top ten violent human events in percentage of world population killed ("Population"). Toulmin argues that these events mark the failure of humanist toleration and an era of such economic, social, scholarly, and spiritual turbulence that many intellectuals sought a place of intellectual certainty that was neutral. The Enlightenment emerged from this search for certainty and neutrality, beginning the modern era. Rationality was key to identifying certain human knowledge, foundational principles, and perceptions that would be free from the tumult and violence of emotions that had devastated European society. Modernism was, in part, a product of the hope to prevent violence through the discovery of certain and objective knowledge untainted by extreme and violent emotion.

It is challenging to characterize the diverse currents of intellectual thought in the past 100 years that have questioned modernism. While one cannot do justice to its range and complexity, it is important to present some major ideas and theories that offer alternatives to modernist theories of ethics. If coercion and violence are embedded in modernist thinking, it may also be embedded in modernist theories of ethics. If so, decision makers using modernist theories of moral rights or utilitarianism may unknowingly rationalize harms caused by covert or overt violence. This possibility makes it important that we seriously consider what alternatives to modernist theories contribute to our personal practice of communication ethics, whether it is to incorporate them into our personal ethical standard or use their criticism of modernist concepts and theories to identify rationalizations in our ethical reasoning.

Postmodernism

Postmodernism is an effort to break away from patterns of modernist thinking which postmodernists claim produce inequality, oppression, and violence. Postmodernism is difficult to characterize because of the range and diversity of ideas, and disagreement among postmodern thinkers. There are some commonalities. Postmodern thinkers share skepticism about modernism's focus on legitimate or certain knowledge and how best to think. Modernist thinking values objectivity, rationality, and universality as standards for evaluating knowledge and theory, all of which contribute to a(n) (emotional) sense of certainty. Postmodernists are willing to consider alternative forms of knowledge and thinking as legitimate and reasonable (Connor 3–6; Sim 3–4). Some postmodernists reject theorizing. Generally, they reject the idea of progress as a universal ideal. Although it is difficult to identify a preeminent postmodern theory, there are three themes relevant to communication— the decentered self, knowledge, and power. As you read about each theme, think about how the ideas present an alternative way to think about your ethical commitments and how you practice communication ethics.

Decentered Self

Postmodernists reject modernist assumptions that we are impartial, autonomous actors exercising free will (Eaglestone 184). They claim that our decision making always has a point of view that comes from our position in our relationships. This position shapes what we accept as knowledge and influences how we exercise power. Postmodernism challenges us to think of ourselves as persons in relationships who have incomplete and partial understanding of others and the world around us. Because knowledge exists only in relation to others, our knowledge is always situational. Exploring our partial understanding is one focus of postmodernism, particularly regarding knowledge and power, the two other postmodernist themes explored in this section.

Ideas of **Emmanuel Levinas**, a philosopher and survivor of Nazi prison camps, can help us better understand the postmodern idea of the Self. Levinas argues that **the Self** arises out of our relation to others (*Ethics and Infinity* 85–9; "Meaning and Sense" 51–7). The Self depends upon the **call of the other**. Your understanding of your Self, your knowledge, and your ability to act as a human being depend upon your responsiveness to this call. The call of the other comes before knowledge of the other. How each person recognizes and responds to this call raises questions of ethics. Because the call of the other comes before our ability to know the other, Levinas claims that questions of ethics are the fundamental questions of life and philosophy.

To act ethically requires being responsive to the call of the other (Hyde; Levinas *Otherwise* 10–1). So much interferes with our ability to be responsive to this call, or to recognize it. Our consciousness and attention are focused on our Self, putting our Self at the center of our relationships. When we do recognize an other, too often we treat her as **the Same**, explaining or containing the other within our viewpoint. This encourages us to act as if we know everything about the other. We are not open to what we do *not* know, what Levinas calls **the infinity of the other** that exceeds our understanding or consciousness. The other is more than we can ever know. Recognizing the infinity of the other calls our consciousness into question (Levinas "Meaning and Sense" 54–7).

The communication act of acknowledgment is based on Levinas's call of the other (Hyde). In acknowledgment, a communicator focuses her consciousness on the other, going beyond recognition that the other exists. When she acknowledges an other, she decenters and opens her Self to the infinity of the other, understanding that there is more to the other than she could possibly ever know. Acknowledgment is a response of receptivity that treats the other as a subject, not an object. When we assume that we already know and understand what another person thinks or feels, we treat that person as an object and put our Self at the center of our relationships. How might the call of the other occur in everyday communication? Think of a situation at work, at school, with friends, or in your family where your needs or ideas were not recognized or acknowledged by others. Applying the decentered Self, we would say that no one was ethically responsive to your call, because they did not recognize or acknowledge that their understanding of you was partial or incomplete. They focused on *their* understanding and placed themselves at the center of their relationship with you.

Everyday Communication Ethics

❖ *When do you recognize that others exceed your knowledge of them? How does this recognition affect your communication practices?*

Levinas challenges us to think about how we have placed our Selves at the center of our relationships. At our relationships' center, we dominate others

150

with our certainty that we know or understand. To practice the **decentered Self**, we focus our attention on the other and ask ourselves whether we have been responsive to the other's call. In the chapter's opening case, President Wick's challenge is to be ethically responsive to the call of the protesting students, to acknowledge that these students are not the same as him. If he presumes that he understands the students, he cannot recognize that the students are more than he can ever know or understand. When we do not understand that the other is not the same as our Self, we cannot understand that our knowledge is incomplete and partial. With certainty about who the other is, we cannot be ethically responsive to the other.

Levinas challenges us to move ourselves out of the center of our relationships and the reciprocity of interpersonal relationships. Levinas is not interested in mutually responsive communication, but with our responsibility to be responsive to the infinity of the other (Arnett; Levinas *Ethics and Infinity*, 96–7; Lipari "Listening" 126–7). **Ethical responsiveness to the infinity of the other** requires setting aside interpersonal fairness based upon the moral emotion of the equality bias. For Levinas, the stakes are too high for interpersonal fairness. When we are not ethically responsive to the other, we deny her humanity, turning her into an object that can be abused, even killed. Turning others into objects also denies our own humanity, because we exist in relation to others. When we treat others as less than human, we become less human as well. Only by moving our Self from the center of our relationship through ethical responsiveness, is it possible to affirm the humanity of the other and make possible our own humanity.

Postmodern Truth as Justified Truth

Questioning what we traditionally consider knowledge is the second major theme in postmodernism. Postmodernists argue that truth is limited and open to multiple interpretations (Roseneau 77–91; Sheehen 22–5). Postmodern truth is not universal knowledge. It is local and variable, "close to the ground" in what people do and experience. Partial and multiple interpretations characterize local knowledge. Many postmodernists are more comfortable discussing meaning and interpretation than discussing knowledge and truth. Meaning, how we interpret the truth of facts or our experiences, is rarely, if ever, completely obvious and clear. Some degree of ambiguity and uncertainty typically characterizes meaning.

Think about a conversation with your roommate or family member, where you said something like "I meant exactly what I said!" You may have been surprised by her different interpretation of your message, because you were certain you were clear about what you said. Your certainty, however, does not guarantee that your listener's alternative interpretation could not be found in your words. Confidence in your intentions and certainty of the care you took in selecting words does not guarantee that the interpretations of others will coincide exactly with what you intended. Your certainty does not deny the legitimacy of a listener's alternative interpretation. A postmodernist approach to this conversation would ask you to acknowledge the legitimacy of this alternative interpretation alongside your intentions, even if this disrupts achievement of your communication goals.

Everyday Communication Ethics

❖ *How often do you ask the second and third recurring questions of ethical reasoning—"What do I not know and can find out" and "What do I not know and cannot find out?"*

The ideas of **Richard Rorty** help explain how there are multiple interpretations of truth. Rorty rejects the idea that truth is universal or unconditional, because people simply do not act that way (15–7). People act as if the truth varies for many reasons, such as differences between situations, special circumstances, or differences among people. Rorty rejects correspondence between reality as it exists and some universal truth. Instead, he observes that people always talk to one another explaining, justifying, and exploring what they believe to be true. There is always someone, somewhere, who would not be convinced by your justification, no matter how certain you are that your claim is true and how much evidence you present. Because people do not act as if truth is universal and certain, Rorty proposes that we focus on justified truth. **Justified truth** is established by discussions in which people present their justifications of truth for examination by others. Justifications are supported by evidence drawn from their experiences and individual knowledge. If you find a justification convincing, you accept this truth. The challenge is that different justified truths about the same topic or issue can exist simultaneously. In applying Rorty's ideas to the chapter's opening case, President Wick participates in a discussion of who should be memorialized on campus. If he recognizes that the protesting students' viewpoint can be justified, he acknowledges that what is true for the protesting students may differ from what is true for others on and off campus.

Rorty wants us to be careful about how we conduct discussions that involve different interpretations of truth, because standards for justification can vary (5–8). **Standards for justification** are criteria used to evaluate or test whether a statement is reasonable or valid. Discussions about science are different from discussions about politics or religion, because the standards for justification of the truth for science are different from those for politics or religion. People with different political or philosophical viewpoints may use different standards for justification. People from non-Western cultures use different standards for justifying truth than do people from Western cultures. Rorty advocates striving for as broadly democratic discussions about truth as possible, despite difficulties of different interpretations and standards for justification. He claims that if we promote freedom in our discussions and deliberations, the truth will take care of itself (Mendieta).

Recognizing that there are different approaches or standards for justification can stimulate your moral imagination. Knowledge becomes less absolute and certain. Different interpretations in the roommate conversation mentioned above could exist because you and your roommate use different approaches or standards for justifying the truth of your experiences as roommates. Calling one justified truth wrong and the other right would be ethically incorrect, because both are true according to their respective standards. Modernist certain knowledge treats this as a logical impossibility, because both/and claims are confusing, irrational, and even unethical. The postmodern concept of justified truth encourages us to think about how we can recognize and include different justified truths in our conversations with others, using both/and thinking to stimulate our moral imaginations as we deliberate about problems and issues. A challenge of using justified truth is discerning how to broaden the communication process to incorporate different standards while also discerning if there should be limits to how far these standards should be broadened.

Rhetorical scholar Jason Hannan argues that Rorty's argument about justified truth, especially when combined with his argument that by protecting individual freedom the truth will take care of itself, discards truth as a relevant communication value (xix–xxii). Deception, even falsehood becomes acceptable. Yet, without some notion of truth—whether we understand truth as absolute, relative, or partial—communication becomes meaningless. "In throwing out the concept of truth, Rorty throws out speech altogether" (Hannan xxiii), making deception and honesty indistinguishable equals. An unintended consequence of Rorty's concept of justified truth is that it undermines the trust needed to communicate. If there is no difference between truth and lies, why should I trust anyone?

Point to Ponder

❖ *Are there limits to including different standards for justification in public discussions? What justifies these limits?*

Some commitment to honesty is fundamental to communication. Without a communication standard of honesty, trust in relationships, groups, and communities does not develop (Bok). The interrelationship of honesty and trust exists because of the interrelationship of the content and relational dimensions of communication. This interrelationship, however, does not undermine justified truth's criticism of modernist certainty. When we act with a sense of certainty (in contrast to confidence) that we are right, believing that our knowledge and understanding *cannot* be disproven or shown to be limited, we weaken our curiosity. We become less willing to explore and investigate the world around us. As an emotional response to knowledge and understanding, certainty shares a harm of cynicism, an inability to recognize truth. Like cynicism, certainty that we know what is true allows us to rationalize not listening to others who disagree with us, even withdrawing from relationships with them. Competent and ethical communication is a process for exploring, examining, discussing, and debating truth in its many forms. These are communication practices of human curiosity that rely on honesty in examining the truthfulness of facts and claims.

Justified truth encourages us to examine our thinking for rationalizations that produce *over*confidence in what we think or understand, making others automatically wrong. It points out limits to our knowledge and understanding. When we lose sight of our limits, our capability to recognize and understand truthful communication shrinks, sometimes dramatically. Justified truth also highlights the importance of understanding how our standards for evaluating truth work in comparison to the standards of others. If we do not make these comparisons, we will be unable to understand how different standards for truth promote or do not promote human survival and thriving.

Postmodern Power

Power, knowledge, and self are interrelated concepts in modernist thinking. When individuals make informed decisions, they exercise the power of knowledge to achieve a goal. Certain knowledge encourages quick, decisive, perhaps aggressive decision making. For postmodernists, this relationship is more complicated. Our knowledge is partial and incomplete. When we consider alternative viewpoints and recognize our limitations, we realize that our power also is limited and incomplete. Decision making can become more complex and time-consuming. In the chapter's opening case, if President Wick considers his understanding and knowledge partial rather than complete, his deliberations about removing the memorial would take the time to seriously consider the perspectives of the protesting students, as well as other stakeholders.

Postmodernists recognize that there are many different types of power, ranging from overt physical force and violence to subtler power that covertly establishes what we believe is true. Postmodernists are interested in the power of language and discourse practices that prompt us to mindlessly accept social conventions and discourage us from considering alternative interpretations or knowledge. The partial and local nature of knowledge can promote power struggles over what is considered legitimate and true. When knowledge is understood as certain and universal, it contributes to the creation of a comprehensive or **grand narrative**, a story that attempts to explain how everything fits together (Lyotard 14–41). The power of a grand narrative depends on its capacity to explain as much experience as possible, often with little or no critical reflection. A grand narrative maintains social conventions and identifies socially acceptable knowledge and action. Communication and other social practices maintain a grand narrative in the face of alternative narratives that present different interpretations of experience, knowledge, and truth.

The work of **Michel Foucault** is prominent in postmodern discussions of power. Foucault claims that the operation of power determines what a society considers legitimate (*Power* 326–48). Knowledge and power are inseparable. **Power** organizes relationships that create knowledge (Foucault *Politics* 86–109; Rouse). Relationships are not limited to people, but include relationships between organizations, rules, laws, and even objects, like machinery. Relationships and the power that organizes them produce knowledge. Power is always part of knowledge. It is impossible to have a society without power. While Foucault acknowledges the operation of **power as a creative force** that makes alternative knowledge and choice possible, his theory and analysis often focus its operation as a disciplinary force. When **power functions as a disciplinary force**, it determines what is recognized as knowledge; what is ignored is delegitimized. Power relationships determine who gets to create or decide what knowledge is. Foucault draws our attention to how power can subtly coerce us to accept one set of practices as true, right, and good, while rejecting another set of practices (*Power* 118–25).

Everyday Communication Ethics

❖ *What social norms do my communication practices depend upon? Which are practices of overt power? Covert power?*

The disciplinary force of power is not clearly associated with an institution, such as government or a corporation. Its disciplinary force is subtly exercised in discourse practices that constitute knowledge and relationships that we perceive as normal. Questioning and resisting disciplinary power requires questioning practices that construct relationships of power. While resistance can be an ethical response to disciplinary power, resistance also is an exercise of power. Knowledge is always enmeshed with the exercise of power. We cannot avoid power. The chapter's opening case is about power and how to use it—the complex power of institutional racism, the culturally accepted public erasure of women, the resistance of protesting students, the power of the office of the president, the collective power of the campus community, and the authoritative symbolic power of a historical marker.

Once we recognize covert disciplinary power, the grand narrative and its social conventions become less absolute and certain. We become open to alternative stories and forms of knowledge. We have a chance to move away from either/or to both/and thinking.

155

Concluding Thoughts on Postmodernism

This section has discussed three themes of postmodernism relevant to practicing communication ethics—the decentered Self, justified truth, and power. The decentered Self encourages us to think radically about others before Self. The decentered Self recognizes that each person's humanity depends upon someone recognizing her call and being responsive *before* thinking about Self. Justified truth encourages us to recognize that our knowledge is limited and partial. This prompts us to think more critically about claims to certain truth or universal knowledge. We must be careful, however, not to use alternative standards for truth to rationalize intentional deception or falsehood. Our commitment to truthfulness promotes interpersonal trust that is necessary for human survival and thriving. Postmodern power encourages us to recognize how power is embedded in all our relationships and communication practices. Power's creative and disciplinary forces cannot be avoided, although our communication choices may emphasize one force or the other. When we are mindful of how power functions covertly and overtly, we become more attentive to consequences of our actions that may promote survival and thriving or unintentionally harm others.

There are several criticisms of postmodernism. Skeptical critics claim postmodernism is simply a new version of relativism in the absolutism-relativism debate. Sympathetic critics observe that while postmodernism identifies important limitations of modernist approaches to practicing ethics, it does not offer new practices that do not have these limitations. How can we resolve disagreements when two or more sides are certain that their point of view is legitimate and correct? Without some shared standard, how can we address the problems we face within diverse communities or across cultural boundaries? How can we communicate without exercising disciplinary power or turning the other into an object? These criticisms identify the **paradox of postmodernism**, that a postmodern attitude heightens a communicator's sensitivity to ethical issues and her sense of responsibility, while simultaneously discouraging ethically responsive communicative action, because communicating will only perpetuate harms or create new ones.

A **paradox** is a special type of contradiction in which two ideas exist simultaneously, but it is logically impossible for these two ideas to exist simultaneously. One response to paradox is to stop and think about the logical impossibility. As we think about its mutual contradictions, we become paralyzed because we cannot figure out how to act. Every option for action is wrong, except doing nothing. The classic paradox in ethics is "This sentence is a lie." If the sentence is a lie, it is true. However, if it is true, it is not a lie. The more you think about a paradox, the more immobilized you become because you cannot figure out what is true or how to respond. Some people become so fascinated with a paradox that they study how the mutually inconsistent statements affect thinking. Other responses to paradox are walking away and forgetting about it, denying that the paradox has any significance, or cynically doubting everything because the truth of the paradox makes everything meaningless and irrelevant.

Postmodernism makes important criticisms of modernist thinking. In questioning modernist assumptions of certain knowledge, rationality, and progress, postmodernism identifies rationalizing tendencies of modernist certainty. Certainty is vulnerable to rationalization, because "I already know everything I need to know." Listening becomes less important, even stops, prompting withdrawal from communication processes, even relationships. Postmodernism does not provide clear suggestions for how to communicate ethically that does not perpetuate in different ways modernism's harms. If postmodernism is the primary ethical alternative to modernism, the paradox of postmodernism limits communicators who wish to avoid harming others to two options—withdrawing from their relationships or public life to avoid difficult situations entirely, or listening to understand.

Point to Ponder

❖   *What role does curiosity play in practicing communication ethics?*

How much guidance does postmodernism provide for practicing communication ethics? Levinas offers some insight. He claims that his work is not a program or practice of ethics, but an ethical ground of meaning (*Ethics and Infinity* 90). Postmodernism draws our attention to limitations of modernist thinking that foster the overconfidence and certainty that promotes dehumanizing or other harmful communication practices. Recognizing and acknowledging limits of what we know, considering and valuing the perspectives of others, using both/and thinking, and being sensitive to power dynamics of our communication practices are important in imagining the impact of our decisions on others. Understanding postmodernism as a criticism of modernism does not require us to reject moral rights, such as the right not to be tortured, or to reject commitment to do the greatest good for the greatest number. Postmodernism encourages us to become more mindful and examine our thinking for the rationalizing tendencies of modernism. In fact, postmodernist thinking encourages us to be more rigorous in applying utilitarian impartiality, for example, and be honest about potential consequences of our decisions. When our ethical reasoning is characterized by a postmodern awareness of our limitations, our moral imaginations face a new, non-paralyzing paradox—that our limitations free us to create and explore in new ways what is ethically good, right, or virtuous.

Textbox 7.2

Postmodern Cynicism, Despair, and Hope

Some credit postmodernism with increasing awareness of ethical issues in society. Others argue that postmodernism promotes cynicism and even despair, as people recognize ethical problems but feel powerless to do anything that will not exacerbate those problems or create new harms. In response to this cynicism and despair, some scholars and social activists advocate that we embrace hope. Hope is a belief that good may happen but also recognizes and accepts the evidence that good may not happen. Hope is not optimism, which is an unwarranted certainty that the best will happen. Optimism contradicts cynicism, setting up an either/or binary. Hope is a third alternative. Communication based on hope acknowledges that the problems and difficulties that cynics identify are real, but responds to them with the belief that good is possible, if we work for it.

Dialogue

Have you ever had a conversation in which someone really understood what you were saying? It probably is easier to recall conversations in which someone *mis*understood you. Add to this list conversations in which you misunderstood another person, although at the time you thought you understood. One goal of competent communication is understanding and being understood by another person. Unfortunately, misunderstanding is all too common. Moments of mutual understanding seem rare. They are **dialogical moments**. In the chapter's opening case, there is great opportunity for misunderstanding between President Wick and the protesting students. There is equally great opportunity for the mutual understanding of dialogical moments, if both parties commit to the effort.

There is no precise definition of dialogue, no checklist that guarantees a dialogical moment will occur. Dialogue is a slippery form of communication, difficult for scholars to recreate for study and research (Anderson, Baxter, and Cissna 1–2). If you work too hard at dialogue, you will never experience it. Yet, if you never work at it, dialogical moments may never appear. In dialogue, you are open to the possibility that mutual understanding can develop. Such a moment is pivotal to everyone who experiences it, shaping their understanding of each other, the relationship, and possibility. **Dialogue** is a communication practice characterized by willingness to continue to communicate with an Other with an openness for mutual understanding. Mutual understanding is not agreement or consensus. In fact, mutual understanding may be grounded in passionate disagreement and debate. Whether dialogic moments emerge from agreement, disagreement, or a bit of each, mutual understanding of dialogue involves mutual respect. When communicators understand one another in dialogue, they acknowledge and affirm each Other as human beings. Sometimes dialogue leads to agreements and shared decisions. In fact, it is critical for collaborative decision making. Dialogue, however, does not guarantee reaching a mutually satisfying decision. The goal of dialogue is mutual or shared understanding that affirms each Other's humanity, not to make decisions or resolve disagreements.

Philosopher and theologian **Martin Buber** described dialogue as communication that creates an I-Thou relationship. **Monologue**, in contrast, creates an I-it relationship. An I-Thou relationship exists when communicators recognize and affirm the humanity and wholeness of each other as human beings. In an **I-Thou relationship**, each person communicates with the Other as a Subject who is an equal, deserving respect (Buber *I and Thou* 59–69). In an **I-it relationship**, a person communicates monologically, using an Other as an object to be examined or to achieve some goal (82–5). In I-Thou relationships, we experience our humanness and mutually recognize and acknowledge each Other as Subjects, rather than objects. While experience of being understood in an I-Thou relationship is critical to becoming human, Buber considers both dialogical and monological communication important (Friedman 57–60; Buber *I and Thou* 96–107). If cashiers at a grocery store, for example, began to take time to communicate dialogically rather than monologically with customers, most of the store's usual customers would be unable to make purchases. If this dialogue continued long enough, the store could close because it would lose so much business, depriving all its customers this source of groceries and its employees their jobs. I am not claiming that dialogical moments should never develop in a checkout line at a store, but that monological communication has an important place in our lives. Without monologue, we cannot accomplish daily tasks and much of the work needed to sustain our lives. What monological communication cannot do is help us develop into human beings. A challenge of practicing dialogue is discerning how to communicate so dialogical moments can sometimes develop out of monological communication.

Everyday Communication Ethics

❖ *Describe a time when you experienced an I-Thou relationship.*

Richard Johannesen describes dialogue as an attitude with which communicators "best nurture and actualize each individual's capabilities and potentials, whatever they are" (56). A dialogical attitude exhibits three essential qualities—presentness, tensional mutuality, and authenticity[1]. These are values of a dialogical ethic of communication. **Presentness** is an attitude of focusing our attention on the immediate *now* of communication, rather than the past or future. If we think about what to say next or how to achieve our personal goal, we are not present (Friedman 58 and 82–3). If we think about whether we understand our communication partner or appreciate the quality of our understanding, we have stopped practicing presentness. Instead, we have begun to treat an Other as an object to be examined, creating an I-it relationship. Practicing presentness requires being *in the communication moment* with an Other. Presentness helps explain why following a set of guidelines for resolving a conflict can create a sense of detachment to the conflict and the people involved. Communication guidelines or checklists can prompt us to make judgments about the "correctness" of a conflict, rather than being present to our conflict partner. In the chapter's opening case, if either President Wick or the protesting students follow a script or checklist, whether it is for conflict management with students or on how to protest the administration, they will not practice presentness and no dialogical moment will emerge.

Presentness is not an attitude that anything goes. When we are dialogically present, we are open to what develops with the flow of communication in a way that acknowledges the humanity of the Other. Instead of mindlessly following communication rules about timing, turn taking, or thinking about what happens next, presentness opens ourselves to the Other in the moment. Lisbeth Lipari's idea of "listening others to speech" encourages us to think about presentness as attuning our listening to Others and "the dance of circumstance" ("Ethics" 89). When two or more communicators are dialogically present, a dance of mutually responsive presentness emerges. This contributes to the reciprocity of dialogue. If you *expect* reciprocity, presentness disappears. This is Levinas's criticism of dialogue (Lipari "Listening") and a key point of the decentered Self, that in responding to the call of the Other reciprocity is beside the point[2]. If your goal is to create *reciprocal* dialogue, you are not present because you expect or perhaps demand the Other be present to you. Presentness focuses on the Other, *not* on what you want or expect from the Other. With mutual presentness, communicators acknowledge each Other, promoting practice of the second value of dialogue, tensional mutuality.

Everyday Communication Ethics

❖ *In your experience, how might the practice of reciprocity interfere with the emergence of dialogical moments?*

Tensional mutuality requires recognition that the shared understanding of dialogue cannot exist without an Other, whose feelings and thoughts are different from your feelings and thoughts. Tensional mutuality is characterized by tension and the cooperation. A challenge of its practice is being open to an Other, while also being true to how you are different from the Other (Buber *Way of Response* 112). Dialogue creates an environment in which mutual understanding acknowledges differences between your Self and an

Other. When we deny differences to create agreement needed to achieve a communication goal, we do not communicate dialogically. Communication practices that give us a sense of strange otherness for our communication partners promote tensional mutuality (Cissna and Anderson "Ground" 14). An attitude of **strange otherness** requires that we not presume we know or understand everything that an Other means, even when the Other is a family member, friend, coworker, or conflict partner in a recurring disagreement. As we imagine how familiar Others are strangers to us in some way, we begin to listen more attentively for what we do not understand or know. An attitude of tensional mutuality also encourages communication of our tentative understanding of an Other, because we recognize that an Other knows what she feels or means better than we do. As we practice tensional mutuality, we begin to practice the third value of dialogue, authenticity.

Many assume that if a person is honest, he is authentic. Yet, if we define authenticity as simply telling the truth, especially the truth of our feelings, we miss other important dimensions of authenticity for dialogue. **Authenticity** in dialogue is honesty in communicating who we are to an Other, while being genuinely open to understanding and acknowledging the Other (Buber *Between* 4–6, 19–21). The authenticity of dialogue is risky and fragile. Being misunderstood is an obvious risk of authentic communication in either monologue or dialogue. Dialogic authenticity has two additional risks—it can transform both relationships and communicators. First, a dialogic practice of authenticity helps transform the relationship between communicators from an I-it to an I-Thou relationship. When your partner communicates an authentic understanding of you that does not deny her Self, she values and accepts you as a human being. When we communicate our authentic understanding in return, a dialogical moment may emerge. Dialogic authenticity is fragile, because it depends on risking our self-interest to be open to the Other. When we focus only on our Selves to communicate what we think and feel, we are not authentically open to the Other and accepting of the Other's humanity. Yet, if we focus on the Other and do not also acknowledge how we are different, we are not authentically ourselves.

The second risk of authentic dialogue concerns whether a communicator accepts responsibility for the consequences of dialogically understanding an Other for understanding her Self. Our understanding of who we are in our relationship with the Other changes, as we recognize that we have misunderstood an Other. Buber's terminology of the I-Thou/I-it relationships helps illustrate. Dialogue is an experience of mutually authentic and present communication between fully human Subjects who are different from one another. A dialogic moment recreates this relationship, transforming it from an I-it to an I-Thou relationship. In a dialogical moment, we are no longer a certain and powerful Subject in an I-it relationship, becoming instead a mutually equal Subject in an I-Thou relationship. Recognition of the contrast between a moment of dialogue and our history of communicating with the Other can stimulate understanding how our past communication created misunderstanding or dehumanized the Other as an it. The impact of dialogic understanding can dramatically affect our relationships, as we set aside certainties and presumptions about Others and ourselves. If we have been previously treated as an object in an I–it relationship, a dialogical moment transforms us from an object into a Subject in this relationship. It empowers and humanizes us as communicators.

The chapter's opening case illustrates the importance of authenticity for dialogue. If President Wick and the students authentically communicate their feelings and thoughts about the Swisshelm marker and their understanding of each other, mutual understanding is possible. Dialogic authenticity disappears when there are hidden agendas or strategies to achieve an advantage. If President Wick or the students withhold information and ideas or express feelings for strategic advantage, their unauthentic communication creates I–it communication.

Practicing dialogue is not easy. It is like standing on a narrow ridge where it is easy to fall (Friedman 3–10). Dialogue is not about finding a middle ground for agreement or consensus, but risks opening ourselves to the passionate differences, contradictions, and paradoxes of human life. Practicing dialogue is living with *both* the mutuality *and* contradiction of our relationships. There is similarity between Buber's narrow ridge of dialogue and ideas of dialogical theorist **David Bohm**. Bohm approaches dialogue from a background in theoretical physics and philosophy rather than communication (*Wholeness*). He is interested in dialogue as a practice of creative problem solving. **Dialogue as a practice of creative problem solving** occurs when we use dialogue to live with the paradoxes and contradictions of our mutual problems (*Dialogue* 63–95). He urges us to resist solving them too soon, because living with contradiction and paradox is important for understanding difficult problems and issues. An example from physics, Bohm's professional area of study, illustrates living with paradox (*Wholeness* 163–76). Physicists often study problems using contradictory theoretical principles, such as the contradictory idea that energy acts as a particle and a wave at the same time. Both statements are true. At any one moment, a physicist may "see" energy as a particle, while understanding energy is also a wave, or a physicist may "see" energy as a wave, while understanding it as a particle[3]. Bohm argues that only by living with the truth of contradiction and paradox can we develop an understanding that promotes creative problem solving.

Everyday Communication Ethics

❖ *How can you practice presentness in your communication? Tensional mutuality? Dialogic authenticity?*

Bohm's concept of dialogue as creative problem solving encourages us to understand and live with Others whose ethical values and commitments are different from our own. When we avoid contradiction and paradox created by communicating with people who have different ethical commitments, we diminish our moral imaginations and reduce opportunities and resources for creative ethical problem solving. When we avoid the contradiction and paradox, we step off the narrow ridge of dialogue. Dialogue is a communication practice for ethically responding to paradoxes and contradictions of human life so we understand them as best we can. We do not try to manage problems and challenges with halfway solutions that paper over meaningful differences between our Selves and Others.

Textbox 7.3

Living the Tension

The Supreme Court is final arbiter of legal conflicts in the US legal system. Most public communications of justices occur when they ask questions during oral argument and in the written legal opinions explaining the court's decisions. Internal discussions and deliberation about specific cases are secret. News reports typically focus on questions or comments during oral argument and divided votes as signs of disagreement, even opposition among the justices. This creates an image of nine people in intense debate and conflict. This image is one reason why a eulogy for conservative Justice Antonin Scalia by liberal Justice Ruth Bader Ginsberg caught many by surprise. In her eulogy, Ginsberg credits Scalia's pointed criticisms and disagreements with making her opinions better, making her a better Supreme Court justice. She also explains how this vigorous opponent was her best friend.

The momentary nature of dialogue leads some sympathetic critics to conclude that dialogue is too idealistic and fragile to be practical. A society that places a high value on competition values individual success too much to sustain a practice of dialogical communication. With the speedup and overload of digital communication, there are fewer opportunities for thoughtful and intentional dialogue. Practicing dialogue would be nice, if we only had the time. Other critics doubt the willingness of individuals to risk being authentic in genuine dialogue. Other critics question the willingness of individuals, groups, or organizations to practice tensional mutuality and risk setting aside certainty in their rightness and the wrongness of others.

Another criticism of dialogue is that it does not adequately address issues of power (Hammond, Anderson, and Cissna). These critics question whether power imbalances make dialogue impossible. Can there be genuine dialogue between a student and teacher, a child and a parent, or a client and a therapist? For years, Buber argued that genuine dialogue emerges only between equals. After a public dialogue with psychologist Carl Rogers, Buber concluded that with a communicator sensitive to issues of power, dialogue could emerge between a psychologist and a client (Cissna and Anderson *Meeting* 123–4). Buber's conclusion, however, does not address social and cultural inequities based upon differences in race, ethnicity, class, gender, or sexual orientation. Dialogue assumes a relational equality that does not exist for everyone. For less powerful groups and communities, participation in dialogue may acknowledge and affirm cultural, political, or social structures that keep them unequal. A challenge for practicing dialogue is creating communication practices that are relationally just.

Some leaders have used public dialogue to address significant disagreements within their communities as a form of public engagement (Pearce and Littlejohn). Besides power imbalance between participants, public dialogue poses an additional challenge in achieving mutual respect that characterizes the I-Thou relationship. **Italo Testa** argues that mutual or equal respect is a potential outcome of public dialogue, not a starting point. If participants require being respected in order to participate in public dialogue, no dialogic moments will emerge. Requiring respect interferes with presentness, by focusing attention on identity. Identity is not the point of dialogue, understanding is. Being present to the ideas and arguments of the Other in order to understand, creates a foundation for respecting an Other. Testa's argument parallels David Bohm's concept of dialogue as creative problem solving. In dialogic communication, mutual respect develops when communicators are present by authentically engaging with each other's ideas, feelings, and arguments in a way that truthfully honors their similarities and differences. Mutual respect emerges from a truthful and authentic understanding of how each other agrees and disagrees.

Dialogical moments are important for creating our humanity and for understanding the contradictions and paradoxes of human life. Consider how your practice of communication ethics would change if you practiced dialogic ethics.

Ethical Care

Pat, a pseudonym, was a student in one of my classes. Pat was either late to class or absent at least once a week. When she attended class, she was often distracted. It was no surprise that she did poorly on assignments early in the term. She did not follow study suggestions for the first exam and failed it. I saw Pat as a student not interested in being in class for some unknown reason. When making another appointment to talk about an assignment, Pat mentioned that she was unavailable on Friday afternoons because her guardians would be picking her up for the three-hour drive home, as they did every weekend. She disclosed that they did this so she would not have to spend the weekend in town, because being around students who went out partying and drinking was too great a temptation for a recovering addict. This began a conversation that changed my perception and understanding of Pat and changed our relationship into a more caring student-teacher relationship. An ethic of care focuses on how we act in concrete ways that meet the needs of individual people. It focuses our attention on the real lives of specific people in our relationships. Pat was my student, but she also was a person with a history, her own needs and goals, and her own personal struggles. As I learned more about Pat, my growing understanding shaped our student-teacher relationship. Practicing an ethic of care focused my moral imagination and discernment about Pat and her story, as Pat and I created our relationship that term.

An ethic of care may seem familiar. Care is based on the experience of caring and being cared for in our personal relationships. When you were a young child, your parents, family members, and caregivers cared for you. As you grew older, you may have cared for a sick family member or a friend. The experience of caring and being cared for is **natural caring** (Noddings 43). It arises spontaneously from the affection that exists in our close personal relationships. Feelings of affection (or lack of affection) toward someone guide our responses to the needs of that person. Natural caring is not sufficient to create an ethic of care. **Ethical care** is practiced by discerning and deliberating about how to care responsively and competently for the specific needs of another.

Moral psychologist Carol Gilligan first drew attention to care as an ethical value. She argues that some people use care as an alternative to justice in their ethical reasoning. Reasoning with justice requires that we think abstractly about whether a person is being treated fairly or unfairly. For example, we use the universal principles of distributive justice or moral rights to make judgments about what would be fair in a classroom or a workplace. Reasoning with care, we focus on how to meet the individual needs of a person, such as my student Pat, rather than apply an abstract principle of fairness, moral rights, or justice. My relationship with Pat and my student-teacher interactions with her developed out of my understanding of her needs as a student *and* as a recovering addict. Learning facts about the lived experience of a person helps us understand a person's actual needs. Practicing ethical care involves understanding a person in context, within the story of her life, her relationships, and her situation.

Imagine you notice that one of your friends appears agitated and absent-minded. You start a conversation, hoping to discover the source of your friend's discomfort. Whenever you do something like this, you practice care. Your care may end with this conversation, if you discover that you are unable to do more to meet your friend's needs. Even if you decide that you can do something more, your friend may not respond positively to your care. Sometimes we are surprised by how others respond to our care. We often idealize or romanticize care, creating unrealistic expectations about how to care or how others will respond. The practice of care involves tension and, sometimes, conflict. The example of caring for a friend who appears agitated can illustrate one tension of practicing care, that the needs of the person receiving care are incompatible with the care provided. Your friend may be agitated and distracted because of a long separation from a romantic partner. Your practice of care cannot substitute for your friend's absent partner. A more difficult tension is when the needs of the person receiving the care conflict with the needs of caregiver. This can be a source of ongoing tension and even conflict in long-term caring relationships. A conflict about needs may develop as a caregiver realizes that she is caring so much that it harms her, including her capacity to be a caregiver, because she no longer has the emotional, physical, or financial resources to meet the needs of the other. A subtler, but no less significant tension is when the caregiver and those receiving care have different perceptions about what care is needed. The cared-for may not appreciate or want the care given. Sometimes what the caregiver provides does not meet the cared-for's needs or even harms her. Good intentions do not guarantee that the care given will meet the cared-for's needs.

Caregiving is not the same as ethical care. Practicing care without ethical discernment and deliberation lacks integrity. Feminist scholar Joan Tronto identifies the qualities that comprise the holistic practice of ethical care (127–37). When care is practiced holistically, it creates a relationship that is ethically responsive to the needs of the cared-for and to the capacity of the caregiver to meet those needs. The **holistic practice of ethical care** has four phases (105–8)—recognizing the need for care (caring about), taking responsibility for the need and figuring out how to respond to it (taking care of), directly meeting the needs (caregiving), and responding to an act of care (care-receiving). There are four practices of ethical caregiving—attentiveness, responsibility, competence, and responsiveness—that are applied in the four phases of care. While each of these practices of care is distinct, they combine with each other to create integrity for the practice of care (136–7).

The holistic practice of ethical care requires being **attentive** by recognizing the needs of another person. You cannot care for someone, unless you recognize her need. You cannot be attentive to the need of a person, until you recognize that she exists. We often do not practice ethical care because we do not recognize a person in need, until he does something to attract our attention. Practicing attentiveness requires setting aside personal goals and concerns and becoming aware of the existence and needs of others around you. Attentiveness, however, is more than recognition of a need of another person. The communication act of acknowledgment (Hyde) elaborates the practice of attentiveness. Attentiveness involves recognizing and acknowledging another's feelings and thoughts, responding "Here I am" to the cared-for's call "Where art thou?" Attentiveness involves acknowledging the circumstances and relationships that create the fabric of the cared-for's life, which may include how you and your practice of care are part of the fabric of her life.

The second practice of holistic care is a **responsibility** to respond to that recognized need with an act of care. The responsibility of the holistic practice of care is created by your relationship with the person in need. When we are not attentive to the existence of another person, we cannot recognize our relationship or our responsibility. The interpersonal responsibility of ethical care develops as communication creates relational connection with others. Communication that creates relationships, such as making a new friend, becoming neighbors, hiring an employee, or becoming parents simultaneously creates responsibilities to practice care in those relationships in ethically responsive ways. Responsibility in the holistic practice of care is more flexible and responsive than obligation or duty. Responsibility exists within a specific relationship, rather than as an abstract duty to practice care in every relationship. If you were to practice holistic care, your responsibility to meet the needs of the other would grow out of a relationship and your attentiveness to that person. When you are attentive to a person, you can identify which of your personal abilities or resources might address her need. You may conclude, for example, that you do not have the abilities or resources to meet a specific need of a friend or family member. Different people may meet different needs of the same person. Whatever our abilities or resources, the holistic practice of care encourages us to understand how the responsibility to care grows out of our relational connections with others.

Everyday Communication Ethics

❖ *Describe a time when someone who had a responsibility to care for you was inattentive. Describe a time when you were inattentive to someone for whom you had a responsibility to care.*

The third practice of holistic care is competent care. Not all caring is competent. Good intentions are insufficient to create a holistic practice of ethical care, even when the caregiver correctly identifies the need. **Competent care** is about providing good care that meets the needs of the cared-for. If our care is not competent, the needs we are responding to will not be met (Tronto 133). Well-intentioned, caring people can frustrate the cared-for and themselves when care is incompetent. Incompetent care may also create harm, if there are inadequate resources, the caregiver lacks the knowledge and training to care competently, or her motivation falters. Caregivers should acknowledge when their care becomes inadequate, so that care can become competent. A caring and well-intentioned teacher, who lacks the knowledge to teach mathematics but is assigned to teach a math course, cannot care competently for her students.

The fourth practice of an ethic of care is responsiveness. Responsiveness is crucial to the holistic practice of care. Needs of the cared-for make her vulnerable, whether her need is for education, emotional support, physical care, money, or something else. When the cared-for becomes dependent on the caregiver to meet her needs, she may lose her capacity to make choices or act. Because of this vulnerability, caregivers must be sensitive to the potential for abuse of power in caregiving. **Responsiveness** is being attentive to the cared-for, including the cared-for's viewpoint. Focusing our attention on the person receiving our care instead of ourselves—acknowledging her, being aware of and sensitive to the context of our relationship with the cared-for—are communication practices of responsiveness that help us better understand a cared-for, her needs, and what she thinks. When a caregiver is ethically responsive to the cared-for, the caregiver is better able to assess if she is offering competent care.

The chapter's opening case can illustrate each practice of holistic care. The students' protest signals the needs of these students, creating an opportunity for President Wick to acknowledge his relationship with them and recognize their need. Ignoring or minimizing the protest would be inattentive and uncaring. When we do not recognize the need for care, we cannot practice ethical care. As the leader of the campus community, the president has a responsibility to care for the needs of all students on campus, alongside those present before him. Whether the protesting students receive competent care from President Wick would depend on several factors, such as the communication and leadership skills of the president and available campus resources. By meeting with the students and listening to them, President Wick has an opportunity to be ethically responsive to their needs.

An ethic of care challenges us to identify practices of communication that acknowledge the importance of relationships, emotions, needs, and the complexity of individual circumstances. Ethical care rejects one-size-fits-all guidelines for its practice, focusing on responsibilities to care created by our relationships. Because needs and individual circumstances vary, the practice of ethical care often is not consistent from person to person, raising questions about the fairness or justice of caregiving. A modernist practice of care is arguably more just because it encourages thinking more universally about how to practice care. Modernist care, however, would be less responsive to individual need, potentially causing harm in the name of fairness.

Point to Ponder

❖ *Which types of justice could you incorporate in your practice of ethical care?*

An important criticism of care is that the needs of the cared-for can be used to rationalize caregivers sacrificing their needs to practice care (Wood 162–9). A caregiver who consistently sacrifices her personal needs to meet the needs of the cared-for can undermine the holistic practice of ethical care, as well as harm herself. When caregiving is not responsive to the needs of the caregiver as well as the cared-for, care becomes less competent. The film *The Theory of Everything* shows how competent care can deteriorate into incompetent care. The film portrays the courtship and marriage of Jane Wilde Hawking and theoretical physicist Steven Hawking, who had ALS (Lou Gehrig's disease). The film portrays the challenges of ethical caregiving, showing how repeated sacrifice of the caregiver's needs undermines the holistic practice of ethical care.

Textbox 7.4

Communication Ethics in Popular Film: *Harry Potter* and Ethical Care

The *Harry Potter* books by J.K. Rowling, and films based on the books, provide an extended case study of natural caring and ethical care. Harry is alive because of the sacrificial care of his mother. Harry and his friends, Ron and Hermione, learn how to practice caregiving and care-receiving throughout the series. We watch them and other characters such as Dumbledore, the headmaster of Hogwarts School of Magic, struggle with the complexities and difficulties of practicing ethical care—how to distinguish between need and desire, who to care for when many different people need your care, and the role of honesty and truth in the practice of ethical care. Each of these challenges of ethical care appears in the first book and film, *Harry Potter and the Sorcerer's Stone*, and is explored throughout the series.

Distinguishing between a Need and a Desire

The ethical practice of care involves being responsive to a person's needs. A need is important or critical for a person's survival and capacity to thrive. A desire, in contrast, is something a person longs for. While needs and desires may overlap, they do not always. Some desires are easily satisfied, such as longing for a particular drink, while other desires are long-lived, such as Harry's desire for his parents. In *The Sorcerer's Stone*, Harry's desire to know his parents makes him vulnerable to the Mirror of Erised, which shows the deepest and most desperate desire of the viewer's heart. Harry needs a family. The Mirror of Erised shows him the object of his desire, his parents. By focusing on his desire, the Mirror does not meet Harry's immediate need to make friends and his long-term need to become part of a new family. Dumbledore, recognizing and responding to Harry's needs, hides the Mirror of Erised from him.

Deciding Who to Care For

As headmaster of Hogwarts School of Magic, Dumbledore struggles repeatedly with the question of who to care for. His many relationships create multiple responsibilities of care. A recurring dramatic tension is Dumbledore's different and sometimes contradictory responsibilities to care for others. As headmaster, he must care for his students. Because of his relationship with Harry's parents, Dumbledore has a responsibility to care for Harry. Yet to care competently for Harry and for other students, Dumbledore must address the threat of Voldemort, a powerful wizard committed to the destruction of this magical society. To care for his students by protecting them from Voldemort, Dumbledore must also involve himself in caring for the needs of the broader magical community, and in later books, this develops into a responsibility to care for non-magical society. The problem Dumbledore faces throughout the series is that his responsibilities to practice care in these different relationships often conflict with one another. Meeting one person's needs requires ignoring another's needs, whether it is the needs of a friend, a teacher at Hogwarts, some other person in Dumbledore's personal network of relationships, or the relational networks that create magical society. In *The Sorcerer's Stone*, Dumbledore's efforts to care by addressing the growing threat of Voldemort put Hogwarts students in danger. Throughout the series, the complexity of Dumbledore's and other characters' responsibilities to care makes it difficult at times to judge whether someone is practicing ethically responsive care.

Truthfulness and Practicing Care

A common practice in caring is to tell children white lies, because children are not considered capable of understanding the truth. Because the *Harry Potter* series begins when Harry is a young boy, Harry's age arguably justifies Dumbledore withholding a portion of the truth about Voldemort, simply because children would not understand this threat. Withholding some or all of the truth makes care easier, because there is less explaining to do. In *The Sorcerer's Stone*, Dumbledore and the teachers of Hogwarts use secrecy to hide a powerful magic at Hogwarts, in an initial attempt to protect the magical society from Voldemort. Their efforts fail. The *Harry Potter* series explores the relationship between care and honesty, and the challenges of being honest when those you care for do not believe you or when the desires or needs of those you care for affect their capacity to understand the truth. The interplay of secrecy and truthfulness in *Harry Potter* makes it difficult to identify at key points who is practicing ethically responsive care and who is not.

Because the *Harry Potter* series follows Harry and his friends from childhood to early adulthood, the books and films provide an extended example of the challenges and complexities of ethical caregiving and care-receiving

Another criticism of care is that it rationalizes the social status of power-less or less powerful members of society (Wood 99–103). This criticism is based upon observations about how society distributes the responsibilities or burdens of caregiving and the benefits of being cared for. Race, ethnicity, gender, and social status influence the social distribution of caregiving and receiving care. People of color, women, and the working poor are employed in greater proportions in caring or service professions such as nursing, child-care, or housekeeping, than do high status persons who tend to be males or Euro-Americans. This has led some critics to observe that care is a practice of the powerless that contributes little to addressing social concerns about fairness and justice. Many of those who consider care an ethically important value agree that society's distribution of caregiving and care-receiving merits examination. They argue, however, that this is not a criticism of the holistic practice of ethical care. Rather, it is evidence of issues of distributive justice in flawed *social* practices of caregiving and receiving care.

Point to Ponder

❖ *Is ethical care a virtue? If yes, what are the excess and deficiency of care?*

Concerns about justice are the basis of another criticism of an ethic of care, that care is insufficiently rational. An ethic of care focuses our moral imagination on discerning the needs of individuals in our personal relation-ships. Emotional understanding and affection, not objectivity and reason, are important in personal relationships. Objectivity and reason are arguably not relevant in ethical care. When answering the question, "Who do I care for?" some critics charge that an ethic of care encourages us to give special treatment to those we know and for whom we have positive feelings, instead of objectively examining the needs of others for care. Do we have an ethi-cal responsibility to care for others who are not personally related to us? A parent's care for a child can illustrate the challenge of practicing fairness in caregiving. It is generally accepted that parents have greater responsibility to care for their own children than they do a stranger's child. What happens when parents who are ethically responsive to their child's needs use so many resources that other parents no longer have access to resources that meet their child's needs for special or gifted education, after-school care, vaccinations, or well-child medical examinations? An ethic of care gives little guidance for answering questions about distributive justice in society with its focuses on care in personal relationships.

Tronto's practice of holistic care encourages us to shift the focus of our attention away from our Self to an Other. The practice of ethics involves discerning the weight to place on my legitimate interest to survive and thrive relative to the legitimate interests of others to survive and thrive, a weight that is good, right, and virtuous. In an individualistic society that promotes acting on self-interest, natural caring begins to shift the focus of our attention away from our Selves to an Other. Yet, natural caring is vulnerable to becoming incompetent care, either by the caregiver presuming she knows what the cared-for needs when, in fact, she does not or by the caregiver sacrificing herself to the needs of the cared-for. Practices of ethical care must involve some practices of justice that encourage responsiveness to needs to survive and thrive of those who are cared for and those who give care.

Conclusion

Postmodernism, dialogue, and ethical care offer alternatives to modernist theories of moral rights and utilitarianism. Postmodernism challenges practices of modernist certainty, rationality, and objectivity. Nontraditional theories of ethics discussed in this chapter highlight how our understanding is always incomplete and partial and is shaped by our relationships. Whether you decide to include any of these alternative concepts or approaches in your personal ethical standard, studying them expands your moral imagination, providing additional resources for ethical discernment and deliberation. Questions raised by these concepts and theories merit your consideration.

Vocabulary

Cases for Discussion

Directions: Use postmodern concepts of the decentered self, meaning, or power, dialogical ethics, or the ethics of care to identify ethical issues in each case. Include in your deliberations the three recurring decision points of communication.

1. After a Long Silence

Brooke ended the phone call, "Goodbye, Dad." But this was not "dad." It was Steve. Twenty years ago, Steve was married to Brooke's mom.

They divorced before Brooke was 2. She had no memory of Steve and grew up without a father. Brooke had not talked to anyone from Steve's family in years. She did not know much about Steve, except that he moved out west after the divorce. It was just Brooke and her mom until Brooke was 12, when her mom married her current husband Bill. There are four of them now, Brooke, Mom, Bill, and her 10-year-old stepsister Carla. Today, out of nowhere, Brooke gets a phone call from Steve wanting to talk and make plans to get together with his daughter. Brooke is curious, but she is not sure she wants to meet Steve.

What and how should Brooke communicate?

2. Surprise at Work

For years Izabella had enjoyed her job. Work was interesting and her coworkers were fun to be around, and even caring. Several coworkers she considered friends and spent time with them outside of work. A lot can change in six months. Izabella had heard about dinners and outings that she was not invited to. Work had been so busy, she had not noticed that there were fewer invitations for coffee and lunch. Then the surprise at today's department meeting: Dan suggested a reorganization of the department that would eliminate half of her job description, without mentioning any new responsibilities for her. After the meeting, Izabella had talked to Jessie, her first friend in the department. Jessie told her that she had developed a reputation of being distant and hard to work with. About a month ago, Christine suggested that some job responsibilities, like Izabella's, do not fit the department's strategic plan and that the department needed to be reorganized. A few people volunteered to brainstorm about reorganizing.

Izabella did not know what to say. She had helped write the plan and knew that her job not only fit the plan, but was necessary to meet department goals. She should have been included in any discussion of reorganization.

What should Izabella do?

3. Caring Too Much or Too Little

Ivan, age 71, lives alone at Parkside, an assisted living center. His three children, Karl, Louise, and Pat moved him there over his protests two years ago. Because of his dementia, Ivan would forget to take his heart medicine or that food was on the stove. Ivan eventually settled into Parkside's routine and made friends. Although Ivan's dementia progressed, in conversations with strangers his dementia is not immediately obvious. He still recalls the names of his children, but has trouble remembering grandchildren's names, especially younger ones. He is not capable of making financial or health-care decisions. Karl has power of attorney with legal responsibility for making these decisions.

Ivan has had a mild heart attack. He already eats a low-fat diet and exercises. The doctor said the only treatment is implanting a heart pacemaker to regulate the electrical system of his heart. Because of Ivan's dementia, the doctor wants Ivan's family to carefully make this decision. Karl, Louise, and Pat want to make the decision together. Ivan does not have a health-care directive clearly stating his wishes. Karl, Louise, and Pat are all concerned whether Ivan understands the significance of this decision.

Karl remembers traveling with Ivan as a young boy, to visit Ivan's mother in a nursing home. She was in the advanced stages of dementia. Karl cannot remember his grandmother ever recognizing anyone, including his father. What he remembers are conversations driving home, when his father said that he would never want to live like Grandma, lying in bed, not recognizing her own son, and waiting to die. Karl does not want the doctor to implant a heart pacemaker in Ivan, because this is not what Ivan would want if he were capable of understanding the significance of this decision.

Louise is not so sure. Her father seems happy. Even though he does not recognize some of his grandchildren, he soon warms up to them, playing checkers and asking questions about school. She says, "Dad may have felt that way when he saw Grandma in the later stages of dementia, but he's nowhere near that bad. He enjoys his life at Parkside and his family. If we could have a conversation with Dad where he could really understand the issues, implanting a pacemaker would be what he would want. I can see him telling us to implant the pacemaker, if it means he would have more time with us."

Karl and Louise turn to Pat. What and how should Pat communicate?

Notes

1 Cissna and Anderson; Johannesen; and Stewart, Zediker, and Black identify a more extensive list of qualities of dialogue. I suggest that the practice of dialogical communication develops from these three essential qualities.

2 The biographical context Ron Arnett provides in his analysis of Levinas's philosophy helps us understand Levinas's concern about reciprocity in dialogue. Any expectation, even a goal of reciprocity shifts the focus of a communicator's attention away from the Other, to one's Self. Presentness disappears.

3 Understanding how the statements that "energy is a particle" and "energy is a wave" are simultaneously true developed quantum mechanics ("Wave-Particle Duality."). See also Bohm (*Wholeness*).

References

Anderson, Rob, Leslie A. Baxter, and Kenneth N. Cissna. "Texts and Contexts of Dialogue." *Dialogue: Theorizing Difference in Communication Studies*. Thousand Oaks, CA: Sage, 2004. 1–17.

Arnett, Ronald C. *Levinas' Rhetorical Demand: The Unending Obligation of Communication Ethics.* Carbondale, IL: Southern Illinois UP, 2017.

Bohm, David. *On Dialogue.* Ed. Lee Nichol. New York: Routledge, 1996.

Bohm, David. *Wholeness and the Implicate Order.* New York: Routledge, 1980.

Bok, Sissela. *Lying: Moral Choice in Public and Private Life.* 1978. New York: Vintage Books, 1989.

Buber, Martin. *I and Thou.* Trans. Walter Benjamin. New York: Scribners, 1972.

Buber, Martin. *Between Man and Man.* Trans. Ronald Gregor Smith. 1947. New York: Macmillan, 1965.

Buber, Martin. *The Way of Response: Martin Buber—Selections from his Writings.* Ed. N.N. Glatzer. New York: Schocken Books, 1966.

Caputo, John D. "Heidegger's Scandal: Thinking and the Essence of the Victim." *The Heidegger Case on Philosophy and Politics.* Eds. T. Rockmore and J. Margolis. Philadelphia, PA: Temple UP, 1989. 265–81.

Cissna, Kenneth N. and Rob Anderson. "Communication and the Ground of Dialogue." *The Reach of Dialogue: Confirmation, Voice and Community.* Eds. Rob Anderson, Kenneth N. Cissna, and Ronald Arnett. Cresskill, NJ: Hampton Press, 1994. 9–30.

Cissna, Kenneth N. and Rob Anderson. *Moments of Meeting: Buber, Rogers and the Potential for Public Dialogue.* Albany, NY: SUNY P, 2002.

Connor, Steven, Ed. *The Cambridge Companion to Postmodernism.* New York: Cambridge UP, 2004.

Eaglestone, Robert. "Postmodernism and Ethics Against the Metaphysics of Comprehension." *The Cambridge Companion to Postmodernism.* Ed. S. Connor. Cambridge: Cambridge UP, 2004. 182–95.

Farais, Victor. *Heidegger and Nazism.* Eds. J. Margolis and T. Rockmore. Trans. P. Burrell, et al. Philadelphia, PA: Temple UP, 1989.

Foucault, Michel. *Politics, Philosophy, Culture: Interviews and Other Writings, 1977–1984.* Ed. Laurence D. Kritzman. Trans. Alan Sheridan, et al. New York: Routledge, 1988.

Foucault, Michel. *Power. Vol. 3. The Essential Works of Foucault, 1954–1984.* Ed. James D. Gaubion. Trans. Robert Hurley, et al. New York: The New Press, 2000.

Friedman, Maurice. *Martin Buber: The Life of Dialogue.* 3rd ed. Chicago, IL: Chicago UP, 1976.

Gill, Kathleen. "Should These Stories Be Saved: Reflections on the Construction of Public History." Unpublished manuscript.

Gilligan, Carol. *In a Different Voice: Psychological Theory and Women's Development.* Cambridge, MA: Harvard UP, 1982.

Haidt, Jonathan. *The Righteous Mind: Why Good People Are Divided by Politics and Religion.* New York: Vintage Books, 2012.

Haidt, Jonathan and Craig Joseph. "Intuitive Ethics: How Innately Prepared Intuitions Generate Culturally Variable Virtues." *Daedalus* 133.4 (Fall 2004): 55–66.

Hammond, Scott C., Rob Anderson, and Kenneth N. Cissna. "The Problematics of Dialogue and Power." *Communication Yearbook 27.* Ed. Pamela J. Kalbfleisch. Mahwah, NJ: LEA, 2003. 125–57.

Hannan, Jason, Ed. *Truth in the Public Sphere.* Lanham, MD: Lexington Books, 2016.

Hyde, Michael J. *The Life-Giving Gift of Acknowledgement.* West Lafayette, IN: Purdue UP, 2006.

Johannesen, Richard L. *Ethics in Human Communication.* 5th ed. Prospect Heights, IL: Waveland, 2002.

"Justice Ruth Bader Ginsberg Eulogy of Justice Antonin Scalia" *CSPAN,* 1 March 2016. www.youtube.com/watch?v=jb_2GgE564A. Date accessed: 15 October 2017.

Levinas, Emmanuel. *Ethics and Infinity.* Trans. Richard A. Cohen. Pittsburg, PA: Duquesne UP, 1985.

Levinas, Emmanuel. "Meaning and Sense." *Emmanuel Levinas: Basic Philosophical Writings.* Eds. Adriaan T. Peperzak, Simon Critchley, and Robert Bernasconi. Bloomington, IN: U of Indiana P, 1996.

Levinas, Emmanuel. *Otherwise Than Being or Beyond Essence.* Trans. A. Lingus. 1981. Pittsburg, PA: Duquesne UP, 1997.

Lipari, Lisbeth. "Listening for the Other: Implications of the Buber-Levinas Encounter." *Communication Theory* 14.2 (2004): 122–41.

Lipari, Lisbeth. "Ethics, Kairos, and Akroasis: An Essay on Time and Relation." *Philosophy of Communication Ethics: Alterity and the Other.* Eds. Ronald C. Arnett and Pat Arneson, Madison, NY: Fairleigh Dickinson UP, 2014. 75–93.

Lyotard, Jean-Francois. *The Postmodern Condition: A Report on Knowledge.* Trans. Geoff Bennington and Brian Massumi. Minneapolis, MN: U of Minnesota P, 1984.

Mendieta, Eduardo, Ed. *Take Care of Freedom and Truth Will Take Care of Itself: Interviews with Richard Rorty.* Stanford, CA: Stanford UP, 2006.

Noddings, Nel. *Caring: A Feminine Approach to Ethics and Moral Education.* Berkeley, CA: U of California P, 1984.

Pearce, W. Barnett and Stephen W. Littlejohn. *Moral Conflict: When Social Worlds Collide.* Thousand Oaks, CA: Sage, 1997.

"Population Control Marauder Style: Data Points." *The New York Times.* 5 November 2011. www.nytimes.com/2011/11/06/opinion/sunday/population-control-marauder-style.html. Date accessed: 15 October 2017.

Rorty, Richard. "Universality and Truth." *Rorty and His Critics.* Ed. Robert B. Brandon. Malden, MA: Blackwell, 2000. 1–30.

Roseneau, Pauline Marie. *Post-Modernism and the Social Sciences: Insights, Inroads and Intrusions.* Princeton, NJ: Princeton UP, 1992.

Rouse, Joseph. "Power/Knowledge." *The Cambridge Companion to Foucault.* Ed. Gary Gutting. New York: Cambridge UP 1994. 92–114.

Rowling, J.K. *Harry Potter Series.* New York: Arthur A. Levine Books, 1998, 1999, 2000, 2003, 2005, and 2007.

Sheehen, Paul. "Postmodernism and Philosophy." *The Cambridge Companion to Postmodernism.* Ed. S. Connor. Cambridge: Cambridge UP, 2004. 20–42.

Sim, Stuart, Ed. *The Routledge Companion to Postmodernism.* 1998. New York: Routledge, 1998.

Stewart, John, Karen E. Zediker, and Laura Black. "Relationships Among Philosophies of Dialogue." *Dialogue: Theorizing Difference in Communication Studies.* Eds. Rob Anderson, Leslie A. Baxter, and Kenneth N. Cissna. Thousand Oaks, CA: Sage, 2004. 21–38.

Testa, Italo. "The Respect Fallacy: Limits of Respect in Public Dialogue." *Rhetorical Citizenship and Public Deliberation.* Eds. Christian Kock and Lisa S. Villadsen. University Park, PA: The Penn State UP, 2012. 69–85.

Theory of Everything (The). Dir. James Marsh, Prods. Tim Bevan, Eric Fellner, Lisa Bruce, and Anthony McCarten. Universal Pictures, distr. 2014.

Toulmin, Stephen. *Cosmopolis: The Hidden Agenda of Modernity.* 1990. Chicago, IL: U of Chicago P, 1992.

Tronto, Joan C. *Moral Boundaries: A Political Argument for an Ethics of Care*. New York: Routledge, 1993.

"Wave-Particle Duality." *Chemistry LibreTexts*. 28 September 2015. https://chem.libretexts. org/Core/Physical_and_Theoretical_Chemistry/Quantum_Mechanics/09._The_ Hydrogen_Atom/Atomic_Theory/Electrons_in_Atoms/Wave-Particle_Duality. Date accessed: 5 March 2018.

Wood, Julia. *Who Cares?: Women, Care and Culture*. Carbondale, IL: Southern Illinois UP, 1994.

Part III

FOUR CONTEXTS OF
ETHICAL COMMUNICATION
PRACTICE

8

COMMUNICATION ETHICS AND DIGITAL COMMUNICATION

As Jarron watched, Carlson set his mobile phone on the table to record their dinner. Jarron remembered earlier times when they would take pictures of each other, the food and drinks they ordered, and then post pictures in their different social media accounts. There was an informal competition to see which posts got more followers or likes. Now Carlson live streams video whenever he goes out with friends, checking posts all evening. It's not the same. Most of the time Carlson looks at the camera and rarely speaks directly to friends, unless it is for the audience watching his video stream. When Tom is part of the group, he tries to get on camera with Carlson. Txuci won't go out with the group anymore. He says Carlson is more interested in his live stream than his friends at the table with him. Carlson's voice interrupts Jarron's thoughts, "Jarron, check your phone. How does it look?"

Most people reading this book grew up using digital platforms and mobile devices. I grew up before digital communication, when many homes did not have a typewriter. Today, I belong to a group that uses digital technology to meet and write about teaching communication ethics. We call ourselves a "virtual department." Digital technology is a recent innovation in the history of communication. Inventions of writing, the printing press, broadcasting technologies of film, radio, and television, and digital communication with its expanding number of platforms, added technologies that not only influenced *how* we communicate (Turkle; Walther "Technological"), they changed how we think (Thompson). When each technology was new, its novelty prompted excitement and concern. This diminished as people became familiar with the new medium and standards for using

181

the technology stabilized and became routine. Socrates's warnings about the new communication technology of writing in the fifth century BCE are like warnings today about digital communication (Plato). Clive Thompson points out that each new technology offers opportunities, if we develop practices and literacies for its competent use. New technologies also present challenges, including ethical challenges. To explore some of the ethical issues raised by digital communication technology, this chapter will discuss two qualities of digital communication that exist across digital platforms, highlighting how these qualities influence communicators and communication dynamics. This will be followed by a discussion of ethical issues of freedom and truth in digital communication.

Qualities of Digital Communication

Kenneth Burke's definition of humanity highlights the importance of studying technologies humans have created, because humanity is "separated from his [sic] natural condition by instruments of his [sic] own making" (*Language* 16). Technologies we invent change us. Clive Thompson identifies ways human thinking changed as different communication technologies became routine. The technology of writing created physical records that reduced the need to memorize everything you need to know, while the telegraph quickly sent messages across great distances using Morse code, stimulating development of weather forecasting. Each new communication technology requires new skills and standards for competent communication. **Literacy** is a baseline proficiency, developed through education and practice, of the skills required for competent use of a technology. New technologies change individual communicators by developing new skills, practices, and ways of thinking. New technologies also change society. The printing press mechanized the creation and distribution of written communication in pamphlets, newspapers, and cheap books. This created larger audiences for written communication than did expensive, handwritten books and documents. Some of the earliest popular pamphlets presented Martin Luther's criticisms of the Catholic Church to a much larger audience than did his initial, handwritten criticism. In creating a larger audience for Luther's criticisms, the printing press facilitated the Protestant Reformation and the violent religious conflict that followed[1].

Digital communication transforms messages into a binary sequence of 1s and 0s that is transmitted through an infrastructure of digital software, hardware, and networked systems. Digital communication technology is changing how we communicate, including what it means to be a competent and ethical communicator. This section briefly explores how two qualities of digital communication influence individual communicators and the dynamics of digital communication—1) digital technology's influence on a communicator's experience of time, space, and physical reality, and 2) digital

182

filtering. Studying fundamental qualities of digital communication, instead of specific software or hardware platforms (e.g., social media or email), helps identify qualities of digital communication technology that influence communicators and communication dynamics (Walther "Technological").

Time, Space, and Physical Reality

Digital technology influences our sense of space, time, and physical reality. In **face-to-face (f2f) communication** you are physically close enough to hear your friend speak. You see your friend's body and observe her nonverbal cues, including how she responds to what you say and how you listen. Digital communication, in contrast, allows you to communicate with friends located in other physical places. Have you ever wondered where digital communication occurs? There are different names for the digital alternative to physical reality, such as "cyberspace" (Horsfield), "virtual reality," or "between screens" (Soukup)[2]. I will use the terms "virtual reality" and "between screens" in this chapter.

Digital platforms also vary in their use of time. Some platforms, such as email, social media, texts, or stand-alone podcasts and video are **asynchronous,** because messages are exchanged at different times, instead of waiting for real-time communication. Real-time platforms, such as Carlson's live video stream in the chapter's opening case, are **synchronous**, with communicators exchanging messages in a real-time flow. Digital processing speed has increased to the point that communicators may experience asynchronous platforms as if they are synchronous, if receivers respond to messages immediately.

The ease and speech of digital communication have changed our sense of space and physical reality. Physical distances appear shorter, even nonexistent. In digital communication, we experience people who are physically distant as physically close, creating **virtual proximity**. When virtual proximity is novel, we recognize that our conversational partner is physically distant and that the time needed for messages to travel has shrunk. As virtual proximity becomes routine, our experience of faster speed and compression of space becomes ordinary and expected, speeding up our daily routines. The chapter's opening case raises a question of whether Carlson experiences people watching his live video stream as being as close or closer than his friends sitting with him.

Our communication experiences create our sense of reality. If f2f exists in physical reality, where does digital communication exist? One answer is that it occurs in perceptual and cognitive space in a communicator's mind (Saunders et al.), creating a virtual reality that exists alongside physical reality (Horsfield). You may be familiar with virtual reality from computer games where players create avatars that represent themselves. Virtual reality is achieved by what digital software and hardware designers call telepresence. **Telepresence** is a psychological state in which a communicator does not recognize that her experience is filtered through or generated by a man-made technology (Lombard and Ditton). When your digital experiences feel *as if* they were occurring in physical reality, you have experienced telepresence. Yet, it is *not* the same, because digital platforms filter out, to varying degrees, nonverbal communication cues present in f2f communication. In the chapter's opening case, the quality of Carlson's live video filters out some nonverbal cues of his voice, face, and body. It also filters out the context when he responds to people off screen. Carlson receives almost no nonverbal cues in the real-time likes and posts to his video. Differences between digitally mediated and f2f nonverbal cues can influence communicators and communication dynamics.

Joseph Walther developed his **social information processing theory** to study how communicators adapt their communication practices when using digital communication technology ("Computer-Mediated"; "Technological"). Digital communication platforms restrict, in varying degrees, nonverbal communication cues that accompany verbal messages. Nonverbal cues provide significant information about a communicator's feelings and emotions that often are not clearly expressed with words (Pearson, et al. 78–100). Because digital communication platforms filter out nonverbal cues, the emotional content of digital messages is diminished in comparison to f2f communication. In the early years of digital communication, this difference caused some to assume interpersonal relationships could not develop between people who only communicated digitally. Studying email message exchanges, Walther found that relationships could develop using only digital text, although they took four times longer to develop than with f2f communication. When we receive digital messages from people we have never met f2f, a desire to reduce uncertainty motivates us to overinterpret the nonverbal communication messages not digitally filtered out, such as how quickly we receive a reply to our message. Overinterpretation of nonverbal cues not filtered out is one characteristic of hyperpersonal relationships. **Hyperpersonal relationships** develop when communication practices create relationships characterized by feelings of intimacy and trust greater than those in f2f relationships. Not all digital personal relationships become hyperpersonal.

Sherry Turkle studies how reduced nonverbal cues of digital communication, especially reduced facial cues and eye contact, psychologically influence children and adults. She has found that many people express a preference for digital over f2f communication, as evidenced by checking mobile phones during f2f conversations, meals with family or friends, or while caring for children. In the chapter's opening case, Jarron fondly remembered friends using digital communication in a friendly competition, alongside f2f communication around a restaurant table. Now, Carlson streams video during meals with friends, using his friends as props.

Repeatedly checking her digital device distracts a communicator from physically present conversation partners, creating continuous partial attention. **Continuous partial attention** is where communicators are physically present to a conversation, but their attention is distracted by their technology. Research shows that the presence of digital devices will prompt distraction from f2f conversation (Przybyliski and Weinstein). Possible interpretations of the presence of digital devices may range from mild rudeness of the owner of the digital device to intentional insults or disrespect to either an individual communicator or the relationship (Miller-Ott and Kelly). In the chapter's opening case, Carlson has continuous partial attention for his physically present friends, because he is distracted by creating streaming video. Continuous partial attention interferes with attentive listening, reducing our understanding of what friends, family, and coworkers say. An ethical consequence of continuous partial attention is that dialogic presence, discussed in Chapter 7, may be impossible when digital devices are present.

Everyday Communication Ethics

❖ *Keep a record for 24 hours of how you use digital technology, listing every device you use and how long you use it. Note your multi-tasking. Calculate how much time you were digitally connected and unconnected.*

Turkle is interested in how continuous partial attention impacts family communication. Families play a critical role in modeling to children how communication works. When parents are continuously distracted by technology during conversations with their children, they model distracted listening, demonstrating that being understood is not important in f2f communication (105–7). For babies and young children, the effects of continuous partial attention may prove more significant. Child development research shows that babies and children need f2f interaction with adults for healthy cognitive, emotional, psychological, and moral development (see Tompkins *in press*). F2f interaction is important for developing a child's empathic capacity, which is critical for communication and moral development. Without attentive f2f communication, babies, children, and adolescents lack opportunities to develop competence in interpreting the emotional content of nonverbal cues, which stimulates development of cognitive forms of empathy such as perspective-taking. Turkle asks, but does not answer whether routine practices of digitally distracted communication by adults contributes to the increasing number of children who exhibit behaviors associated with Asperger's syndrome, such as lack of eye contact when speaking, lack of empathic behaviors, and social withdrawal. Finding answers involves research on the effects of digital technology use on a generation of children raised with digital technology from birth.

You may be asking, "Why don't adults set aside or restrict digital technology around children?" Digital software and hardware are designed for habitual use (Fogg) which encourages our mindless dependence on digital devices (Wang et al.). Turkle does not argue for deactivating our digital devices, but advocates *mindful and competent* use of digital technology. We need to be aware of how our digital practices affect us, our relationships, and communities. Clive Thompson, who argues that digital technology can develop how we think in new and productive ways, warns that multitasking and mindless use of digital technology are both incompetent. Turkle recommends regular digital vacations to disrupt mindless digital habits and stimulate awareness of how our digital practices affect us and our relationships. Mindful use of digital technology is important for discovering competent digital communication practices. As a society, we have yet to agree on what skills or knowledge comprise competent or ethical digital communication.

Everyday Communication Ethics

❖ *After telling friends and family your intention, unplug for 24 hours from **all** digital devices. Be sure to plan how to use your time, e.g., playing board or card games, spending time with family or friends, playing a musical instrument, playing a sport, doing homework, or taking a nap. After 24 hours of unplugging, describe how you felt, what was more difficult, and what was easier. How did your communication change?*

Digital Filtering

Digital communication has affected our lives, even when we are not communicating digitally. This is apparent in business. Using digital technology, you can invest in any stock market around the world any day and any time. In many industries, a business workday is 24 hours and for many companies the workweek is seven days (24/7). In a 24/7 world, sleep is a luxury and time is precious. Email is too slow, in comparison to texting or social media. Consider whether you have patience for handwriting a letter, dropping it in a mailbox, and waiting for a response days or weeks later. We receive more messages at a faster rate than ever before, creating **digital communication overload**. Adding to this overload are mobile and wearable devices that connect us everywhere we go, perhaps 24/7. Digital communication overload contributes to our sense of never having enough time, whether it is time to read or respond to our messages, complete our work, spend time with family or friends, or sleep.

Textbox 8.1

Multi-tasking and Managing Digital Communication Overload

While humans multi-tasked long before invention of the computer, the multiple screens and mobility of digital technology offer new forms of **multi-tasking**, augmenting the human tendency to do two or more things at the same time (MacKinnon; Nass).

Multi-tasking advocates claim these advantages:

- *More efficient* use of time
- *Greater productivity* in accomplishing tasks
- *Relieving boredom* by stimulating the mind
- *More creativity* because of access to multiple resources.

Digital multi-tasking critics claim multi-tasking is about the quality of human attention while working on a task. Multi-tasking reduces mental focus and increases distraction, creating the following disadvantages:

- *Distracted work* decreases task efficiency and productivity. The greater activity of multi-tasking creates a sense rather than actuality of productivity and efficiency.
- *Novelty that relieves boredom is misjudged as creativity.* Digital multi-tasking is about being open to interruptions that draw attention away from one task to a different task. Compared to the original task, interruptions are stimulating because they are different, but nothing new is created.
- *Boredom increases creativity* by allowing the mind to wander without interruption, exploring thoughts and ideas as they arise. Creativity arises in this focused wandering. Continual interruption decreases boredom with distraction, decreasing creative potential.

Clive Thompson, who argues that digital technology can improve ways humans think, identifies multi-tasking and digital distraction as incompetent uses of digital technology that undermine its benefits.

Research shows that **uni-tasking**, minimizing distractions to focus attention on accomplishing one task, increases productivity and efficiency. Uni-tasking involves turning off your mobile phone or closing social media programs while working on a digital or non-digital task. Uni-tasking could involve working with more than one program or device, *if* these actions are focused on completing a single task or goal while eliminating other sources of distraction.

Digital filtering manages message flow with software that opens access to messages we wish to receive and blocks messages with characteristics we do not wish to receive. Digital filtering is the primary strategy for managing digital communication overload, other than uni-tasking or turning off digital devices. Filtering is not a new factor in human communication. Human perception filters messages, along with other sensory data, helping us understand the world in which we live by selecting, organizing, and interpreting sensory stimuli (Alberts, Martin, and Nakayama 26–48). Whenever we seek someone out for conversation or choose not to listen in f2f conversation, we are filtering available messages to customize the messages we receive.

Digital enhancement of the filtering capacities of human perception makes digital communication highly customizable. **Intentional digital filters**, such as setting up contacts or privacy settings, could open access to messages about potential jobs or block messages about a relationship breakup. In the chapter's opening case, people who know Carlson could customize program settings to receive a text notification whenever he is live streaming. By customizing messages we receive, intentional digital filtering influences how we experience our relationships and social world. Using a search engine is another example of intentional filtering. Eli Pariser has demonstrated how if you and a friend compare your separate searches using the same search engine and search terms, there will likely be different search results, sometimes very different. This example reveals the existence of unintentional digital filters. **Unintentional digital filters** are procedures created by digital code called algorithms, that use calculations to produce knowledge for users, without most users realizing this is happening (Gillespie). Algorithms are not limited to search engines. They are used in software, hardware, and networking to manage communication overload by using our past digital practices as guidelines for managing message flow.

Algorithms are written by people using digital code to create calculations that sort through databases to determine what data or messages are relevant for you to receive. Algorithms produce and certify what counts as knowledge for us without our realizing it is happening, unless we are somewhat familiar with coding language, hardware design, or computer networking. Algorithms search for information in databases that also includes data about communicators; "every click, every query" (Gillespie 173) is collected by software and hardware to create a digital dossier on each of us. Algorithms search your digital dossier to make predictions about what messages you want to receive. If you watch live stream video, algorithms would send you a message suggesting you watch Carlson's live stream. The capacity of algorithms to change in response to user practices is what enables websites, software programs, and hardware to continuously update and send customized messages to users. This is how customized advertising appears on your social media or news feeds (Skeggs and Yuill).

Everyday Communication Ethics

❖ *Watch Eli Pariser's Ted Talk on filter bubbles at* www.ted.com/talks/ eli_pariser_beware_online_filter_bubbles.

Repeat Pariser's experiment with a friend whose interests or political viewpoints are different from your own.

One way to think about computers is as algorithm machines that process massive amounts of data using calculations created by computer code. The calculations of algorithms identify what data or messages count as knowledge. Tarleton Gillespie is concerned with what he calls **public relevance algorithms** whose calculations for producing and certifying knowledge have political implications. These implications involve how algorithms include and exclude data to create knowledge, in contrast to how impartial yet knowledgeable human experts would evaluate this data. Businesses, governments, institutions, and the very wealthy can use algorithms to create digital advertising, political, or other campaigns. Because the average digital communicator is unaware of algorithms and how they work, algorithms can be used to create "calculated" publics. Algorithms create **calculated publics** by identifying a common characteristic of individual communicators, most of whom do not know of each other's existence, and then send messages to create digital connections between them. How calculated publics will influence society's understanding of itself is an open question (Gillespie 168). Algorithms filter data in digital processes, both large- and small-scale, creating what many people consider neutral and objective knowledge, without most digital users realizing what is happening or how it happens.

Learning the basics of digital code is a form of digital communication literacy that creates awareness of the political and ideological nature of public relevance algorithms (Gillespie). Algorithms are "unstable" because they change in response to the changing practices of digital users (including hackers). Understanding the logic of digital code, even without moderate or high-level coding abilities, could allow a communicator to change or disrupt how algorithms work, promoting more mindful digital communication. You could disrupt an algorithm by becoming mindful of your routine digital practices and then changing them, because algorithms are designed to be responsive to patterns in your habitual digital practices. This is what Chinese activists did in 2012, as part of large-scale protests about environmental consequences of the government's economic policies. The Chinese government used extensive digital filtering to block dissent by searching for banned words, and then deleting identified posts. In response, activists posted pictures as messages, which the digital censoring algorithms could not easily identify and delete. The China Media Project found that in four days there were 5.25 million postings about the protest on Weibo, the Chinese version of Twitter, that government censors did not delete (Thompson 245–9).

As powerful unintentional filters of digital messages, algorithms influence communicators and communication dynamics. Digital filtering enhances human perceptual filtering. This becomes apparent when we compare the influences of f2f and digital filtering on communication dynamics. The ideal dynamic of f2f communication is symmetrical interaction. **Symmetrical communication** is a relatively balanced message exchange between senders and receivers, with both having mutual responsibility for the quality of messages exchanged and the communication process. In f2f communication, individual perception is the primary method of filtering. Competent (literate) communication involves recognizing and understanding how individual psychological processes of selecting, organizing, and interpreting perceptions can promote or undermine perceptual accuracy that affects how communicators understand or misunderstand each other. Communication skills of mindful listening and perception-checking promote perceptual accuracy (Alberts, Martin, and Nakayama 100–19). Mindful listening and perception-checking also facilitate symmetrical communication, by helping a communicator shift her attention solely from herself and her goals to her communication partner, creating a starting point for mutual understanding. The physical proximity of f2f interaction offers an important, though not absolute, advantage for mindful listening and perception-checking. Nonverbal cues in f2f communication offer opportunities to check the consistency between verbal and nonverbal messages. In comparison to digital communication, there is more opportunity to see or hear immediate consequences for understanding or misunderstanding messages and communication practices such as listening or turn taking.

When communicators use digital filtering to customize the messages they receive, they enhance the filtering capabilities of their perceptual system to manage digital communication overload. Instead of promoting the more symmetrical dynamics of f2f communication, intentional digital filtering facilitates a more unbalanced process of **asymmetrical communication** that reinforces the perceptual systems of receivers. Unintentional digital filtering of algorithms, which significantly enhances customization of digital messages received, can further reinforce perceptions. This is significant for communication ethics, because the moral imagination is stimulated by exposure to alternative viewpoints.

Digital filtering influences communication dynamics in two ways. First, with intentional filtering receivers exercise more power to limit messages they receive, than in f2f communication. This can be ethically good when blocking spam or messages from a bully, or opening access to senders with different viewpoints. However, intentional digital filtering also promotes a shift in responsibility for the quality of communication dynamics. In the relatively balanced exchange of messages in symmetrical communication, senders and receivers *share* responsibility for the quality of the communication flow. Intentional digital filtering encourages delegation of this responsibility to receivers—"if-you-don't-want-it-block-it" thinking. This nudges digital communication dynamics from a symmetrical to a more *a*symmetrical message exchange.

A second way digital filters influence communication dynamics is when software, hardware, and infrastructure filter out, to varying degrees, nonverbal cues. This is a key point of Walther's social information processing theory ("Computer-Mediated"; "Technological"). While he studied the influence of digital filtering of nonverbal cues on relational development, this discussion focuses on the influence of digital filtering on the general dynamics of message exchange. Your nonverbal facial expression, tone of voice, or shift in body orientation can signal agreement or disagreement with a friend. In f2f communication, ambiguous or contradictory nonverbal cues can prompt perception-checking by receivers, *because* senders are physically present. Of course, this depends on the receiver noticing the cues, but in digital communication you have significantly less access to nonverbal cues, because they are filtered out. There are fewer opportunities for you to recognize when your conversational partner understands, misunderstands, is unsure, agrees, disagrees (perhaps passionately), is happy, or upset, and then to check your perception with mindful listening. If you are attentive, especially in interpreting the timing of messages, you may recognize something is amiss. However, without sufficient nonverbal cues or specific verbal messages communicating emotions, there is more uncertainty and less information in digital than in f2f communication. With this uncertainty, the tendency to overinterpret or misinterpret the few nonverbal cues communicators receive is not surprising.

Everyday Communication Ethics

❖ *Think of a f2f conversation and compare a digital conversation with the same person. What is the same and what is different? How much do you rely on your understanding of f2f communication with this person to understand this person's digital communication?*

How could the asymmetrical dynamic of digital filtering influence the mindless practices of digital communicators? Nonverbal cues convey a significant portion of the emotional content of communication messages that can stimulate empathic and perspective-taking responses. In digital message exchange, there is less opportunity for nonverbal cues to stimulate empathy and perspective-taking. Understanding the asymmetry of mindless digital communication offers some insight into the pattern of Twitter messages sent by Justine Sacco. Sacco was fired from her job because of backlash to a racist Tweet she sent before boarding a plane to South Africa at London's Heathrow airport—"Going to Africa. Hope I don't get AIDs. Just kidding. I'm White!" (Bates). While the Africa Tweet was the most egregious, examination of her account revealed a series of insulting, demeaning, and generally questionable Tweets. These messages show no evidence of Sacco's adaptation to others, evidence of awareness of others, or efforts to consider what others would think or feel after reading her Tweets. While her messages are self-centered, it is overstatement to claim that Twitter caused Sacco's self-centered communication. Rather, the digital platform promoted a receiver-oriented communication dynamic that reinforced Sacco's view of the world. Beyond an emoticon or explicit verbal message, nonverbal cues that could signal the extent of disagreement, hurt, or sadness were filtered out. Verbal messages communicating disagreement could have been sent, but not necessarily received if a sender was blocked. Dissenting messages that made it through could be ignored, until the number became overwhelming, as they did in response to Sacco's last racist Tweet.

A less immediate consequence of digital filtering is how it influences the abilities of communicators to competently interpret and respond to nonverbal messages. Because nonverbal messages are more effective in conveying emotion than verbal messages, digital filtering influences the ability of communicators to competently interpret and respond to the emotional content of messages. This is a focus of Turkle's criticism of how we use digital communication technology. Continuous partial attention characterizes the experiences of children raised by digitally distracted parents. These children are not exposed to the variety of nonverbal messages found in *un*distracted f2f communication, especially eye contact and facial gestures. They are less likely to learn how to interpret emotional content of nonverbal cues, such as happiness, sadness, joy, or anger, because they lack practice in f2f interaction with digitally *un*distracted adults. This impacts a child's ability to empathize or take the perspective of others, both of which are critical for competent communication and moral development. Turkle also is concerned with using digital technology to avoid f2f communication in difficult conversations, because digital communication is emotionally easier than f2f communication. Filtering out nonverbal cues filters out the messiness of emotions. Emotions are an important part of our humanity, who we are as individuals. Moral emotions play an important role in our development as ethical communicators. When we use digital technology as a buffer to filter out emotions that make us uncomfortable, we can more easily deny our fellow communicators' humanity. It also becomes more difficult to recognize ethical issues.

The two qualities of digital communication discussed in this section—how digital communication influences our sense of time, space, and physical reality and the processes of intentional and unintentional digital filtering—are not inherently good or bad or even ethical or unethical. Because digital technology is a relatively new medium of communication with relatively novel communication practices, we are trying to understand how digital communication affects us. As Burke suggests (16), we need to understand how each of us, our relationships, and our communities are being changed by instruments of our own making. While some of us are concerned about the dangers of mindless or distracted digital communication, others are excited about how digital technology creates new opportunities, including how digital communication is influencing how we think (Thompson). As a society, we have not identified or agreed upon what are practices of competent digital communication. David Gunkel points out that too often our discussions are shaped by polarized judgments that digital communication is inherently good or inherently bad. Binary logic makes it difficult to recognize the both/and qualities of digital communication. Thompson, who is encouraged by how digital technology can promote collaborative public thinking, also acknowledges that digital distraction and multi-tasking undermine these benefits (135–8). While Turkle is concerned about our preference for digital communication because it is "emotionally easier" than f2f communication, she does not advocate deactivating our digital devices. She agrees with Thompson that mindfulness is critical for competent digital communication. She also advocates that we carefully examine how digital technology is changing us and our children, as we identify what are competent digital communication practices.

The next two sections will explore some of the ethical issues of freedom and truth, which are recurring areas of ethical concern in digital communication.

Issues of Freedom in Digital Communication

Digital communication excites our imaginations because it liberates us from the limitations of time, space, and physical reality, especially the physical reality of our bodies. You have freedom to meet people anywhere in the world, discover ideas and information, even create alternative identities and worlds. Chapter 4 examined freedom using the metaphor of a musical chord consisting of three different notes—personal, sovereignal, and civic freedom (Patterson 3–5). This section uses these notes to examine issues of freedom in digital communication.

The most dramatic characteristic of personal freedom in digital communication is liberation from physical reality. Limitations of space, your body, and time are reduced, and sometimes disappear entirely. You have the personal freedom to go anywhere, meet anyone online, or assume a virtual identity. In digital gaming, a virtual identity is called an **avatar**, a digitally created icon that represents you online that may be a person, animal, or object. Physical characteristics of your body—gender, height, age, weight, skin color, physical ability or disability—are irrelevant, unless you include them in your avatar. Gaming avatars can be helpful in thinking about digital virtual identity, if you create digital identities that are different from who you are in physical reality. This is possible because digital technology allows you to practice freedom of anonymity. **Freedom of anonymity** exists when people you communicate with do not know who you are in physical reality, unless you tell them. Sometimes specific software, such as an email system at work, requires you to use your physical world name so you are identifiable. Most software allows you to choose which, if any, of your characteristics in physical reality will be revealed in your digital communication. Digital anonymity empowers personal freedom for persons discriminated against in physical reality.

Digital anonymity also contributes to the second note of sovereignal freedom. Sovereignal freedom is the freedom to exercise power over others, sometimes to the point of harming them (Patterson 403–4). There is no accountability for practices of sovereignal freedom. Because physical reality may have little or no relationship to a digital identity, the consequences of your digital communication may have little impact on you in physical reality. Anonymous digital communicators can create an identity that communicates hurtful or harmful messages to others, such as digital bullying, trolling, or malicious hacking with few or no negative consequences for themselves in physical reality, because they are not reachable in physical reality (Nissenbaum "Anonymity" 556–8). No reachability equals no accountability.

Digital filtering also promotes freedom from the immediate emotional consequences of digital messages, because digital platforms filter out, to varying degrees, nonverbal cues of hurt, fear, joy, or happiness that could stimulate empathic responses. This makes it emotionally easier to mindlessly exercise sovereignal freedom. Turkle's concerns that some people use digital platforms instead of f2f communication because it is "emotionally easier" can be evidence of choosing to be free of the emotional consequences of their messages. If filtering nonverbal cues makes it easier for a shy person to participate in online discussion, digital filtering promotes personal freedom. Yet, digital filtering of nonverbal cues of happiness, joy, sadness, hurt, or anger may *unintentionally* promote sovereignal freedom, when cues that a receiver has been hurt or harmed by a message are filtered out. Competent and ethically responsive digital communication involves mindful listening and perception-checking to reduce unintentional practices of sovereignal freedom.

Everyday Communication Ethics

❖ *When has your use of digital communication been emotionally easier than f2f communication? How has it been easier?*

There are limits to digital anonymity. While anonymity can exist among communicators exchanging messages, it begins to dissipate at the systems or network level. Here, anonymous communicators are more reachable. The digital dossiers collected about every computer user are compiled in large databases. Algorithms allow systems administrators or security analysts to analyze databases for patterns and characteristics of both messages and users. As Lawrence Lessig observes, the software code and digital architecture that create the internet can be designed either to create the freedom of relatively unrestricted digital communication, including anonymous digital communication, or it can be designed for surveillance, to monitor and restrict communicators (6–7 and 60). The challenge is to find a competent and ethical balance between these two extremes.

Passwords are one method of **digital surveillance** or tracking. The passwords you create to protect your privacy also are a form of surveillance. When you use a personal password, security questions, or two-step verification, you authenticate who you are to the network so you can access your personal data. Tracking use of a password is a simple form of surveillance to maintain online privacy and security, such as keeping malicious hackers from changing your personal profile. This is what happens when you receive a notice that your password has been changed. Online privacy and security are important in e-commerce, especially online banking and financial services. If you do not trust that your digital communication is private and secure when you want it to be, you are less likely to make online purchases (Nissenbaum "Trust Online").

Another simple form of surveillance occurs whenever you visit a web page. The site's software places a marker called a cookie on your internet browser, which algorithms track ("No Hiding Place"). Using algorithms, website designers analyze cookies to improve website navigation or customize digital advertising for you. Even if you delete cookies from your browser, you unintentionally provide data for algorithms to analyze. Cookies and other digital markers make the internet less anonymous. Hackers may use digital markers to identify targets for installing malicious programs. These programs find you by piggybacking on free downloads (Stafford) or when you click on links in an infected message ("Virus Basics").

Data mining is a more complex form of internet surveillance. **Data mining** uses algorithms to search a digital database to answer questions (Fulda; Gillespie). Everything you do on digital devices adds to databases that can be mined. There is an ethical and legal issue of whether you or technology companies own your personal digital data, including whether it can be sold. Data mining is an important tool in monitoring fraud and other criminal activity, including terrorism (Monash). Some consider data mining a threat to individual privacy, while others consider it the price we pay for online safety and security. Although the sheer quantity of activity online makes it challenging to monitor specific accounts for system efficiency, security, illegal activity, or terrorism, improvements in digital processing capacity, computer code, digital architecture, and software make large-scale monitoring and surveillance more a reality than a possibility (Lessig 209–25). Data mining itself is neither good nor bad. The ethical question is how is it used. The environmental protests in China discussed earlier in this chapter (Thompson 245–9) are an example of the hacking of data mining algorithms. The Chinese government used algorithms to mine databases of social media messages for key words to identify messages to censor. Simple hacking of algorithms, as the Chinese protestors did using pictures instead of words for social media messages, resisted this surveillance. Since these protests the Chinese government has increased its digital censorship efforts (King, Pan, and Roberts 2013; 2017).

Surveillance is monitoring by large-scale institutions or organizations of less powerful individuals and groups. Digital surveillance uses algorithms to monitor text, numbers, pictures, or video. Networked cameras have expanded surveillance to physical spaces—airports, government buildings, and city streets—to search for illegal or terrorist activity. Video surveillance is commonplace, with cameras mounted in or on buildings or at intersections in major and medium sized cities throughout North America and Europe. Improvements in algorithms and processing capacity allow analysis of ever increasing video databases. In contrast to this top down video surveillance by institutions and organizations, video and still cameras in mobile phones allow ordinary people to record and monitor their daily lives, like Carlson in the chapter's opening case. They also can record and monitor powerful people, institutions, and organizations. Surveillance is when government or businesses monitor or record daily activity of people from above (*sur* is French for above). Ordinary people observing and monitoring the world around them, including monitoring the powerful, is **sousveillance** (Bakir), monitoring from below (*sous* is French for below). Posting pictures of protests of the Chinese government's environmental policies (Thompson 245–9) is an example of sousveillance. Regulations requiring police to wear body cameras is a form of sousveillance that raises interesting questions, because persons with power (police) are recording their own activity which government officials and average people may view.

Point to Ponder

❖ *What are the consequences of routine digital surveillance and sousveillance for communication practices?*

Ethical issues of personal and sovereignal freedom arising from practices of anonymity and surveillance are complex, neither entirely good nor bad. Anonymity makes communicators more unreachable in physical reality. Anonymous digital communication can be a source of personal growth, facilitating communication without the restrictions of stereotypes and expectations found in physical reality (Turkle 201). Anonymity also allows digital trolls and bullies to post hostile and hateful digital messages, while avoiding accountability in the communities where they live in physical reality. At the network level, ethical issues of anonymity begin to shift from exercising personal and sovereignal freedom to questions about restricting personal freedom by surveillance. Unobtrusive or covert surveillance of communicators at the systems level raises ethical issues about privacy and restricting moral rights of freedom, as discussed. Sousveillance may expand or protect personal freedom of individuals by monitoring powerful individuals and institutions. Yet even sousveillance can limit personal freedom when harassers or stalkers use pictures and video to intimidate their victims.

The third note of freedom is the civic freedom (Patterson 4–5 and 404–6) to participate in governance of our digital and non-digital public life. Digital communication's capacity to transcend space and time makes it possible for people to create virtual communities and govern themselves. Michele Wilson defines **virtual community** as a digital form of postmodern community where each person has greater freedom and flexibility than ever before (206–10). In a **postmodern community**, you can choose when and for how long to be a community member. In a traditional f2f community, you belong from birth. The freedom to choose to be a community member is a characteristic the postmodern community shares with the modern community. The difference is that a modern community has more limited choices. Membership in a religious community illustrates these differences. With a traditional religious community, you are born into your family's religious community and never leave. In a modern religious community, you may choose not to be a member of your family's religious community, if they have one, instead choosing from whatever religious community is available in your local physical community, or none. Virtual digital communities allow for greater choice, as you search online for virtual communities more compatible with your spiritual beliefs and interests. Religious or spiritual virtual communities may be more specialized, focusing on the interests and needs of the hearing impaired, LGBTQ persons, a specific ethnic group, or less widely practiced religions such as Wicca. Traditional, modern, and postmodern communities exist simultaneously, and sometimes overlap one another (Wilson 39–48). In a virtual community, communicators experience community as being part of an interconnected whole that is disembodied, extending beyond physical reality (11–20).

The variety of virtual communities expands civic freedom beyond political interest groups. Virtual communities can be about anything—Reiki, mixed martial arts (Ultimate Fighting), bow hunting, live action role-playing, or British punk music. Virtual communities are customizable and can be self-governing. You can search for a community that fits your interests, join it, participate as little or as much as you wish, and leave whenever you wish. If you cannot find a virtual community that suits you, you can create one and invite others to join you.

Digital communication also creates more opportunities to become politically involved at the local and national levels of traditional politics (Rice and Katz). Peter Dahlgren argues that in political processes there is a merging of traditional and digital media, with digital media providing alternative paths for those frustrated with standard forms of democratic participation. For example, the US Occupy Wall Street protests used social media alongside traditional media to encourage participation, because organizers recognized a need to reach potential supporters not active on social media (67–87). Evidence of digital technology as an alternative path to political participation, alongside more traditional non-digital paths appeared during the early 2010s in protests around the world. In the Arab Spring of 2010 protesters in multiple countries used social media to promote demonstrations against governments (Lutz and du Toit), which eventually resulted in protests and riots, and in some countries political coups and civil wars. While many identified social media as the instigator of these wide-scale activities, participants in the movements themselves pointed to the importance of traditional methods of political communication and organization for their successes. In the Arab Spring, the note of sovereignal freedom also is evident alongside the note of civic freedom, as governments used new forms of digital surveillance to censor and suppress protest, alongside violent forms of physical suppression (Al-Khawaja; DeVriese; Reed 125–7). Similarly, demonstrations in Russia during the Duma elections of 2011 pointed to the potential of social media to encourage civic participation; however, in later elections the Russian government responded by tightening digital control, essentially neutralizing political opposition (Gainous, Wagner, and Ziegler). Similar patterns are evident in China (King, Pan, and Roberts 2013; 2017).

Practices of digital communication raise complex ethical issues of freedom. To address these issues, it is important to avoid binary evaluations of digital communication practices as either ethical or unethical. While anonymity may help a person of color, a woman, or a GLBTQ person participate in an online political or professional discussion, it also empowers the sovereignal freedom of a predatory adult who pretends to be an 11-year-old boy in messages to other children. While digital communication facilitates exercise of our civic freedom, algorithms increase governmental and institutional resources for surveillance and censorship of citizens. Yet, without some forms of surveillance, e.g., for illegal or terrorist activity, proliferation of malicious software, harassment, or illegal activity, severe disruption of online processes we expect or depend on will occur with greater frequency (see Owen).

Issues of Truth in Digital Communication

Practices of digital communication raise ethical issues of truth, specifically what is the truth and how to recognize it. Virtual reality challenges our understanding of truth, encouraging us to think about truth that does not exist in physical reality. Virtual reality is not limited to the digital. There are other realities existing separately from physical reality such as the dreamtime of Australian Aborigines, visions or vision quests of various cultures, or personal dreams (Horsfield). The concept of telepresence, discussed earlier in the chapter, highlights how digital virtual reality is different. Telepresence involves experience and interactions that are so engaging that you psychologically experience virtual reality as if it were physical reality, while not realizing the experience is filtered through man-made technology (Lombard and Ditton). In the early years of digital communication, some viewed virtual reality as a utopian space for human interaction, while others were skeptical about its "reality"—what is in virtual reality does not really exist, so what happens there is irrelevant, or at least not as important as what happens in physical reality. Debates generated by the essay "A Rape in Cyberspace," challenged these assumptions, in its description of a digital rape in an early multi-player digital platform (Tompkins, "Telepresence"). What happens in digital virtual reality has consequences in physical reality (Lievrouw; Sterne).

Digital technology expands our understanding of what is real and true. Clive Thompson argues that it offers us new ways of thinking, new ways of creating and understanding what is true. The logic of algorithms (Gillespie), combined with the brute force of digital processing power, can augment human cognition, making possible new levels of human excellence in cognitive diversity and public collaborative thinking (Thompson). In his ethnographic study of practices of navigating between the screens of our digital devices, Charles Soukup observes that "between screens" is a place where communicators can make sense of the reality of their complex, digitally fragmented lives. Arguably, this liminal space between screens is where cognitive diversity and public collaborative thinking materialize. Interestingly, in the conclusion of *Exploring Screen Culture,* Soukup describes the importance of solitude, a digital sabbath from his fragmented, hypermediated life, for developing his analysis of life "between screens."

Whether we consider the reality of our digital experiences as cyberspace, virtual reality, or between screens, discerning the truth can be more complicated in digital communication. Sisella Bok's distinction between truth and truthfulness is helpful in thinking about digital communication. She acknowledges that while we may not be able to know the truth, especially the complete truth, what is easier to discover is whether communication is truthful (6–13). Truthfulness is important for digital communication, as technology filters out nonverbal cues that could trigger a communicator's skepticism about the truthfulness of a message.

The research of Judee Burgoon in **interpersonal deception detection theory** shows that when deceivers communicate f2f, any differences in the communication behaviors of liars and truth tellers at the beginning of an interaction almost disappear by its end. The observable communication behaviors of liars and truth tellers eventually mirror one another, as liars modify their communication behaviors to reflect those of their communication partners. In digital communication, the asynchronous quality of communication combined with its anonymity filters out nonverbal cues that could raise suspicion about deception. Digital communication also provides greater opportunity for deceivers to plan and edit their messages than does f2f communication (16). Nonverbal differences that would be evident in an initial f2f exchange of messages are digitally filtered. In addition, there are ample resources for deceivers to tailor their digital messages, especially when a receiver is communicating mindlessly.

Communicators who mindlessly use communication scripts are especially vulnerable to deception, even nonhuman deception. Burgoon presents an example of a man named Barry who spent 13 days trying to develop an intimate relationship with Julia, a software bot. Artificial intelligence programs known as **chatterbots**, or bots for short, simulate human interaction. Julia provided truthful answers to Barry's questions, including telling him where she is located—"Maas-Neotek Robot User's Guide—Information Services" (15). Barry, however, was mindlessly stuck in a communication script of developing an intimate virtual relationship, and so was deceived. It is reasonable to question how much Julia the bot deceived Barry and how much Barry deceived himself. Julia told the truth, although Barry did not recognize it. As software for bots continuously improves, it becomes more difficult to recognize when you are communicating digitally with a bot or another human being. The social media platform Instagram has struggled with how to enforce its rule that bots cannot be used because they generate "inauthentic" likes and posts. On some digital platforms people use bots to generate followers or likes to "give a sheen of legitimacy to small businesses or aspiring social media influencers" (Maheshwari). Bots can game or hack digital platforms, producing deceptive messages that are difficult to detect.

Everyday Communication Ethics

❖ *What can you do to check whether a digital message is true or false?*

Different issues of truth and truthfulness were raised in recent UK and US political campaigns in which communication patterns, especially in digital communication, appeared to downplay, even denigrate the use of accurate and reliable facts in creating or interpreting messages (Barnett; Erlanger and de Freytas-Tamura; McCoy). These false messages became known as **fake news.** One quality of fake news stories is expression of authentic emotion, such as betrayal, fear, or anger, while presenting inaccurate or false information. When evaluating emotion, such as anger, is substituted for evaluating the accuracy of information, we become more vulnerable to making impulsive or risky decisions (Kligyte et al.), in addition to making decisions based on false information. During these campaigns, many communicators became aware that some news stories, especially on social media, were intentional or unintentional fake news (Pew). An understandable defensive response to confusion about the truthfulness of messages is to be skeptical, assuming many messages present false facts, whether intentionally or not. Repeated skepticism in response to deceptive communication has the potential to become a cynical attitude that everyone deceives. Cynicism makes it difficult to recognize a truthful and honest message in news stories, discussions, or debates. Arguably, a more "positive" strategy for evaluating messages is to focus on the honesty of a communicator's feelings. If we cannot evaluate the accuracy of facts, then at least we can evaluate the authenticity of a communicator's expressions of anger or betrayal. Listening for feelings *as well as* facts and ideas is critical to understanding others, especially how they think and reason (Nussbaum). When we assume that facts are irrelevant or that others are dishonest, our capacity to understand diminishes. When we cynically dismiss accurate and reliable facts as untrustworthy, we increase the odds that our decisions will cause more harm than good. Unfortunately, the asymmetrical receiver orientation of digital communication dynamics reinforces a receiver's certainty that her cynicism is correct. If we are to work with others to address our mutual problems, especially those with whom we disagree, we need to be truthful and at some point risk trusting the truthfulness of others. A commitment to truthfulness is a key element of the National Communication Association's *Credo for Ethical Communication*. Without a personal commitment to be truthful and trust in the truthfulness of others, we cannot understand each other. When we stop trusting the truthfulness of others, especially those whose viewpoints differ from our own, opportunities for dialogic communication diminish, as do opportunities for creative problem solving that dialogue makes possible (Bohm).

It would be rash to condemn digital communication for being inherently deceptive and, thus, unethical. When we communicate mindlessly, we make ourselves more vulnerable to deception and more easily deceive ourselves. A healthy dose of skepticism, including skepticism about what we initially consider true, is one way to minimize being deceived. An ethical challenge of digital communication is being skeptical about the messages from your communication partners, while also being open to their truthfulness (Tompkins "Telepresence"). Being simultaneously skeptical and open requires both/and thinking, rather than polarized either/or thinking. This is an example of "thinking otherwise" about digital communication, as Gunkel encourages us to do. To be both skeptical and open in your communication involves not prejudging your communication partner, but also considering how you could be deceived, by your communication partner or your own communication practices. Both/and thinking requires mindfulness about your digital communication practices and a basic understanding of the dynamics of digital communication.

Conclusion

This chapter has explored digital communication as the latest technology in the history of human communication. It identifies two qualities of digital communication that exist in varying degrees in all digital platforms. First, digital communication allows us to transcend the limitations of time, space, and physical reality. Second, digital filtering augments how selective perception influences the dynamics of digital communication processes. Intentional filtering of messages by communicators and digital algorithms creates customized messages that promote asymmetrical communication dynamics that reinforce perceptions of receivers. When this asymmetrical dynamic is combined with distracted or mindless communication practices, this combination discourages mindful listening and perception-checking, two practices that promote symmetrical communication and mutual accountability for the quality of communication processes, including the truthfulness of communication messages.

When a digital platform is relatively novel, we are more sensitive to ethical issues. As digital practices become more routine and mindless, we have more difficulty discerning issues of communication ethics, for example, how digital practices of anonymity promote both personal and sovereignal freedom or how our digital practices could make it difficult to recognize false messages. Whether we judge a specific digital communication practice as ethically good or bad depends upon mindful consideration of digital communication dynamics and practices, which are part of the facts and circumstances of a digital situation. Ethical reasoning is no different for addressing ethical issues of digital communication than for other communication contexts. It involves examining the facts and circumstances of a situation, and identifying stakeholders and their interests to reveal significant ethical issues. Yet, it differs from ethical reasoning about f2f communication, because the communication dynamics have shifted. The intentional and unintentional digital filtering by software, hardware, and networking nudges the dynamics of communication from symmetrical to more asymmetrical exchanges that reinforce the perceptual biases of digital receivers. A further complication is digital filtering of nonverbal cues that minimizes receiver access to information that could stimulate moral emotions, moral imagination, and ethical reasoning. With mindless or distracted digital communication practices, it is more challenging to be an ethically responsive digital communicator.

It is important that we are mindful of qualities of digital communication which exist across digital platforms that influence our communication practices. Mindfulness of digitally influenced communication dynamics better prepares us to be competent and ethically responsive digital communicators. The ethicality of our digitized relationships and social worlds depend upon our digital communication practices.

Vocabulary

Algorithms 188
Asymmetrical communication 190
Asynchronous 183
Avatar 193

Cases for Discussion

Directions: Use the process of ethical reasoning to identify an ethical communication response for each of the cases. Identify the qualities of digital communication that influence the ethical issues of each case. Identify possible communication practices that are responsive to the experience of asymmetrical communication in each case. Include in your deliberations the three recurring decision points of communication.

1. "I don't understand."

Mark drove over as soon as he could after his sister, Diane, called. Mark's nephew Jason, age 11, had posted on social media a topless picture of a girl, Lara, in his class. He admitted he did it, and did not understand why it was wrong. The school's no tolerance policy for bullying meant an automatic suspension. Diane and her husband were shocked and angry. They are considering suspending all computer privileges for six months, except for school work. Jason is an avid online gamer. Mark remembered when he was Jason's age how hard it was for him to talk to girls. "I made so many mistakes. I was lucky I only looked foolish and wasn't suspended. It must be harder for Jason. He spends so much time online. He doesn't have many friends at school who aren't gamers."

Mark turned to Jason. "I hear there's some trouble. What happened?" Jason explained that he and Lara had been texting each other for several weeks. This was his "first relationship" with a girl. They exchanged pictures of themselves. She sent a picture of herself without a top. Jason thought she looked good and wanted to share it, so he posted it. "Just like all those other pictures of people online. I did what other people do all the time. Why am I being punished?"

What should Mark say?

2. Campus Free Speech

Marty reads the comments on the university programming board's (UPB) social media page about the speaker coming to campus next week, Elizabeth Dillman. Marty is chair of UPB's speaker's committee. The committee organizes four to six speaking events each year. At least one speaker presents on a controversial topic to meet UPB's and the university's mission of promoting freedom of speech on campus. For speeches on controversial topics, UPB organizes follow-up campus discussions.

Elizabeth Dillman is known for her criticism of what she calls "faint-hearted feminists" who, she says, treat women as weak and vulnerable, always needing protection from men. Her criticisms of "rape culture" and her proposal that police and not campus administration should investigate charges of sexual assault and harassment are controversial.

Looking over the online comments, Marty reads, "Stephens advocates a 'boys will be boys' mentality about rape." Another comment states that Dillman has said that a woman who has passed out from drinking too much has given her consent. Marty thought, "I've read several of Dillman's essays and speeches. She says rape is a crime, which is why the police and not the university should investigate charges of sexual assault and harassment. Though, I can understand why some people think she's soft on punishing rapists on campus." Marty reads the next online comment. "Anyone saying 'rape is OK' shouldn't be allowed to speak on our campus." The next four comments agree that Dillman's invitation should be rescinded. What should Marty do? What should UPB do?

3. Social Media and a Close Friend

Sydney knew she spent too much time checking social media, but it was nothing like Amanda. Amanda did not comment on their friends' pictures or posts, but she always knew what was going on. Sydney noticed that Amanda missed classes about once a week. She seemed sadder. Sydney could not remember the last time Amanda had made a joke, and her joking was legendary among their friends. But you would not know Amanda was sad, if you knew her only from her social media accounts. Her pictures and posts are like the old Amanda, making jokes and having fun. "Amanda will snap out of it soon," thought Sydney. "I wonder . . ." What should Sydney do?

Notes

1 The initial, small audience for Luther's printed writings were those who read handwritten manuscripts. For the illiterate general population, pamphlets with pictures, created with woodcuts, communicated Luther's ideas. As Luther's ideas were popularized, more people were motivated to learn to read. Printed communication of Luther's ideas is considered a major factor in the Peasant's Revolt in Germany (1524–1525) and later the Thirty Years War (1618–1628) (Minneapolis Institute of Art, 154, 283, 297–357; "Word and Image.")

2 The terms "cyberspace" and "between screens" (Soukup) are attempts to identify a location for this alternative reality. "Cyberspace" emphasizes a *location* other than physical reality somewhere, while "between screens" emphasizes the perceptual and cognitive nature of virtual reality.

References

Alberts, Jess K., Judith N. Martin, and Thomas K. Nakayama. *Communication in Society.* New York: Pearson, 2011.

Al-Khawaja, Maryam. "Crackdown: The Harsh Realities of Nonviolent Protests in the Bahraini Civil Conflict." *Journal of International Affairs* 68.1 (2014): 189–200.

Bakir, Vian. *Sousveillance, Media and Strategic Political Communication.* New York: ontin-uum, 2010.

Barnett, Neil. "Who Funded Brexit?" *The American Interest.* 26 July 2016. www.the-american-interest.com/2016/07/26/who-funded-brexit/. Date accessed: 1 July 2017.

Bates, Daniel. "'I Am Ashamed': PR Exec who Sparked Outrage with Racist Tweet Apologizes after She's Fired and Her Own Father Calls Her an 'Idiot.'" *Daily Mail.* 22 December 2013. www.dailymail.co.uk/news/article-2527913/Justine-Sacco-tweet-Going-Africa-Hope-I-dont-AIDS-causes-Twitter-outrage.html. Date accessed: 26 June 2017.

Bohm, David. *On Dialogue*. Ed. Lee Nichol. New York: Routledge, 1996.

Bok, Sisella. *Lying: Moral Choice in Public and Private Life*. New York: Vintage Books, 1989.

Burgoon, Judee K. *Truth, Lies and Virtual Worlds*. Carroll C. Arnold Distinguished Lecture 2005. Boston, MA: Allyn and Bacon, 2007. www.natcom.org/sites/default/files/annual-convention/NCA_Convention_Video_Archive_2005_Arnold_Lecture.pdf. Date accessed: 29 December 2017.

Burke, Kenneth. *Language as Symbolic Action: Essays on Life, Literature, and Method*. Berkeley, CA: U of California P, 1966.

Dahlgren, Peter. *The Political Web: Media, Participation and Alternative Democracy*. Basingstoke, UK: Palgrave Macmillan, 2013.

DeVriese, Leila. "Paradox of Globalization: New Arab Public? New Social Contract." *Perspectives on Global Development and Technology* 12 (2013): 114–34.

Erlanger, Steven and Kimiko de Freytas-Tamura. "Godfather of 'Brexit' Takes Aim at the British Establishment." *The New York Times*. 20 January 2017. www.nytimes.com/2017/01/20/world/europe/arron-banks-brexit-britain.html?emc=eta1&_r=0. Date accessed: 4 April 2017

Fogg, B.J. "A Behavior Model or Persuasive Design." *Persuasive '09*. 26–29 April 2001. www.bjfogg.com/fbm_files/page4_1.pdf. Date accessed: 25 June 2017.

Fulda, Joseph S. "Data Mining and Privacy." Spinello and Tavani 471–5.

Gainous, Jason, Kevin M. Wagner, and Charles Ziegler. "Digital Media and Political Opposition in Authoritarian Systems: Russia's 2011 and 2016 Duma Elections." *Democratization*. 25 April 2017. http://dx.doi.org/10.1080/13510347.2017.1315566. Date accessed 2 July 2017.

Gillespie, Tarleton. "The Relevance of Algorithms." *Media Technologies: Essays on Communication, Materiality, and Society*. Eds. Tarleton Gillespie, Pablo J. Boczkowski, and Kirsten A. Foot. Cambridge, MA: MIT Press, 2014. 167–93.

Gunkel, David J. *Thinking Otherwise: Philosophy, Communication, Technology*. West Lafayette, IN: Purdue UP, 2007.

Horsfield, Peter. "Continuities and Discontinuities in Ethical Reflections on Digital Virtual Reality. *Journal of Mass Media Ethics* 18. 3 and 4 (2003): 155–72.

King, Gary, Jennifer Pan, and Margaret E. Roberts. "How Censorship in China Allows Government Criticism but Silences Collective Expression." *American Political Science Review* 107.2 (2013): 326–43.

King, Gary, Jennifer Pan, and Margaret E. Roberts. "How the Chinese Government Fabricates Social Media Posts for Strategic Distraction, Not Engaged Argument." *American Political Science Review* 111.3 (2017): 484–501.

Kligyte, Vykinta, Shane Connelly, Chase Thiel, and Lynn Devenport. "The Influence of Anger, Fear, and Emotion Regulation on Ethical Decision Making." *Human Performance* 26 (2013): 297–326.

Lessig, Lawrence. *Code: Version 2.0*. New York: Basic Books, 2006.

Lievrouw, Leah A. "Materiality and Media in Communication and Technology Studies: An Unfinished Project." *Media Technologies: Essays on Communication, Materiality and Society*. Eds. Tarleton Gillespie, Pablo J. Boczkowski, and Kirsten A. Foot. Cambridge, MA: MIT Press, 2014. 21–54.

Lombard, Matthew and Theresa Ditton. "At the Heart of It All: The Concept of Presence." *Journal of Computer Mediated Communication* 3 (1997). Retrieved 1 April 2000 from www.acuse.org/jcmc.index.htm. Date accessed: 3 March 2007.

Lutz, Barend and Pierre du Toit. *Defining Democracy in a Digital Age: Political Support on Social Media*. New York: Palgrave MacMillan, 2014.

MacKinnon, Matthew. "The Myth of Multitasking: Why Your Brain Lacks the Capital to Pay Attention to Two Things at Once," *Psychology Today*, 5 January 2016. www.psychologytoday.com/blog/the-neuroscience-mindfulness/201601/the-myth-multitasking. Date accessed: 20 October 2017.

Maheshwari, Sapna. "How Bots are Inflating Instagram Egos. *The New York Times*. 6 June 2017. www.nytimes.com/2017/06/06/business/media/instagram-bots.html. Date accessed: 1 July 2017.

McCoy, Terrence. "For the 'New Yellow Journalists,' Opportunity Comes in Clicks and Bucks." *The Washington Post*. 20 November 2016. www.washingtonpost.com/national/for-the-new-yellow-journalists-opportunity-comes-in-clicks-and-bucks/2016/11/20/d58d036c-adbf-11e6-8b45-f8e493f06fcd_story.html?tid=ss_mail&utm_term=.15ee8d525faf. Date accessed: 1 July 2017.

Miller-Ott, Aimee E. and Lynne Kelly. "A Politeness Theory Analysis of Cell-Phone Usage in the Presence of Friends." *Communication Studies* 68.2 (2017): 190–207.

Minneapolis Institute of Art, The Morgan Library and Museum. *Martin Luther. Treasures of the Reformation: Catalogue*. Dresden, Germany: Sandstein Verlag, 2016.

Monash, Curt A. "Data Mining Ready for a Comeback." *Computerworld*, 11 September 2006. 45–7.

Nass, Clifford. "How Multi-Tasking Is Affecting the Way You Think," YouTube. 3 October 2013. Available: www.youtube.com/watch?v=MPHJMIOwKjE. Date accessed 20 October 2017.

National Communication Association. *Credo for Ethical Communication*. Approved by Legislative Council November 1999. Available: www.natcom.org. Date accessed: 4 March 2018.

Nissenbaum, Helen. "The Meaning of Anonymity in an Information Age." Spinello and Tavani 555–60.

Nissenbaum, Helen. Securing Trust Online: Wisdom or Oxymoron?" *Boston Law Review* 81.3 (2001): 635–64.

"No Hiding Place." *The Economist*. 23 January 2003. www.economist.com/node/1534283. Date accessed: 5 March 2007.

Nussbaum, Martha C. *Upheavals of Thought: The Intelligence of Emotions*. Cambridge: Cambridge UP, 2001.

Owen, Taylor. *Disruptive Power: The Crisis of the State in the Digital Age*. Oxford: Oxford UP, 2015.

Pariser, Eli. "Beware Online 'Filter Bubbles.'" *Ted: Ted2011*. March 2011. www.ted.com/talks/eli_pariser_beware_online_filter_bubbles. Date accessed: 18 April 2017.

Patterson, Orlando. *Freedom: Vol. 1. Freedom in the Making of Western Culture*. New York: Basic Books, 1991.

Pearson, Judy, Paul Nelson, Scott Titsworth, and Lynn Harter. *Human Communication*. 2nd ed. Boston, MA: McGraw Hill, 2006.

Pew Research Center. "Many Americans Believe Fake News Is Sowing Confusion." Pew Forum on Journalism and Media. 15 December 2016. www.journalism.org/2016/12/15/many-americans-believe-fake-news-is-sowing-confusion/. Date accessed: 1 July 2017.

Plato. "Phaedrus." *Plato: The Collected Dialogues, including the Letters*. Eds. Edith Hamilton and Huntington Cairns. Trans. R. Hackforth. Bollingen Series LXXI. Princeton, NJ: Princeton UP, 1961. 475–525.

Przybyliski, Andrew K. and Netta Weinstein. "Can you Connect with Me Now? How the Presence of Mobile Communication Technology Influences Face-to-Face Conversation Quality." *Journal of Social and Personal Relationships* 30.3 (2012): 1–10.

Reed, T.V. *Digitized Lives: Culture, Power and Social Change in the Internet Era.* New York: Routledge, 2014.

Rice, Ronald E. and James E. Katz. "The Internet and Political Involvement in 1996 and 2000." *Society Online: The Internet in Context.* Eds. Philip N. Howard and Steve Jones. Thousand Oaks, CA: Sage, 2004. 103–20.

Saunders, Carol, Ann F. Rutkowski, Michiel van Genuchten, Doug Vogel, and Julio Molina Oreggo. "Virtual Space and Place: Theory and Test." *Management Information Systems Quarterly* 35.4 (2011): 1079–98.

Skeggs, Beverley and Simon Yuill. "The Methodology of a Multi-Model Project Examining How Facebook Infrastructures Social Relations." *Information, Communication & Society* 19.10 (2016): 1356–72.

Soukup, Charles. *Exploring Screen Culture Via Apple's Mobile Devices: Life Through the Looking Glass.* Lanham, MD: Lexington Books, 2017.

Spinello, Richard A. and Herman T. Tavani, Eds. *Readings in CyberEthics.* 2nd ed. Sudbury, MA: Jones and Bartlett Publishers, 2004.

Stafford, Thomas F. "Spyware." *Communications of the ACM* 48.8 (2005): 34–6. Date accessed: 23 February 2009.

Sterne, Jonathan. "'What Do We Want?' 'Materiality!' 'When Do We Want it?' 'Now!'" *Media Technologies: Essays on Communication, Materiality and Society.* Eds. Tarleton Gillespie, Pablo J. Boczkowski, and Kirsten A. Foot. Cambridge, MA: MIT Press, 2014. 119–28.

Thompson, Clive. *Smarter Than You Think: How Technology Is Changing Our Minds for the Better.* New York: Penguin, 2013.

Tompkins, Paula S. "Truth, Trust, and Telepresence." *Journal of Mass Media Ethics* 18.3&4 (2003): 194–212.

Tompkins, Paula S. "Communication and Children's Moral Development." *The Children's Communication Sourcebook.* Eds. Thomas Socha and Narissra Punyanunt-Carter. New York: Peter Lange, in press.

Turkle, Sherry. *Reclaiming Conversation: The Power of Talk in a Digital Age.* New York: Penguin, 2015.

"Virus Basics." *United States Computer Emergency Readiness Team.* U.S. Department of Homeland Security. www.us-cert.gov/publications/virus-basics. Date accessed: 26 June 2017.

Walther, Joseph B. "Computer Mediated Communication: Impersonal, Interpersonal, and Hyperpersonal Interaction." *Communication Research* 23.1 (1996): 3–43.

Walther, Joseph B. "Interaction Through Technological Lenses: Computer-Mediated Communication and Language." *Journal of Language and Social Psychology* 31.5 (2012): 397–414.

Wang, Chuang, Matthew K.O. Lee, and Zhongsheng Hua. "A Theory of Social Media Dependence: Evidence from Microblog Users." *Decision Support Systems* 60 (2015): 40–49.

Wilson, Michele A. *Technically Together: Rethinking Community within Techno-Society.* New York: Peter Lang, 2006.

"Word and Image: Martin Luther's Reformation." *The Morgan Library Online Exhibition.* 2016. www.themorgan.org/exhibitions/online/word-and-image. Date accessed: 16 June 2017.

9

COMMUNICATION ETHICS
AND COMMUNITY

"Not again!" The music is so loud that Roberto feels it from the apartment next door. It is 12:30 a.m. Roberto is in bed so he could wake up in time for a 7 a.m. breakfast meeting with his supervisor. He works 40 hours a week and takes college classes. Roberto tries to be neighborly. At first, he stopped by and asked the couple next door to turn down their music. This worked once or twice. Then he called the building manager, and it was quiet . . . for a short time. A week ago, the building manager contacted Roberto about illegally parking his car. Apparently, his neighbors had complained. And now the music . . .

Like Roberto, each of us lives and works in a community. While many in our communities share our values, interests, and goals, there also are people whose interests, values, or goals are different from our own. Differences that create tension and conflict raise questions of fairness that involve issues of justice. There are at least six different types of justice—corrective, retributive, procedural, distributive, restorative, and harmonic. Each of these types of justice can be important in discerning the ethically responsive communication practices of a community.

Communication of community members creates their community. By examining a community's communication practices, we can better understand how fairness is experienced by its members. For example, when you listen to someone's concern about a problem, cut off someone expressing an idea, or ignore this person entirely, you influence the experience of fairness and the practice of justice within this group and its broader community. In some situations, practicing communication justice can be as simple as attentive listening. In a different situation, it may be one of the more difficult and complex challenges of communication ethics you face. Practicing justice might involve finding the courage to acknowledge publicly someone your community ignores or despises or discerning how to address an ethical dilemma as fairly as you can, knowing that whatever decision you make will create significant harm for some community members.

This chapter explores some challenges of practicing communication justice within communities. It begins with a brief discussion of how dialectical tensions of community shape issues of communication justice for both community members and outsiders. It then presents an analysis of two different communication strategies for managing dialectical tensions of community and issues of justice that emerge from practicing these strategies. As you read, think about how these ideas apply to the communities where you live and work.

Dialectical Tensions of Community

In the chapter's opening case, both Roberto and his neighbors want to feel at home where they live, to be accepted by others. Dialectical tensions of community develop out of the human need for acceptance. Communicating with others who think as you do is a powerful appeal of acceptance, because it confirms by tacit or explicit agreement that your ideas and values are right and good. Roberto's and his neighbors' verbal and nonverbal behaviors disconfirm each other, communicating that the other does not belong in the apartment's community. Their messages of disapproval also communicate approval and acceptance to neighbors who share their viewpoints, helping construct two different communities, one wanting quiet at night and one wanting to socialize. Communication that accepts or includes persons simultaneously excludes others who are seen as different. Ron Arnett observes that the simultaneous inclusiveness and exclusiveness that constitutes community is a basic contradiction of community life (29–32). This fundamental contradiction or paradox is the source of two dialectical tensions of community—1) similarity and difference, and 2) the individual and community.

Dialectical Tension of Similarity and Difference

Each of us experiences the **dialectical tension of similarity and difference** whenever our communication identifies us as an outsider. When you start a new job your communication marks you as someone "not from around here." One strategy for fitting in is learning the vocabulary and nonverbal cues that identify community members. Acceptance is important, because other community members recognize you as having a legitimate interest in community life. Using distinctive communication practices, however, may not be enough for your acceptance, because community members see their identity as different from your identity.

Community members construct a distinctive identity using shared symbols and communication practices. Distinctive communication practices and symbols of a **community identity** signal that the communicator has experienced key events of a community's shared life and has accepted its understandings and values. Distinctive communication practices such as speaking a common language, dialect, or slang, or wearing distinctive clothing help community members identify each other and distinguish them from outsiders. Hasidic Jewish communities have maintained their distinctive identity, in part because their verbal and nonverbal communication practices make clear distinctions between insiders and outsiders. The Amish, a Christian community in the US, also makes clear distinctions between insiders and outsiders in their verbal and nonverbal communication practices, transportation, and use of technology, which help monitor or limit the interactions of members with outsiders. Interaction with outsiders has the potential to influence a community's shared understandings and identity. For example, members of Amish communities still wear plain clothes, ride horses, and do not use electricity in their homes, but you can find Amish salsa for sale online. Because of interaction with outsiders, some accepted practices of Amish community life have changed to benefit from digital communication technology while maintaining the distinctive Amish identity. Variations in nonverbal artifacts such as clothing also can signal differences within a community, including the existence of different subcommunities. Although wearing a veil can identify women as Muslim, not all Muslim women wear the same type of veil or wear a veil at all. These differences signal the existence of different subcommunities within the broader Muslim community who may have different beliefs and practices of Islam (see Pew "US Muslims Concerned"). The same is true for the Jewish and Christian communities. Every member of the Jewish community does not dress and believe as Hasidic Jews do, just as every US Christian does not dress and believe as the Amish do.

Distinctive dress and community identities are not limited to religious communities. Wearing a sports jersey or colors of a football team identifies team members or fans of a sports community. Wearing colors of a national flag identifies the wearer as a community member who embraces the ideas and values symbolized by the flag. Nonverbal communication practices that maintain community identity manage the dialectical tension of similarity and difference by helping identify who are insiders and who outsiders.

Everyday Communication Ethics

❖ *Think of a situation where you were excluded from a group because of a nonverbal cue. Think of a situation where you excluded a person from your group of friends because of a nonverbal cue.*

Excluding outsiders as a strategy for maintaining community identity raises questions of justice. In the 17th century, the English policy of plantation (colonization) of Protestants in Ulster, Ireland replaced Irish Catholic communities with English Protestant communities. British historian Norman Davies characterizes the physical separation of Irish Catholics from English Protestants in enclaves of the worst agricultural land, as a practice of extreme exclusion called apartheid (478–82). In the late 19th and early 20th centuries, the US government's policy of forcing Indian children to attend boarding schools was to prevent these children from learning the behavioral and communication practices that created their tribal community identity (Adams). Teachers in government schools gave the children Anglo first names, cut their hair, and taught them to speak English as part of a curriculum designed to "save" them by making them members of the white Anglo community.

Recent controversies about the dress of Muslim women in Western societies are conflicts about community identity, raising questions of inclusion and exclusion. In Europe controversies have included banning various forms of the Muslim headscarf, and in France an unsuccessful effort to ban the burkini, a swimsuit that covers the entire body allowing Muslim women to swim on beaches while maintaining their modesty ("Islamic Veil"). While the US does not ban headscarves, Muslim women wearing them have been harassed. In one instance, two men were killed when intervening in the harassment of a Muslim woman wearing a headscarf (Victor). The increasing numbers of Muslims in Western societies through conversion and immigration have raised questions for some community members about who can be legitimate members of Western communities, heightening the dialectical tensions of similarity and difference.

Practices for maintaining a community identity sometimes use violence to exclude persons labeled outsiders to maintain an idealized community identity. Sometimes this exclusion culminates in killing those who are different. The practice of lynching in the 19th and 20th centuries helped maintain the policy of racial separation of African-Americans from white Americans in the US, as well as maintain an idealized "white" identity of supremacy (Pfeifer 67–8). Kidnapping, torture, and murder by South Africa's government security forces and police supported the late 20th century policy of racial apartheid, which forced black and colored Africans into physically isolated homelands and impoverished townships (see Tutu). The most infamous 20th century community that physically excluded and then killed those who were different is Nazi Germany, which segregated, transported, and then exterminated Jews, gypsies, GLBT persons, and the mentally disabled. The Nazi community rationalized these atrocities as protecting the purity of Aryan identity. What is both interesting and disturbing about these examples is that each community labeled as outsiders, community members who differed in some way from an idealized community identity. Once labeled outsiders, it became easier to develop arguments, explanations, and stories that rationalized unfair and violent treatment of these now unrecognized community members. Their new identity as outsiders supported arguments that rationalized claims that they did not deserve to be treated with standards of fairness as community members or human beings.

A community's strategies for managing the dialectical tensions of community life help create a community's practices of justice. These strategies assist in answering **three questions for practicing justice in a community**— "What is a legitimate interest?," "Who has a legitimate interest?," and "What are the most important or significant legitimate interests in this situation?" Answering these questions helps community members identify what is fair, who deserves fairness in a situation, and which factors identify who deserves the most fairness. Answering the first question—"What is a **legitimate interest**?"—identifies what is fair in a basic sense. Interests are created by the impact or consequence of a decision, action, or a set of circumstances. Not all impacts or consequences raise issues of fairness. Legitimate interests are created by impacts and consequences that affect the interest of community stakeholders to survive or flourish. Individual community members, institutions, or the entire community can be stakeholders. Creating a work schedule at your place of employment illustrates issues of justice in a community. The number of hours worked affects how much money an employee earns. Since surviving and flourishing depends upon money, the number of hours of work is a legitimate interest of everyone in the workplace. Conflicts between work and college class schedules can create harm by reducing potential earnings for individual employees, creating issues of justice.

Once decision makers identify benefits and harms that affect legitimate interests, they need to identify whose legitimate interests are affected by a specific act, decision, or set of circumstances. This is the second question to answer in practicing justice in a community—"Who has a legitimate interest?" Stakeholders who deserve fairness are those whose capacity to survive or flourish would be benefited or harmed by a decision, action, or set of circumstances. All employees in a workplace have a legitimate interest in the number of hours worked, because it affects how much money they earn to pay their bills. A company also has a legitimate interest in scheduling its employees, because it affects the company's profits, part of which is paid to employees. When employees who work productively are on the same shift, the workplace community is more profitable, giving both the company and employees a chance to prosper. A company may need more employees to work at certain times of the day and has a legitimate interest in scheduling them accordingly. Generally, a company's legitimate interest to survive and flourish is compatible with its employee's legitimate interests. Sometimes they are in tension or conflict. By answering questions about who has a legitimate interest, decision makers can identify issues of justice when legitimate interests of community members are in tension or conflict.

A community's identity can influence decisions about who has a legitimate interest. The more similar the affected stakeholder is to the community identity, the greater the likelihood that decision makers will judge that stakeholder's interest as legitimate. Continuing the workplace example, an employee who follows the company dress code and other rules and procedures would be seen by management as having a greater legitimate interest than an employee who does not do these things. When an interest of a stakeholder is not recognized as legitimate, that interest will not be considered in answering the third question of practicing justice—"What are the most important or significant legitimate interests in this situation?" This is an important question when community resources are limited. How decision makers identify what are legitimate interests and who has a legitimate interest are critical elements of a community's practice of justice. Broadening the example of a work community to the larger social community illustrates this. Because earning money is necessary to survive in Western societies, many Western governments have employment laws to ensure that employees who are different in some way (e.g., ethnicity, disability, gender, race, or religion) but also are skilled and competent in doing a job, are not treated as outsiders and discriminated against in the workplace. Practicing communication justice is difficult because practices of acceptance can rationalize treating unfairly those who are different from the ideal community identity. Decision makers may overlook or ignore legitimate interests of nonconforming community members or outsiders, even their legitimate interest to survive.

The paradox of community life is that when some people are accepted into a community others are simultaneously excluded. This is why communication justice is so important. This paradox is also why communities need to repeatedly deliberate about how to practice justice. As facts and circumstances of community life change, the dialectical tensions among community members shift in large and small ways, changing and renewing issues of how to practice justice.

Everyday Communication Ethics

❖ *Some claim that the greatest test of a community's ethics is how it treats strangers. Describe how strangers are treated in your hometown.*

Your personal ethical standard may guide your practice of justice, especially when you interact with people who differ from the generally accepted or ideal identity of your community. In addition, several ethical concepts presented in earlier chapters offer resources you may find useful. These concepts can stimulate your moral imagination and challenge you to identify rationalizations for ignoring the legitimate interests of nonconforming community members or outsiders, especially rationalizations based upon poorly examined social conventions of community. The Golden Rule, identified in Chapter 3, prompts us to imagine how those we consider different are actually similar to us in important ways and, thus, deserve to be treated humanely[1]. The second version of Kant's Categorical Imperative (96) to treat another person never simply as a means to achieving a goal but always at the same time as an end, discussed in Chapter 5, challenges us to examine whether we have recognized and honored the capacity of all persons to reason and make decisions, whatever their community membership. Political toleration of differences (Sacks *Home*), discussed in Chapter 5, also applies to the dialectical tension of similarity and difference. Nonconforming community members who comprise a minority today may become the majority in the future. Rigid imposition of community identity sometimes leads to conflict that weakens the community, even to the point of civil war that threatens to destroy the community (Sacks *Not in God's Name*).

Philosophical theories offer ideas for managing the dialectical tension of similarity and difference. Recognition of human dignity is a fundamental assumption of the moral rights approach to communication ethics, discussed in Chapter 6. Whether a person is an insider or outsider is irrelevant to the fundamental human interests of moral rights, because moral rights are based upon a quality of humanness inherent in each person. The concept of utilitarian impartiality, also discussed in Chapter 6, encourages a practice of justice in which our personal interests are no more important than the personal interests of others. Whether a person is a nonconforming community member is irrelevant. Finally, Levinas's "call of the other," discussed in Chapter 7, encourages us to examine how our community's shared understandings and communication practices may interfere with our ability to recognize the call of the other, including the call not to be killed. Incorporating concepts like these into your personal ethical standard can help you better recognize the legitimate interests of persons who differ from your community's identity.

Dialectical Tension between the Individual and Community

The fact that community members are individuals while simultaneously being part of the community creates the second dialectical tension of community. At first, this appears to be a variation of the dialectical tension of similarity and difference. The chapter's opening case illustrates both dialectical tensions of community. The conflict between Roberto and his neighbors raises an ethical issue of toleration of different legitimate interests of community members to thrive, to relax by socializing or having the quiet needed to sleep at night. Toleration of his neighbors' late night music does not address Roberto's legitimate interest of getting enough sleep. Roberto is dependent on his neighbors to be quiet enough for him to sleep at night, so he can meet his responsibilities at work. Roberto's neighbors also have a legitimate interest to relax and socialize in their home, and are dependent on their neighbors tolerating their music and other activities for relaxing. Both are in an interdependent relationship as physically close neighbors in an apartment building, so they experience consequences of each other's choices. Rhetorical listening reveals other relationally connected community members, such as others living in the apartment complex and Roberto's supervisor and coworkers. The **dialectical tension between the individual and community** concerns relational bridges and bonds that connect individuals to other community members and to the community in general (Depew and Peters). The conflict between Roberto and his neighbors is influenced by the degree to which they understand their relational connections to each other as interdependent or loose relational bridges and bonds.

When community members understand their relationships as **interdependent relational connections**, fulfilling relational responsibilities and duties to sustain community life are highlighted. This is a holistic understanding that the network of interdependent relationships of a community is greater than the sum of its individual members. Fulfilling relational responsibilities or duties of community, including communication responsibilities or duties, help maintain the network of relational bridges and bonds that create community. Laws and rules formally recognize some responsibilities and duties and may be enforced with fines and penalties, such as laws about drunk driving or the penalty rules of a sports association. Some may be informal, such as an expectation of service to others by helping a neighbor or volunteering in a local school. Individual members help maintain the network of interdependent relationships that constitute their community, by fulfilling formal and informal relational responsibilities and duties.

When community members understand their relationships as **loose relational connections** between individuals, they value independence and relative autonomy. This promotes the understanding of relationships, responsibilities, and duties as a matter of personal choice. Each community member has value as an individual, independent of others. Members' responsibility to the community is shaped by their individuality, personal integrity, creativity, freedom of thought, or freedom of action. Fostering independence of thought or individual creativity is a valuable source of innovation or growth that sustains a community. An understanding of community life that recognizes the individuality of community members acknowledges that without individual members, there is no community.

Everyday Communication Ethics

❖ *Describe three issues of justice created by dialectical tensions in your hometown.*

In the chapter's opening case, Roberto's and his neighbors' communication has consequences for each other and the broader community, because of the network of their relational bridges and bonds. Their immediate conflict is that their individual legitimate interests differ, Roberto to get enough sleep for his breakfast meeting and his neighbors to relax and socialize. Whether they understand relational bridges and bonds of community as relatively autonomous or interdependent, influences what they are willing to tolerate and how they communicate to manage their differences.

Dialectical tensions of community life make communicating ethically difficult. We create our communities by distinguishing ourselves from others who are different. Without excluding persons who are different in some way, we cannot create human community. The interdependent relationships that create community cannot exist without individuals, yet focusing too much on individuals may weaken interdependent relationships of community. Dialectical tensions exist in all human communities, repeatedly raising issues of justice.

Textbox 9.1

Communication Ethics in Popular Film: Justice and Community—*Munich* and *V for Vendetta*

A sense of injustice is a powerful motivation for action. It also makes a good story. Stories of restoring justice are common themes in film and literature, often celebrating characters who courageously overcome obstacles to achieve justice for innocent victims. Justice, however, is only one of six ethical values of communication. What happens when justice becomes the predominant legitimate interest and justification for action? Could a firm resolve for justice lead to rationalizing ethically questionable, if not unethical action? Considering more than one ethical value can aid our moral imaginations in discerning alternative legitimate interests that arise from the dialectical tensions of community life. It may also help us recognize how the practice of justice sometimes creates new harms, or discern when we have rationalized an ethically questionable decision.

Two films that tell stories of practicing justice in a community are Stephen Spielberg's *Munich* and James McTiegue's *V for Vendetta*. Justice is depicted as the primary or one of the two primary commitments of the main characters in each film. *Munich* is based on the true story of Israeli agents whose job is to administer retributive justice for the kidnapping and murder of unarmed Israeli athletes at the 1972 Munich Olympic Games. The film explores how far these men go in the name of justice for the murdered Israeli athletes and the nation of Israel. The film portrays how characters use justice to explain the personal cost to the Israeli agents who administer retributive justice, raising questions about the impact of a steadfast commitment to justice on the dialectical tension between the individual and community.

V for Vendetta is a fictional story about freedom and justice in a future totalitarian state. V, hiding behind a mask representing a

---

historical radical, challenges the government's control over the public and private lives of its citizens. For V, justice provides the context for freedom. Denial of freedom is unjust, while the practice of freedom is just. The film shows what V sacrifices and requires others to sacrifice to promote freedom and justice for his community. V's steadfast and single-minded focus on freedom raises questions about whether his actions are ethically good, bad, or some combination of both.

Each film raises questions about dialectical tensions between the individual and community in its exploration of characters' steadfast focus on justice and to a lesser extent on freedom. These tensions make a definitive and unambiguous ethical assessment of the characters and their actions difficult. The films raise an important question for examining our practice of communication ethics within our communities, whether the steadfast practice of an ethical value is always ethically good for a community and its members or an issue of justice.

The next section explores a challenge of practicing communication justice in community at this historical moment. Many social critics and researchers have observed that social capital, the resources provided by the network of relationships that constitute community, is seriously weakened and should be strengthened. Communication is one way to strengthen relationships in community. How a communication strategy manages the dialectical tensions of community to strengthen community relationships raises questions of justice.

Managing Dialectical Tensions of Community in Western Societies

In recent years, observers have expressed concern that Western communities are weakening, that the social capital of community relationships is deteriorating. They claim that community members see themselves as more isolated than relationally connected to other community members. This undermines civil society. For the US, the claim that community is weakening is not new. In 1840 Alexis de Tocqueville expressed concern that some practices he observed would eventually weaken US community, putting both individual liberty and democratic government at risk. Almost a century and a half later, Robert Bellah and his research associates concluded that Americans saw themselves as separate and relatively autonomous individuals who had a difficult time connecting to other people in their communities. More recently, Robert Putnam has argued that the social capital of American society is frayed (*Alone*). **Social capital** consists of communication practices and networks of reciprocal social relationships that help create the strength and vitality of a community. Social capital creates and maintains relational bridges and bonds that promote social trust between community members. **Social trust** is the shared expectation that the regular behavior of community members is honest and cooperative. Without relational bridges, there can be no relational bonds that maintain friendships, social groups, even business partnerships. Social trust weakens, even disappears. Social capital for Putnam is not about political parties or large institutions. It is about what people do in relation to other community members, as they go about their daily lives. Social capital focuses on the everyday practices of community by individuals. Putnam argues that US social capital has deteriorated to the point that individuals feel increasingly disconnected and isolated, even when they are physically near other people. He came to this conclusion *before* digital communication became widespread.

Putnam developed his concept of social capital studying community in Italy, to explain differences between the rich north and poor south (*Democracy*). Social scientists in the UK and Europe also study social capital. Paola Grenier and Karen Wright found a decline in social trust in Britain between 1990 and 1995 that paralleled the decline in social trust Putnam documented in the US, although the decline varied by social class. They identified income inequality as a factor in explaining class differences in the decline of social trust. Looking at social capital more broadly, researchers found informal social interaction and trust important for happiness in 25 European countries (Rodriguez-Pose and von Berlepsch). Post-communist countries in Europe offered an environment for studying social capital in societies transitioning to democracy. Dowley and Silver found a correlation between social capital and attitudes toward democracy, especially social trust, but relationship between social capital and democratic practices were mixed, especially for minority groups who may be suppressed by the majority.

In a later work, Putnam revisited his earlier research on the relationship between social capital, wealth, and poverty (*Our Kids*). He studied the impact of US income inequality on social mobility, the capacity of individuals and families to move from poverty to the middle class. This research parallels Grenier and Wright's findings in the UK that the amount of available social capital is influenced by income inequality and social class. Putnam found that the beginning and end of the 20th century exhibited both high income inequality and low social mobility. The middle of the 20th century had the lowest levels of income inequality and highest levels of social mobility. Putnam attributes mid-century social mobility in the US to effects of the economic leveling of the 1930s Great Depression and World War II, combined with lower corporate executive salaries and federal government policies that encouraged college education for World War II veterans. Veterans from poor families could earn a college degree and then get a job that paid a middle-class income. This was the experience of my father, who came from a poor white farming family in Depression-era Kansas. By the early 21st century, it was rare for poor individuals or families to move from poverty to the middle class through hard work, because the poor lacked access to the social capital available to moderate- and high-income families. An interesting exception to this 21st century trend involved a poor family's access to social capital provided by a local church (198–226). Relational bridges and bonds created by relationships within stable local organizations such as churches can provide social capital to poor families and individuals by offering relational resources that promote social mobility.

Everyday Communication Ethics

❖ *Describe the social capital of your hometown. Do different communities in your hometown have different social capital resources?*

Research of social capital in the US, UK, and Europe paint a picture of deteriorating communities, but also possibilities for rebuilding. Without social interaction, social capital is weakened and unstable because there are fewer relational bridges and bonds on which community members can rely. Communication strategies for managing a community's dialectical tensions may help rebuild and strengthen the networks of relationships that create social capital. One resource for developing strategies to strengthen social capital is found in metaphors to describe community. A **metaphor** is a symbol of comparison that organizes understanding and guides action (Lakoff and Johnson). Metaphors of community offer ways to think about relationships among community members, suggesting practices for managing dialectical tensions of community. Metaphors also provide answers to some questions of justice by providing a framework to think about legitimate interests within the community, who has those interests, and what are the most important legitimate interests. One practice of justice is assuring access to social capital for all community members. Two common metaphors of community are friendship and citizenship. Friendship is a personal or psychological metaphor, while citizenship is more social and political, though not in the sense of party or political ideology.

"Friendship" as a Metaphor for Community

The meaning of **friendship as a metaphor for community** seems clear, so its strategy for strengthening community appears obvious. You trust friends, so a community would consist of people you would trust as friends. You trust your friends to treat you fairly, which would strengthen a community's social capital. When we look at the meaning of friendship, however, it is not so clear how to build trust. Disagreements over what a friend is, even among friends, indicate that its meaning is not obvious. The following discussion explores two models of friendship. Each offers different strategies for creating trust and strengthening community relationships, which create different frameworks for justice. The first is Aristotle's model of friendship as striving for the happiness of a friend. The second model is friendship as a relationship of self-actualization.

In Aristotle's *Nicomachean Ethics* friendship and community are interdependent (263–4). Both friendship and community allow people to live lives of excellence. The ideal community is small, creating opportunities for face-to-face communication that encourages friendship. The aim or excellence of both friendship and community is "the good" or happiness which people achieve by living lives of virtue. This parallels social capital research that linked social interaction to happiness in 25 European countries (Rodriguez-Pose and von Berlepsch). To practice **Aristotle's model of friendship**, your goal is to promote the happiness of your friend, rather than your happiness. Friendship is more about loving your friend than being loved by her (271–2), which involves sacrifice of your personal interest for that of your friend. You may be wondering how you can trust a friend in this model of friendship, if you are not looking out for your personal happiness, just a little bit. Aristotle's answer is that your friend strives for your happiness, just as you are striving for your friend's happiness. Friendship is a reciprocal or mutual commitment to do good for the other person. The good or excellence of a community arises when community members mutually strive for the happiness of other people, their friends.

As a strategy for strengthening community, Aristotle's model of friendship requires a shared understanding of "the good" that creates happiness. Aristotle's community in ancient Greece had a shared understanding of the good life, which is not true for social community today. If you ever had a disagreement about what it means to be a loyal or supportive friend, you have experienced disagreement about "the good" of friendship. Questions of fairness arise among friends who have different understandings of "the good" of friendship. Without shared understanding of "the good" of friendship, individuals become less willing to act for the happiness of others and trust one another. Without such an understanding, Aristotle's model of friendship cannot provide a workable or fair strategy for strengthening community.

Point to Ponder

❖ *How big can a community become before community members become unfamiliar, even strangers?*

Friendship as self-actualization offers a different strategy for creating trust and strengthening community relationships, raising different issues of justice. In a self-actualizing relationship one person seeks help and support from another person (Arnett and Arneson 64–71; Bellah, et al. 128–40). In the **self-actualizing model of friendship**, friends use authentic and empathic communication to help each other achieve the legitimate interest of personal self-actualization. You and a friend would communicate authentically to create consensus about how each of you works to achieve personal goals, such as passing an exam, developing an artistic ability, or achieving a career goal. This consensus creates a basis of trust in your friendship. If your personal feelings or needs change enough to weaken this consensus, your friendship may end, unless you and your friend create a new consensus that allows trust to redevelop, because everyone has a right to their feelings and achieving their personal goals. The self-actualizing model of friendship offers interpersonal consensus based on authentic communication and empathy to strengthen community relationships.

Self-actualization is a practice of personal freedom. It promotes practices of justice in recognizing the legitimate interest of others to flourish, including individuals who differ from the community's identity. As a consensual practice of personal freedom, personal self-actualization can exhibit the dialectical tension of similarity and disagreement by excluding those who differ from agreed-upon authentic expressions of feeling and related goals. A focus on self-actualization, authenticity, and empathy also encourages a style of thinking and decision making called emotivism (Arnett and Arneson 55 and 62–3). **Emotivism** is the reliance on personal feelings or personal preferences in decision making. When decision making relies primarily on personal feelings, personal preferences, or self-actualization, it focuses on the decision maker rather than legitimate interests of others in the broader community. Emotivism substitutes authentic feelings or personal preferences for the shared understandings and practices of the larger community. This substitution includes the community's shared understandings and practices of justice. With emotivist thinking, justice is more personal—"Is it fair for me or you?"—rather than the "us" of the broader community. Emphasis on authentic feeling rather than on thinking could nudge a community's practices of corrective justice to be more retributive.

The self-actualizing model of friendship encourages communicators to base their practice of justice on their consensus, with little regard for legitimate interests of persons outside of the friendship. Individuals have little or no responsibility to act fairly toward other community members, beyond being empathetic and authentic communicators, which is easier when people have similar feelings and personal preferences. Even with consensus, discerning what is fair and deserving is subject to changes in feelings or preferences. Practices of what is fair and deserving may vary as the friends' feelings and thoughts about self-actualization change. This analysis is not an argument that self-actualization is never a legitimate interest of a community. When self-actualization focuses on needs and aspirations of community members, this metaphor offers a framework for growth and innovation that benefits a community and its members. However, when authenticity of feeling and consensus on personal preferences become key mechanisms for decision making, this metaphor of friendship can discourage consideration of interests of community members outside of the consensual framework for self-actualization accepted by friends.

Everyday Communication Ethics

❖ *What could you do to build community, beginning with your friends?*

The metaphor of friendship uses the development of interpersonal trust to strengthen the relational bridges and bonds of a community's social capital, as a strategy for strengthening community. At present, Western social communities lack a shared understanding of the good or excellence of friendship needed for practicing Aristotle's model of friendship. It would be unfair to impose a definition of "the good" of friendship, and most likely unsuccessful in democratic societies that value freedom. Although the self-actualizing model of friendship establishes a minimum standard for practicing justice by recognizing the legitimate interest of others to thrive, it also has limitations in strengthening relational connections, the bridges and bonds among community members that create and sustain community. The legitimate interest of self-actualization is met through a fluid consensus created by authentic feeling and empathic communication between friends. If feelings change or consensus ends, trust and friendship end, as do relational connections that create and sustain community. Community members with different feelings or goals can easily be excluded as insufficiently authentic. The self-actualizing model of friendship offers relatively fragile personal support networks for strengthening community. While it offers practices of justice for individuals, there are questions about how far its practices of justice would extend to community members who have different feelings and goals.

"Citizenship" as a Metaphor for Community

Citizenship offers a different strategy for strengthening relationships in a community. **Citizenship as a metaphor for community** has two elements, the political-legal dimensions of citizenship and practices of civic behavior (Gosewinkel 1852). Citizenship is *not* about political parties, although political parties may influence how a community understands citizenship. The metaphor of citizenship encourages us to think about the legitimate interests of community as benefits (political-legal rights and protections) and responsibilities (practices of civic behavior) that maintain the community.

The **legal and political rights of citizenship** provide citizens with benefits that promote the survival and flourishing of the community by encouraging the survival and flourishing of its citizens. The governing body of the community protects citizens by granting them legal rights. Exactly what these protections are would depend upon founding documents such as a constitution and the laws governing the community. In the US, the Constitution and Bill of Rights identifies legal rights that protect citizens and empower them to act within those protections, while in the UK several documents beginning with Magna Carta outline legal rights that protect citizens (Ashley). In France "The Declaration of the Rights of Man and of the Citizen" outlines rights of citizenship, as well as offering a statement of human rights (Heer, Schnieper, and Schwob). In 1996, the Republic of South Africa ratified a constitution that established rights of citizens (*Constitution*). A community's shared understandings, including its community identity, also guide how its institutions provide benefits to citizens, supporting the broader community. Take your education as an example. In the citizenship metaphor, education is a benefit of community life that also maintains the community. Your education has empowered you by teaching knowledge and skills you need to live in the community, facilitating your future personal success. As a productive member of the community your future actions will support other community members, helping maintain the community. Education benefits *both* your individual and the community's legitimate interests.

In a democratic community, legal rights of citizenship include the right to participate in the governance of the community. This is more than the right to vote. Yet, few of us will be elected government officials. In large democratic communities, a more realistic right for the average citizen is participation in public conversations about topics and issues of interest. Legal rights that protect citizens' participation in public conversation include the rights of a free press, speech, and assembly for the ordinary community member, not just government officials, leaders of institutions or businesses, or the wealthy. In this digital age, participation involves access to the internet. Before the internet, participation of ordinary citizens often was limited to local public conversations. With multiple digital platforms, especially social media, anyone can participate in public conversations at local, national, and international levels.

One limitation of the citizenship metaphor of community is that individual citizens have difficulty being heard in public conversations over those who have greater access to communication resources because of their size or wealth. Governments at almost every level and institutions such as media conglomerates, political parties, businesses, and interest groups have become adept at strategically presenting their message and managing communication resources such as digital infrastructure and networks. Digital communication technology and the internet make it easier for average citizens to disrupt government and institutional control of public conversations (Dahlgren). However, digital disruption can be countered by government and institutional use of digital algorithms, data mining, surveillance, and the brute force of digital processing power, which governments or institutions may use to influence or manage individual citizens and their participation in public conversations. Because of continuing developments in digital technology and platforms, we are still trying to understand the impact of digital technology on legal and political rights of citizenship, as well as how to protect citizens' rights, such as the right to privacy and access to digital resources.

Instead of exercising their legal rights to influence government, some community members focus on alternative ways to practice citizenship through community service and involvement (see Loeb). Virtual communities (Wilson; Dahlgren) offer alternative spaces for practicing citizenship that often do not focus on government or institutions. Practices of community service and involvement are part of the second element of citizenship, practices of civic behavior.

Practices of civic behavior focus on actions, interactions, and performances of citizens that promote shared community life (Asen). With practices of civic behavior, citizenship is a form of public *engagement* in a community. Because practices of civic behavior help maintain the existence of a community, including its social capital, the community has a legitimate interest in encouraging these practices. These practices are more responsibilities of membership than duties, although a community could legally require some practices, such as mandatory national service (military or nonmilitary) after graduating from secondary school. Practices of civic behavior integrate individual citizens into the interdependent relationships of the broader community in ways that cross social lines of class, income, ethnicity, race, or religion. These practices highlight how legitimate interests of community members are interrelated to each other. Practices of civic behavior may be more important than the legal protections of citizenship in creating and maintaining community (Gray 5–6, 128–9). Building a common community life involves practices of civic behavior. Jonathan Sacks argues that to build a common community life, we must create or build things with other community members (*Home*).

Point to Ponder

❖ *Issues of justice are part of community life. How do the metaphors of friendship and citizenship differ in their approach to practicing different types of justice?*

Think about the common life of your workplace. Showing up on time for work is a civic practice that supports the organization that hired you. It also supports your job. If you or your coworkers do not show up to work on time, or perhaps do not show up at all, the organization that employs you would not operate efficiently. There is a reciprocal relationship between practices of civic behavior and the maintenance of legal rights and benefits of citizenship. By promoting a shared community life, practices of civic behavior support the maintenance of community relationships and institutions that distribute the legal rights and benefits of citizenship. The civic practice of showing up to work helps maintain the benefits to which you have a legal right, such as wages or health insurance. If you and other employees do not follow the civic practice of showing up for work or arriving on time, the company's effectiveness would diminish. Over time, the financial health of the company could weaken to the point that it could no longer afford to pay the wages or other benefits you have a legal right to. Legal rights and benefits exist because the community exists. If citizens do not maintain their community with practices of civic behavior, the community could eventually deteriorate to the point it cannot provide members their legal rights and benefits of citizenship. Showing up for work on time is a practice of civic behavior that helps maintain your workplace.

The relationship between practices of civic behavior and the legal rights and benefits of community membership also can highlight injustice, especially when the social capital of trust is weakened. The workplace also illustrates this relationship. Imagine an employee whose weekly schedule is two hours short of full-time work status, e.g., 38 of a 40-hour work week, just under the legal minimum needed to qualify for full-time employee benefits, such as health insurance or paid vacations. While technically legal, this civic practice of the workplace community raises questions of fairness among employees. Not answering or offering inadequate answers to repeated questions of fairness can weaken social trust. Recall that questions of fairness are not identical to questions of what is legal. Law and ethics are not the same. A weakened social capital of trust is a sign that there are unaddressed or poorly addressed issues of fairness within a community, which may include unfairness sanctioned by a community's laws.

Public discussion, dialogue, and debate are communication practices of civic behavior. To encourage citizen involvement, sometimes organizations promote formal public engagement events for community members, ranging from candidate forums to meetings where community members learn about, discuss, or debate issues. Rhetorical scholars Adam Lerner and Pat Gehrke propose that public engagement events be organized to align with a local community's preexisting practices of civic behavior. Public engagement on issues based upon a local community's preexisting communication and deliberation practices is **organic public engagement**. Many if not most formalized public engagement efforts employ outside experts or researchers who oversee the conditions and structures of local communities and their already existing practices of civic behavior. When public engagement events are organized with better understanding of local communities, their publics, and their citizenship practices, decisions made in public engagement events are more sustainable. Organic public engagement does not try to control citizens by forcing them to participate in artificial or stilted communication, deliberation, or decision making processes. It is an inclusive communication practice that acknowledges how people in local communities gather to form publics. It encourages citizens, experts, community leaders, and government officials to listen to one another, a practice of harmonic justice (Tompkins). Organic public engagement is risky, because organizers relinquish control to publics in local communities, acknowledging the importance of localized knowledge and civic practices for addressing issues and problems. Outcomes of organic public events are not guaranteed to produce agreement or decisions. But when agreements or decisions do occur, they are more sustainable because they are more trustworthy to community members.

Everyday Communication Ethics

❖ *What might organic public engagement on a controversial topic look like in your hometown?*

An important practice of civic behavior in a democracy is civility (Carter; Eicher-Catt; Hardy and Jamieson). Stephen Carter defines **civility** as "the sum of the many sacrifices we are called to make for the sake of living together" (*Civility* 11). Civility encourages us to consider others as important as and, in some situations, more important than ourselves. It sustains community by creating and maintaining social capital. Practicing civility does not depend on whether you like a person, nor does it require masking our differences.

Democratic community is weakened by highly competitive, uncivil practices of political partisanship. Repeated uncivil political practices can create feelings of animosity that discourage compromise, including compromise with integrity (Benjamin). Highly competitive, uncivil communication practices reject community members who are different, including members with different viewpoints. Extreme practices of political animosity may stimulate physical violence that goes beyond shoving and pushing, such as the 2011 attempted assassination of US Congresswoman Gabrielle Giffords (Nagourney) and the 2016 murder of UK Member of Parliament Jo Cox (Cobain and Taylor). In 2016 the Pew Research Center found that in the US, for those who identified with the major political parties and did not have close friendships with individuals belonging to the other party, political animosity increased significantly (Pew "Political Polarization"). When citizens communicate only with people who think like them, political animosity can increase towards community members who think differently.

Political animosity is not the only challenge to civility as a practice of civic behavior. Because democracy tolerates and encourages disagreement and dissent, it encourages what some people consider incivility. When disagreement or dissent is considered uncivil, it undermines the practice of political toleration, which also is a weakness of the metaphor of community as friendship, discussed above. The logic of emotivism in friendship as self-actualization discourages disagreement, because disagreement upsets the emotional consensus needed for friendship to exist. Emotivism relies more on self-confirmation and the expression of authentic emotion than deliberation about facts and circumstances that challenge a decision maker's point of view. When emotivism becomes an accepted practice of civic behavior, disagreements necessary for democratic deliberation and problem solving can be seen as uncivil (Herbst). This is not an argument that friendship does not have a role in strengthening community, but that community is more than friendship. It is important that our communities include people who are not our friends and are different from us in many ways, including some ways that make us feel uncomfortable.

Civility affirms an individual citizen's relationship to the community by how it manages the dialectical tensions of community, encouraging similarity, difference, and individuality. When you practice civility, you honor how another person differs from you alongside what you share as community members (Eicher-Catt). Civility requires that we recognize the possibility that others might be correct and we might be wrong. It requires checking our perceptions of persons and situations for accuracy and reliability. Civility also requires that when we are convinced that we are correct, we respectfully work to manage or resolve our differences. By respectfully focusing on others who are different, Carter's concept of civility aims to create communication practices that strengthen the interdependent relationships and social capital of community, while also creating room for disagreement and individuality. It is important to note that Carter also offers a definition of integrity, discussed in Chapter 4. Carter's definition (*Integrity*) is to discern what is right, act upon your discernment, and to publicly state why you did what you did so others may understand and examine your action. Civility without integrity can deteriorate into obsequiousness. Without civility, integrity can deteriorate into incivility, even violence.

Point to Ponder

❖ *Brainstorm practices of civility. What practice of civility is most important? Least important? Why?*

There are other important communication practices of citizenship. Consider whether having a **voice** that can be heard in community processes of deliberation is as important or more important than voting. Procedures and issues of fairness for voting are familiar. Procedures for deciding who has the right to have a voice in community discussions and debates are less familiar. Questions of voice raise questions of fairness—who is included or excluded in community practices of public engagement (Hauser and Benoit-Barne). Citizenship does not always guarantee a voice for community members who differ from the ideal community identity. When a community's definition of citizenship changes, some members may gain or lose legal protection or rights that protect their voice. The abolitionist, suffrage, labor union, and civil rights movements in the US and UK created new definitions and practices of citizenship that eventually expanded legal definitions of citizenship, affecting which community members received the benefits of citizenship in these countries, including rights to speak and participate in public conversations. When community members are labeled outsiders or when their behavior differs from either the community's ideal identity or norms for civic practices of citizenship, it becomes easy to question their loyalty and suppress their voice, making them vulnerable to efforts to limit or eliminate their legal rights and protections as citizens. During World War I, American citizens who questioned the military draft or the sale of US war bonds were arrested, tried, convicted, and imprisoned for sedition, because they did not practice the accepted civic communication behaviors of patriotism (Tedford and Herbeck 44–5). During World War II, US citizens of Japanese descent were placed in internment camps, having lost their legal protections of citizenship, property, and livelihoods. Long after the fact, community members may recognize how the community unjustly denied citizens benefits of citizenship, including their right to speak. A challenge we face in practicing communication ethics in the communities where we live and work is recognizing and responding to injustices as they happen. Today, increasing immigration in Europe and North America aggravates the problem of denying rights to citizens, when community members treat citizens who are similar to immigrants as non-citizens and try to exclude them from the community, or deny them basic human rights. An ethical problem you may face is treating with civility, even care, a community member who is harassed because she looks different or voices unpopular ideas.

Textbox 9.2

Voices and Standpoints in Public Conversation

Do the voices in the conversations of a community belong to individual citizens or to diverse standpoints within that community? A standpoint is a different way to think about the dialectical tension of the individual and community. A **standpoint** is a social location within a community's power structure and hierarchy (Collins). It does not belong to a specific individual, because it is a set of experiences created by the relational networks and the social and cultural practices of a community. In larger and more diverse communities, especially those with limited communication resources, answering questions of how to practice procedural justice may depend on discerning the different standpoints that have a legitimate interest in being heard by others, rather than simply giving each person a chance to speak. One challenge is recognizing that people with the same standpoint can have different points of view.

The metaphor of citizenship raises questions about practicing procedural justice in distributing the communication benefits of citizenship—speaking, listening, and being listened to. Small communities can give everyone a turn to speak during community deliberations. Larger and more diverse communities may require different procedures because of time restrictions and limits on communication resources, such as space, access to information, or access to technology. Too often, voices of the powerful or the majority can drown out minority viewpoints to the point that the majority may not recognize the existence of a minority. This is a limitation of utilitarian ethics, discussed in Chapter 6. John Stuart Mill's solution was to protect minority voices, giving them greater opportunity to speak. Important questions to consider in practicing communication justice in a community are "Who gets to speak?," "What voices are heard?," and "How are voices filtered out?" Criticisms of power and privilege in our communities help us better understand how majority and minority viewpoints are and are not recognized, so we can listen more attentively to obscured or silenced voices in difficult public conversations and, so, stimulate our moral imaginations. Because communities typically do not have unlimited communication resources that insure everyone is heard, considering how to practice procedural justice is integral to the everyday practice of communication ethics in community.

At this point, you might conclude that the maintenance of a community depends primarily upon practices of civic behavior. Practices of civic behavior are important, but a community requires many resources to maintain its health. Such resources include economic, agricultural, energy, and health-care resources, alongside the quality of a community's relationships with other communities. In fact, Putnam's analysis of the impact of income inequality demonstrates the importance of these resources for maintaining a community's social capital (*Our Kids*). Practices of civic behavior provide *communication* resources that support the interdependent relationships that create and maintain a community. Communication resources alone are insufficient to create and maintain a community; however, absence of communication practices of civic behavior weakens the social trust communities need to sustain themselves and promote justice for its members.

Conclusion

Most of us hope to find a community that will accept us and has sufficient resources to support our legitimate interests to survive and flourish. Yet, our acceptance by a community exists in a dialectical relationship with the exclusion of others from our community. Out of this paradoxical contradiction of community life, issues of justice develop. A community's strategies and practices for managing the dialectical tensions of community life shape the practice and experience of justice for its members. At this moment in history, social critics claim that the social capital that helps create democratic community in the US, UK, and Europe has deteriorated, weakening community life. A strategy for rebuilding community is using communication strategically to strengthen social trust and networks of relational connections that comprise social capital. The metaphors of community as friendship and community as citizenship offer different strategies for strengthening community in how they manage the dialectical tensions of community. They raise different issues of communication justice.

Whether you agree or disagree with the claim that democratic social community is weakening, the metaphors of friendship or citizenship can be helpful in thinking about justice in the communities where you live and work. These metaphors can stimulate your moral imagination to recognize ethical issues that develop from the dialectical tensions of community life, and for fairly managing those tensions. Because it is impossible for human community to exist without excluding others in some way, issues of fairness, especially in how a community treats outsiders and community members who are different, are central in community life. The metaphor of community you use will influence your understanding of community life and your discernment and decision making about what is ethically good, right, or virtuous for your community.

Vocabulary

Cases for Discussion

Directions: For each of the cases use your personal ethical standard to choose an ethical communication response. As part of analyzing the facts of a case, identify the dialectical tensions of community present in each case and issues of social capital. As part of your deliberation, consider how the metaphors of friendship and citizenship influence your understanding of the facts.

1. Bailing Out

"Really, Carol. You have to do better! When someone is as important as Tom Hergert, you need a good reason for not showing up. Texting 'I'm overwhelmed' is insulting," advised Suzanne. "People who don't matter to you don't need an explanation. If you text you're not coming, that's enough. You're building your network to find a new job. You need to figure out your strategy."

What should Carol consider the next time she thinks about not showing up after promising to?

2. Sportsmanship

Kayla is staying with her brother's family for summer. She is job hunting, after being laid off. She works as a server to keep from going too far into debt, and pays her brother something for living with his family. To fit into family life, she goes with her brother and sister-in-law to her nephew's soccer games at least once a week. Jarrod plays on a seventh- and eighth-grade team named Sorrento that is tied for first place. Tonight is the season's last game before playoffs.

During the last few games, several parents urged more aggressive play. After one game last week, one father went onto the field, loudly complaining to the referee that an "unfair" call cost Sorrento the game. He said there should be a different referee for the playoffs. Soccer referees are volunteers. Most are students who play on the high school soccer team. Kayla saw the play and thought the call was close. She understands why the father disagreed with the call. However, playing a sport is learning how to move on from setbacks, like a bad call or losing a game, and continuing to play your best.

The referee has made several calls against Sorrento. The father who confronted the referee at the last game has shouted several times that the referee is making bad calls.

If you were Kayla, how would you practice your personal ethical standard of communication? If you were a parent of a child playing soccer on Jarrod's team who had watched this father's behavior throughout the season, how would you practice your personal ethical standard of communication?

3. A Group as a Community

Each year Communication Club sponsors a drive to register donors for the National Bone Marrow Donor list. Bone marrow donations are used to treat people with cancers that attack the bone narrow and blood. The registry is a list of people willing to donate their bone marrow, but only to a patient with the same blood type. The more people on the registry, the greater the chance of finding a match. Potential donors complete a simple health screening and screen their blood type. Transplant programs depend upon registry drives to expand the pool of donors.

You are the recruiting chair for this year's drive. The goal is to register 125 students. Recruiting involves giving speeches in classes and making reminder calls about appointments the day before the drive. Each member of the recruiting committee will visit classes and do follow-up. You are concerned about meeting this year's goal, because one committee member, Darryl, has not completed his assignment. He also is not willing to do in-class recruiting. Darryl is well liked by everyone on the committee. He participates at meetings and talks about his commitment to the registry. A member of his family died of cancer.

The date for the registry drive is one week from today. You have just received an email from Darryl saying that he is just too busy to go to classes for the last recruiting effort or to make reminder calls.

How would you practice your personal ethical standard of communication in communicating with Darryl and other committee members? How would you practice your personal ethical standard of communication if you were Darryl?

Note

1 Critics of the Golden Rule argue that it overemphasizes similarity. The Platinum Rule is offered as an effort to recognize human dignity that also acknowledges the ways others are different from us—"Do unto others as they want done unto themselves." The Golden Rule and the corresponding Platinum Rule offer different strategies for managing the dialectical tension of similarity and difference in community life.

References

Adams, David Wallace. *Education for Extinction: American Indians and the Boarding School Experience, 1875–1928.* Lawrence, KS: U of Kansas P, 1995.

Aristotle. *The Ethics of Aristotle: The Nicomachean Ethics.* 1955. Trans. J.A.K. Thomson and Hugh Tredennick. New York: Penguin Books, 1976.

Arnett, Ronald C. "Communication and Community in the Age of Diversity." *Communication Ethics in an Age of Diversity.* Eds. Josina M. Makau and Ronald C. Arnett. Urbana, IL: U of Illinois P, 1997. 27–47.

Arnett, Ronald C. and Pat Arneson. *Dialogic Civility in a Cynical Age: Community, Hope, and Interpersonal Relationships.* Albany, NY: SUNY 1999.

Asen, Robert. "A Discourse Theory of Citizenship." *Quarterly Journal of Speech* 90.2 (2004): 189–211.

Ashley, Mike. *Taking Liberties: The Struggle for Britain's Freedoms and Rights.* London: The British Library, 2008.

Bellah, Robert N., Richard Madsen, William M. Sullivan, Ann Swidler, and Steven M. Tipton. *Habits of the Heart: Individualism and Commitment in American Life.* New York: Harper, 1985.

Benjamin, Martin. *Splitting the Difference: Compromise and Integrity in Ethics and Politics.* Lawrence, KS: U of Kansas P, 1990.

Carter, Stephen L.. *Civility: Manners, Morals, and the Etiquette of Democracy.* New York: HarperCollins, 1998.

Carter, Stephen L. *Integrity.* New York: HarperCollins, 1996.

Cobain, Ian and Matthew Taylor. "Far-right Terrorist Thomas Mair Jailed for Life for Jo Cox Murder." *The Guardian.* 23 November 2016. www.theguardian.com/uk-news/2016/nov/23/thomas-mair-found-guilty-of-jo-cox-murder. Date accessed: 5 March 2018.

Collins, Patricia Hill. "Comment on Hekman's 'Truth and Method: Feminist Standpoint Theory Revisited': Where's the Power?" *Signs: Journal of Women, Society, and Culture* 22.2 (1997): 375–81.

Constitution of the Republic of South Africa. 1996. www.gov.za/documents/constitution-republic-south-africa-1996. Date accessed: 5 August 2017.

Dahlgren, Peter. *The Political Web: Media, Participation and Alternative Democracy.* Basingstoke, UK: Palgrave Macmillan, 2013.

Davies, Norman. *The Isles: A History.* New York: Oxford UP, 1999.

Depew, David and John Durham Peters. "Community and Communication: The Conceptual Background." *Communication and Community.* Eds. Gregory J. Shepherd and Eric W. Rothenbuhler. Mahwah, NJ: LEA, 2001. 3–21.

De Tocqueville, Alexis. *Democracy in America.* 1835, 1845. Eds. and trans. Harvey C. Mansfield and Delba Winthrop. Chicago, IL: U of Chicago P, 2000.

Dowley, Kathleen M. and Brian D. Silver. "Social Capital, Ethnicity and Support for Democracy in the Post-Communist States." *Europe-Asia Studies* 54.4 (2002): 505–27.

Eicher-Catt, Deborah. "A Semiotic Interpretation of Authentic Civility: Preserving the Ineffable for the Good of the Common." *Communication Quarterly* 61.1 (2013): 1–17.

Gosewinkel, Dieter. "Historical Development of Citizenship." *International Encyclopedia of the Social and Behavioral Sciences.* Vol. 3. Eds. Neil J. Smelser and Paul B. Baltes. New York: Elsevier, 2001. 1852–7.

Gray, John. *Post-Liberalism: Studies in Political Thought.* New York: Routledge, 1993.

Grenier, Paola and Karen Wright. "Social Capital in Britain: Exploring the Hall Paradox." *Policy Studies* 27.1 (2006): 27–53.

Hardy, Bruce and Kathleen Hall Jamieson. "Overcoming Endpoint Bias in Climate Change Communication." *Environment Communication.* 2016,

Hauser, Gerard A. and Chantal Benoit-Barne. "Reflections on Rhetoric, Deliberative Democracy, Civil Society, and Trust." *Rhetoric and Public Affairs* 5.2 (2002): 261–75.

Heer, Friedrich, Xavier Schnieper, and Pierre R. Schwob. *Great Documents of the World: Milestones of Human Thought.* New York: McGraw-Hill, 1977

Herbst, Susan. *Rude Democracy: Civility and Incivility in American Politics.* Philadelphia, PA: Temple UP, 2010.

"Islamic Veil across Europe, The." *BBC News.* 31 January 2017. www.bbc.com/news/world-europe-13038095. Date accessed: 28 July 2017.

Kant, Immanuel. *Groundwork of the Metaphysics of Morals.* 1797. Trans. H.J. Paton. New York: Harper, 1964.

Lakoff, George and Mark Johnson. *Metaphors We Live By.* Chicago, IL: U of Chicago P, 1980.

Lerner, Adam S. and Pat J. Gehrke. *Organic Public Engagement: How Ecological Thinking Transforms Public Engagement with Science.* Cham, Switzerland: Palgrave Macmillan, 2018.

Loeb, Paul Rogat. *The Impossible Will Take a Little While: Perseverance and Hope in Troubled Times.* 2nd edn. New York: Basic Books, 2014.

Mill, John Stuart. *On Liberty.* 1859. Ed. Alburey Castell. Northbrook, IL: AHM Publishing, 1947.

Munich. Dir. Steven Spielberg. Prod. Kathleen Kennedy, et al. Universal City, CA: Universal Pictures, 2006. DVD

Nagourney, Adam. "In Gifford's District, a Long History of Tension." *The New York Times.* 10 January 2011. www.nytimes.com/2011/01/11/us/11district.html. Date accessed: 5 March 2018.

Pew Research Center. "US Muslims Concerned about Their Place in Society, but Continue to Believe in the American Dream." 26 July 2017. www.pewforum.org/2017/07/26/findings-from-pew-research-centers-2017-survey-of-us-muslims/. Date accessed: 28 July 2017.

Pew Research Center. "Political Polarization." Publications 2012–2017. www.pewresearch.org/topics/political-polarization/2017/. Date accessed: 11 July 2017.

Pfeifer, Michael J. *Rough Justice: Lynching and American Society, 1874–1947.* Urbana, IL: U of Illinois P, 2004.

Putnam, Robert D. *Making Democracy Work: Civic Traditions in Modern Italy.* Princeton, NJ: Princeton University Press, 1993.

Putnam, Robert D. *Bowling Alone: The Collapse and Revival of American Community.* New York: Simon & Schuster, 2000.

Putnam, Robert D. *Our Kids: The American Dream in Crisis.* New York: Simon & Schuster, 2015.

Rodríguez-Pose, Andrés and Viola von Berlepsch. "Social Capital and Individual Happiness in Europe. *Happiness Studies* 15 (2014): 357–86.

Sacks, Jonathan. *The Home We Build Together: Recreating Society.* New York: Continuum, 2007.

Sacks, Jonathan. *Not in God's Name: Confronting Religious Violence.* New York: Schocken Books, 2015.

Tedford, Thomas L. and Dale A. Herbeck. *Freedom of Speech in the United States.* 6th ed. State College, PA: Strata Publishing, 2009.

Tompkins, Paula S. "Acknowledgment, justice, and communication ethics." *Review of Communication* 15 (2015): 240–57.

Tutu, Desmond. *No Future Without Forgiveness.* New York: Random House, 1999.

V for Vendetta. Dir. James McTiegue. Prod. Grant Hill, et al. Burbank, CA: Warner Home Video, 2006.

Victor, Daniel. "Three Men Stood Up to Anti-Muslim Attack. Two Paid with their Lives." *The New York Times.* 28 May 2017. www.nytimes.com/2017/05/28/us/portland-stabbing-victims.html?_r=0. Date accessed: 28 July 2017.

Wilson, Michele A. *Technically Together: Rethinking Community Within Techno-Society.* New York: Peter Lang, 2006.

10

COMMUNICATION ETHICS
AND INTERCULTURAL
COMMUNICATION

Mahroof, Ghulam, and Mohammed headed to their meeting with the plant supervisor, Mr. Wilson. They represented Muslim employees at Caledonia Industries in discussions with management about allowing them to fulfill their daily obligation to pray at work. Several supervisors had told Muslim employees that they could not be excused to pray, because that would be a special treatment. Who would not like to have a break to pray, meditate, or just collect their thoughts for a few minutes? Management suggested that Muslim employees simply close their eyes and pray silently, like observant Christians do. Muslim prayer, however, requires each person to wash for purification, face Mecca, and pray on a prayer rug. Then there is the operations management problem. If every Muslim on the assembly line prayed at the same time, production would stop. Every time production stops and starts during a shift, the company loses money. Mahroof knocked on the door of the plant supervisor's office. Mr. Wilson opened the door and invited them to be seated.

It is likely that you have communicated with people from a different culture. With increasing immigration caused by war and the effects of climate change, as well as traditional economic factors, communicating with people from different cultures is commonplace. Even without immigration, we communicate in a world created by global economics, global corporations, and global digital communication (Friedman). A customer service call could be answered by someone anywhere in the world or artificial intelligence (Martinez). We live in a world of virtual proximity, where we can speak in real time with people (or artificial intelligence) located in different places in the world as if they are physically proximate or close to us, but they are not.

Intercultural communication involves the opportunities and challenges of communicating with people from a different culture, whether that different culture exists as a subculture within your community or a culture located somewhere else. **Culture** is the shared meanings of symbols, both verbal and nonverbal, held by members of a community. **Intercultural communication** is "the exchange of symbolic information between well-defined groups with significantly different cultures" (Barnett and Lee 276). In their discussion of intercultural conflict, Stella Ting-Toomey and John Oetzel compare culture to an iceberg (Ting-Toomey 9–11). When we communicate with people from different cultures, we tend to notice surface similarities, rather than listening for the underlying beliefs and values of these cultures that are the sources of differences. This ethnocentric attitude creates much intercultural misunderstanding and conflict. It also can create ethical nearsightedness. Another attitude that can create intercultural misunderstanding and ethical nearsightedness is presuming that there are no overlaps between cultures, that cultures are incommensurable. This assumption ignores common human experiences, such as eating, raising children, and dying. It also ignores the biological basis and science of human development, including moral development (Tompkins). Ethically responsive intercultural communication navigates between the binary extremes of seeing people from different cultures as the same as ourselves or presuming they have nothing in common with us.

Intercultural communicators find it helpful to understand what different cultures identify as good, right, or virtuous behavior. The chapter's opening case develops out of different cultural understandings of what is good employee behavior. These understandings are influenced by the different religious or secular traditions of employees. You may have experience communicating in an intercultural situation where there were significant differences between what communicators considered ethically good, right, or virtuous. If you have not, it is likely that you will face such a challenge at work, in your neighborhood, or among friends and acquaintances.

The study of intercultural communication stresses that ethics is more often relative to a culture than universal (Martin and Nakayama 34–5). Intercultural communication specialists discourage making ethical judgments about other cultures and encourage tolerance. Practicing tolerance involves accepting something that makes you uncomfortable, which behaviors and practices that are culturally different often do. Sometimes tolerance involves accepting something that you think is wrong, especially when it violates ethical principles such as truthfulness, justice, freedom, care, integrity or honor. Tolerance is guided by the idea that a communicator's personal ethical standard may not be ethically fitting in every intercultural communication situation. An example might help to illustrate. While truth is a widely recognized ethical value (Jensen; Mieth), people from different cultures may consider the other's practice of truth telling unethical. One culture values truthfulness as candor about personal feelings, observations, or ideas, while the other culture also values a truthful recognition of the interdependencies and relationships that enmesh a person in relationships with others and requires acts of kindness. Both cultures value truth, but understand and practice truth in different ways. A person from a culture that prizes truthfulness as candor may view as deceptive the face-saving communication of a person from a culture that recognizes the truth of relational interdependency. An ethnocentric attitude that truthfulness requires candor in all situations can produce an ethical nearsightedness that does not recognize the truthfulness of interdependent relationships. Tolerance promotes recognition and acceptance of culturally different practices of truth, along with culturally different practices of other ethical values and principles.

Dialectical Tensions of Intercultural Communication

A decision to be tolerant or to initiate a discussion of your ethical concerns would depend on the facts and circumstances of the situation you face. Such a decision involves assessing the dialectical tensions evident in the facts and circumstances of that situation. Chapter 9 discussed issues of communication ethics that develop from the dialectical tensions of community. The dialectical tensions of community—similarity and difference and between the individual and community—are also two dialectical tensions of intercultural communication practice. Dialectical tensions may create or influence ethical issues.

Judith Martin, Thomas Nakayama, and Lisa Flores describe the practice of intercultural communication as a dynamic process influenced by six contradictory dialectical tensions (6–8). A competent intercultural communicator would use the **six dialectical tensions of intercultural communication practice** to understand how these tensions influence communication dynamics. Chapter 9's discussion of communication ethics and community examined two dialectical tensions of community, the dialectical tension of similarity and difference and the relationship between the individual and community/culture. Just as strategies for managing the dialectical tensions of community can develop into recurring ethical issues of justice, strategies for managing the dialectical tensions of intercultural communication may develop recurring ethical issues.

Textbox 10.1

**Dialectical Tensions of Intercultural
Communication Practice—Martin, Nakayama,
and Flores**

Cultural—Individual	A person is a unique individual whose communication is not always determined by culture.
Personal—Social	A person simultaneously communicates from their individual personal identity and social roles.
Differences—Similarities	Similarity and difference coexist within and between cultures. In communication, similarities and differences sometimes work in cooperation, in opposition, or some combination of both.
Static—Dynamic	Cultures include patterns that remain stable and consistent over time and other patterns change.
Present/Future— History/Past	How members understand their culture's history influences how they understand the present, and how they understand their culture's present influences their understanding of their culture's future.
Privilege—Disadvantage	Power differences vary by context and may be in tension within a specific context.

Ethical Issues and Challenges of Intercultural Communication

Because dialectical tensions are present in some form in every intercultural communication situation, intercultural communicators develop strategies for managing these tensions. The remainder of this section will explore ethical issues that can develop from practicing three approaches for managing the dialectical tensions of intercultural communication—negotiating cultural identity, absolutism, and cultural relativism.

Negotiating Cultural Identity

Cultural identity concerns how people define themselves as members of a culture. Intercultural communication theorist Young Yun Kim describes cultural identity as "integral to an individual's identity, offering a sense of historical connection and embeddedness and of a 'larger' existence in the collectivity of a group" (145). The discussion of community identity in Chapter 9 explained its importance for managing the dialectical tensions of community. A community's identity also influences issues of justice for a community. Identity has similar importance for cultural life and managing the dialectical tensions of intercultural communication. Members of a culture share similarities, while also differing from one another, sometimes in significant ways. Some members of a culture may disagree with the values, expectations, or meanings that create their culture's norms and practices. Another way members of a culture may differ is that they belong to different cocultures or subcultures.

A friend of my daughter can illustrate how cocultures and subcultures create dialectical tensions of similarity and difference for identity. Ok Kyu is a Korean middle school teacher who worked with my daughter at a middle school in the Republic of Korea. The obvious dialectical tension of similarity and difference my daughter faced with Ok Kyu was that my daughter is an American while Ok Kyu is Korean. This, however, was only the beginning of differences and similarities that my daughter needed to be aware of, as she worked with Ok Kyu inside and outside of the classroom. Besides being a member of Korean culture, Ok Kyu is a member of the Korean Christian subculture. While she shares the identity of being a Korean with her coworkers in Guanggu province, she does not share their cultural identity of being a Buddhist, although Buddhism is part of her general cultural heritage as a Korean, because Buddhism is Korea's dominant religion.

Another dialectical tension that influences cultural identity is the tension between static and dynamic. Dialectical tensions of stability and change can be evident in cultural identity. Initially, intercultural communication theorists understood cultural identity as stable and uniform, remaining relatively constant and possessed by most members of a culture. Theorists proposed, for example, that there were stable and dominant American, Brazilian, British, Indian, Nigerian, Malaysian, or Korean cultural identities. Today, students of intercultural communication recognize that cultural identity is variable, complex, and dynamic. Cultural identities may change as members communicate with members of other cultures, or share a widespread new experience such as unexpected prosperity, a natural disaster, epidemic, or war. Digital communication can change cultural identity in sometimes unexpected ways (Cheong, Martin, and MacFadyen).

Intercultural communication theorist Stella Ting-Toomey studies identity negotiation. **Identity negotiation theory** presumes individuals acquire their identity through communicating with others. There are ten theoretical assumptions of the identity negotiation perspective. As you read these assumptions, it is apparent that they outline a strategy of inclusion and acceptance for managing the dialectical tension of similarity and difference. For example, core assumption 2 identifies the basic motivations and needs of communicators for "identity security, inclusion, connection and stability" of their identity as persons and as members of ethnic groups or culture (Ting-Toomey 40). Core assumption 5 states "Individuals tend to feel included when their desired group membership identities are positively endorsed . . . and experience differentiation when their desired group membership identities are stigmatized." Core assumption 9 states that "Satisfactory identity negotiation outcomes include the feelings of being understood, respected, and supported" (41). You may recall from the discussion of the dialectical tensions of community in Chapter 9, that the tension of similarity and difference creates the fundamental paradox of community life—communication that accepts and includes some persons simultaneously excludes and rejects others. The tension created by this paradox can develop into ethical issues or conflict about fairness and justice. One challenge of intercultural communication practice is discerning identity negotiation practices of inclusion that are fair and just both for culturally different community members and cultural strangers.

Everyday Communication Ethics

❖ *What community and cultural identities are being renegotiated in your hometown?*

The axioms of Ting-Toomey's identity negotiation theory offer strategies for responding to the paradoxical nature of communication that creates and maintains a culture. How communicators negotiate identity would also influence issues of fairness and justice within a culture. The chapter's opening case illustrates this paradox of culture and the challenges of identity negotiation in a workplace setting. The supervisor must discern a communication strategy that addresses fairly the legitimate interests of employees who have culturally different religious and spiritual traditions, that is also ethically responsive to the legitimate interests of the workplace community to survive and flourish so employees can keep their jobs. If Mr. Wilson practices tolerance of Muslim employees by accepting and including their culturally distinctive religious practices in the work rules, he is trying to correct the unfairness of not respecting cultural identities of Muslim employees. This arguably is an issue of practicing religious freedom. Mr. Wilson might not realize that some practices of corrective justice in the workplace would simultaneously exclude equally legitimate interests of non-Muslim employees, for example, to allow work breaks to pray for one religious group, but not other religious groups. Nonreligious employees do not need a break to pray, so would they then receive no break? What Mr. Wilson decides could create a practice of unfairness for a different cultural group, potentially laying groundwork for a conflict spiral of retributive justice. A challenge of practicing communication ethics in situations where different cultural identities are being negotiated is practicing ethical reasoning to help discern creative ethical communication choices that promote corrective justice, which are as inclusive as possible and also promote practices of toleration and thus minimize or discourage practices of retributive justice.

The different domains of cultural identity, in combination with the dialectical tensions of intercultural communication practice make it challenging to discern what is ethically responsive intercultural communication in a specific situation. Ting-Toomey identifies eight domains of identity, ranging from cultural, ethnic, gender, and personal identities to the situational identities of roles, relationships, face-work, as well as the identity negotiated as we communicate (29–39). Intercultural communicators are challenged to discern the most important differences and similarities for identity negotiation in a specific communication situation. The example of my daughter's communication with the Korean middle school teacher Ok Kyu can illustrate how the different domains of identity may combine with the dialectical tension of similarity and difference. The different domains of Ok Kyu's identity range from her personal role as a friend of my daughter to her social roles as a teacher, woman, wife, and mother. These roles are practiced within the context of Korean culture. Because Ok Kyu and my daughter shared the similarity of their gender role as a woman and their professional role as a teacher, their intercultural communication was characterized by the similarity of their identity domains as middle school teachers, women, and daughters, while their cultural identity domains differed as a Korean woman and an American woman. For my daughter, competent and ethical intercultural communication involved recognizing how differences in Korean and American cultures influence the identity domains of teaching, gender, and family, and how the similarities in the identity domains of teaching, gender, and family influenced her communication with Ok Kyu.

Textbox 10.2

Core Theoretical Assumptions of Identity Negotiation—Ting-Toomey

1. Communication with others forms people's group membership identities and personal identities.
2. Individuals in all cultures have the same basic needs for identity security, trust, inclusion, connection, and stability.

---

3. Individuals tend to experience identity security in a culturally familiar environment and experience identity vulnerability in a culturally unfamiliar environment.

4. Individuals tend to experience identity trust when communicating with culturally similar others and identity distrust with culturally dissimilar others.

5. Individuals tend to feel included when their desired group membership identities are positively endorsed, and experience differentiation when those identities are stigmatized.

6. Individuals tend to desire interpersonal connection through meaningful close relationships.

7. Individuals perceive identity stability in predictable cultural situations and perceive identity change or chaos in unpredictable cultural situations.

8. Cultural, personal, and situational variations influence the meanings, interpretations, and evaluations of identity.

9. Being understood, respected, and supported are outcomes of satisfactory identity negotiation.

10. Mindful intercultural communication emphasizes the importance of integrating intercultural knowledge, motivations, and skills in order to communicate satisfactorily, appropriately, and effectively.

At this point, the challenge of discerning ethical issues of intercultural communication practice may seem overwhelming, between considering the number of different domains of identity and the number of dialectical tensions of intercultural communication practice. Cultural contracts theory of identity negotiation, developed by rhetorical theorist Ronald L. Jackson II, can help in discerning significant ethical issues of identity negotiation. Jackson uses Ting-Toomey's theory of identity negotiation in developing **cultural contracts theory**. He proposes that one result of communication that negotiates identity is a cultural contract that influences how communicators define their identity. Again, Ok Kyu can illustrate. She is a Korean teacher of English who works in a Korean middle school located in a suburb of Seoul, Korea. Besides her friendship with my native English-speaking daughter, she also has English-speaking friends in Australia and the United States. Her communication and the relationships she has developed with people from English-speaking cultures have created cultural contracts for Ok Kyu that are different from the cultural contracts of Koreans who do not speak English or who do not have ongoing relationships with native English speakers. These different cultural contracts create a different worldview for Ok Kyu that incorporates the meanings, expectations, and norms of different English-speaking cultures with the meanings, expectations, and norms of Korean culture. If Ok Kyu negotiated a new cultural contract in a relationship with a Muslim from the Philippines, for example, her identity and view of the world would probably change further. Part of Ok Kyu's personal history is how her communication and relationships with Koreans and native English speakers has influenced her personal identity. Cultural contracts like those that Ok Kyu has negotiated are not legal contracts. Jackson argues that the concept of cultural contracts is a metaphor to help us make sense of how communicating with others influences individual identity and personal history (361).

Everyday Communication Ethics

❖ *What cultural contracts have you been asked to agree to since you began taking college courses?*

Jackson's cultural contracts theory is helpful in discerning ethical issues created by intercultural communication practices that negotiate cultural identity. When we are unaware that our communication is negotiating a cultural contract of identity with others, we may not recognize issues of justice created by our communication. This may be due to mindlessness or an ethnocentric attitude that denies the importance of specific cultural differences within or between cultures. In the chapter's opening case, the supervisors and Muslim and non-Muslim workers are negotiating cultural contracts while addressing a workplace problem. The cultural contracts they negotiate will influence both the spiritual and work dimensions of their individual identities. If the supervisor, Mr. Wilson, does not recognize that he is negotiating work *and* spiritual cultural contracts, he is less likely to recognize important ethical issues of fairness and justice in this situation. Communication issues of justice, in contrast to legal issues, are not limited to the employee right to take a work break. They also include whether the company is ethically responsive to significant similarities and differences in the cultural identities of its employees that influence the workplace.

Cultural contracts theory also helps us recognize ethical issues that develop from other dialectical tensions of intercultural communication practice, such as the dialectical tension of privilege and disadvantage. When communicators are deceived or coerced as they negotiate a cultural contract, there are ethical issues of truthfulness as well as justice. Deception or coercion can have a far-reaching impact on the identity of communicators, particularly when the dialectical tension of privilege and disadvantage is present. For example, significant disparities in the privileges of education or access to information can create situations in which some communicators are deceived or coerced into agreeing to cultural contracts that dehumanize them or undermine their culture. The arguably well-intentioned but nonetheless dehumanizing cultural contracts imposed on Native American Indian children in Indian boarding schools in the US denied generations of Indian children their cultural identity, history, traditions, and language (Adams). At these boarding schools, teachers, staff, and administrators coerced Indian children into speaking English rather than their native language. These children were prevented from practicing their cultural norms and rituals and, instead, they were forced, often physically, to dress and act like Anglo people. While the stated intention was to assure the survival of these children as individuals in a dominant white culture, a consequence of these communication practices were cultural contracts that excluded their native Indian identities and cultures. Today, Indian peoples in the US face the dialectical tension between static and dynamic in their efforts to rebuild their cultures, with some tribes lacking enough elders who can both express their tribal identity in their communication practices and negotiate cultural contracts with the next generation. With losses of their native languages, histories, and traditions, some tribes face significant obstacles in negotiating cultural contracts that pass their tribal Indian culture on to the next generation. These losses have made it more difficult for them to practice their cultural values, including their cultural communication practices of truthfulness, justice, freedom, care, integrity, and honor.

Everyday Communication Ethics

❖ *What dialectical tensions influence negotiating your identity as a college student?*

The dialectical tension of privilege/disadvantage is important for digital communication. Cultures vary in access to digital communication technology and infrastructure (Chen and Dai). When cultural groups lack access, even if they are adept at creating new culturally appropriate digital communication practices, they will be at a disadvantage when communicating with cultures with greater digital access. Ethical issues of negotiating cultural contracts may also exist at the level of international or global communication. Multinational corporations dominate international mass communication using the communication standards of Western industrial culture (Albarran and Chan-Olmsted; McChesney). The concentration of media ownership in a decreasing number of Western corporations globally promotes Western industrial communication practices, discouraging culturally diverse mass media communication practices based upon the values of non-Western or nonindustrialized cultures (Hamelink; Vidal-Hall). Bollywood, the Indian film industry, offers a small but growing alternative to Western media organizations and practices (Punathambekar). By drawing our attention to the dialectical tensions of both similarity and difference and of privilege and disadvantage, critics of global mass media encourage us to recognize situations where the identities of dominant cultures are privileged in international mass media communication practices, disadvantaging local cultural identities.

Even the internet, which may have the greatest potential for helping people who live in non-Western or nonindustrialized cultures participate in mass communication, presumes that communicators are literate and can communicate in a language understood by mass audiences. Many presume this language is English, rather than Chinese or some other language (Kim 130–3). Additional issues of justice become evident as we recognize privileges of literacy and disadvantages of illiteracy. The rural poor and persons living in cultures that do not emphasize written literacy are much less likely to create digital mass media messages. International mass media messages promote acceptance of more Westernized and industrialized cultural contracts, often based on written literacy, in contrast to indigenous knowledge and practices of communication. If non-Western and nonindustrialized cultures are unable to adapt their communication practices to the accepted practices of new mass media technologies, these cultures risk losing their voice in international and global conversations about issues such as climate change, poverty, war, peace, human rights, economic development, and more. An important issue of global intercultural communication ethics at this historical moment involves whether or how the voices of people in non-Western and nonindustrialized cultures will be heard.

Strategies for managing the dialectical tensions of intercultural communication practice raise issues of communication ethics. Awareness of dialectical tensions stimulates our moral imaginations to discern ethical issues that develop from communication practices we use to manage these tensions. Negotiating cultural identity offers a framework for recognizing ethical issues of justice that develop from dialectical tensions of intercultural communication. The next section examines absolutism and relativism as strategies for addressing ethical issues of intercultural communication.

Absolutism and Relativism in Intercultural Communication

Absolutism and relativism are familiar to students of intercultural communication. Intercultural communication scholars consider the practice of cultural relativism one way to develop your competence as an intercultural communicator (see Martin and Nakayama 34–5). Cultural relativism is a form of conventional relativism. In thinking about your practice of communication ethics in intercultural contexts, however, the most useful starting point is not to begin with questions of whether to be an absolutist or relativist, but to understand the role of values in a culture.

Cultural values help members answer important questions such as "What is human nature?," "What is the relationship between humans?," "What is the preferred human activity?," or "What is the orientation toward time?" The shared understandings among members of a culture about how to answer these questions reveal the **value orientation of a culture**. Florence Kluckhohn and Fred Strodtbeck suggest that cultures use different approaches to answer these questions. They suggest that there are three common approaches for answering the question "What is the preferred human activity?"—"action," the "growing or becoming" of inner development, or simply "being" who you are. (10–20). While all cultures have elements of each of the three value orientations toward human activity, one value orientation predominates. When a person from a culture with the preferred activity of "action" or "doing" interacts with someone from a culture with a preferred activity of "being" who you are, differences in value orientations can be a source of tension, misunderstanding, or conflict. A "doing" culture such as the US focuses on results, while the "being" culture, such as a Latin culture of Central or South America, focuses on the flow of interacting that constitutes your "being" with another person. How cultures answer other questions, such as whether human nature is basically good, basically evil, or a combination of both also influence what communicators consider ethical communication. A challenge of practicing ethical intercultural communication is discerning an ethically fitting way to communicate with people who have different value orientations. Yet, when we narrowly focus on a value of a culture, it becomes difficult to see its inner diversity. Using the dialectical tension of history/past and present/future to understand a culture, we often discover eras with a totalitarian approach to values as well as eras of greater toleration within a culture. While examining values is important, a narrow or rigid focus on values can obscure the diversity within a culture and create intercultural misunderstanding.

Point to Ponder

❖ *What are the value orientations of your personal ethical standard?*

The often polarized debate between absolutist and relativist approaches to ethics can make it difficult to discuss ethical issues in intercultural situations. This debate can reduce ethical choices to either absolutist application of cultural values or relativist practice of tolerance. Such conflicts often focus on community identity, especially when an intercultural identity differs from community identity. Absolutists encourage or require that people with a culturally different identity change or leave the community, while relativists are more tolerant, even accepting of cultural differences. Rigid consistency of absolutism can repeatedly justify or excuse harms that result from absolutist approaches to applying a value or principle. While cultural relativism acknowledges and tolerates cultural differences, it may also create harm, as communicators practice repeatedly keeping their ethical concerns to themselves because expressing their concerns would be intolerant. When cultural relativists repeatedly do nothing more than listen when facing a recurring

Table 10.1 Value Orientations of Culture—Kluckhohn and Strodtbeck

Question of Culture	Dominant Value Orientations
What is the human nature?	Evil/Good/Mixture of Good and Evil
What is the relationship between humans?	Hierarchical/Equals/Individualistic/ Collectivistic
What is the preferred human activity?	Being/Becoming/Doing
What is the orientation toward time?	Past/Present/Future

and significant ethical problem, their communication may tolerate a persistent harm or even an atrocity. Ethically responsive intercultural communication often requires creatively addressing the polarized tension between absolutism and relativism.

The debate between absolutism and relativism often makes it difficult to discern when to communicate your ethical concerns and when you should remain silent and practice tolerance. In the chapter's opening case, should management be consistent and absolute (and, thus, fair) in following the established work rules about breaks, or should Mr. Wilson the supervisor practice tolerance (and, thus, practice a different form of fairness) in implementing the request of Muslim employees for prayer breaks? If Mr. Wilson considers issues of negotiating cultural identities discussed in the previous section, he would recognize that if he changes the work rules about breaks to be more accepting of his Muslim employees, he is likely to simultaneously exclude the cultural identities of his non-Muslim employees, whether they are religious or not. Because of the dialectical tension of similarity and difference, a culturally relative response of accepting the request of the Muslim employees simultaneously excludes the cultural identities of non-Muslim employees. Management at Caledonia Industries faces the paradox of culture in an ethical dilemma—if it treats some employees fairly, it simultaneously treats other employees unfairly. Both absolutist and relativist approaches to applying ethical values reinforce this paradox in different ways, perpetuating some form of injustice. David Bohm's concept of dialogue as living with paradox, instead of solving problems too soon, encourages us to think outside of the binary, either/or logic of absolutism and relativism.

Situations like the Caledonia Industries case raise a question of whether there are practices of communication ethics that transcend cultural boundaries. Is there something so basic or integral to human experience that it could provide a basis for a value shared by all human cultures? Sissela Bok notes that "Projects for worldwide ethics litter history like tanks abandoned in the desert" (1). Yet, the scale of the problems that create human misery—climate change and environmental degradation, poverty, disease, war, and terrorism— cannot be addressed without some coordination of efforts between cultures and nations. Instead of identifying theoretically well-developed values that all cultures should share, Bok encourages us to identify minimalist values to guide our conversations about human survival. **Minimalist values** "must represent the simplest, most commonplace forms of mutual support, respect and forbearance necessary for group survival" (53). Identifying minimalist values can be part of a search for common ground across cultural boundaries, providing a basis for intercultural cooperation and problem solving about difficult issues facing humanity. Minimalist values may also provide an approach for addressing the dialectical tension created by the polarized choices of absolutism and relativism.

Are there candidates for a minimalist value for the practice of communication ethics in any of the previous chapters? Levinas's "call of the other," may be a minimalist value of communication ethics, or it may provide insights to help us identify a minimalist value. Levinas's concept of responsiveness to the "call of the other" promotes communication practices that recognize the humanity of other persons. Levinas is making the point that there is always something more to "an other" that calls us to be ethically responsive (Murray; Arnett). When we understand that the other is always more than we already know, we are encouraged to acknowledge the humanity of the other. The communication practice of acknowledgment (Hyde) may be a minimalist communication practice of communication ethics. It is a foundational communication practice for healthy human development, including moral development (Tompkins). Acknowledgment is so fundamental to human existence that it is life giving—"We need acknowledgement as much as we need such other easily taken for granted things as air, blood, and a beating heart. Without the life-giving gift of acknowledgement, we are destined to exist in ways that are marked by the loneliness of what I describe as 'social death'" (Hyde xiv). Acknowledgment may create a starting point for intercultural conversations about ethical issues and problems that recognize *both* cultural similarities and differences.

Clifford Christians and Thomas Cooper offer the idea of a protonorm as an alternative to Bok's concept of minimalist values. A **protonorm** is a foundational belief about what is best for the world which different cultures may express and practice in different ways (Christians and Cooper 59). They explore the protonorm of the **sacredness of life** as the primordial ground from which a culture's ethical values grow. The sacredness of life is found in the natural existence of life that "binds humans into a common oneness" (12) and is drawn from a "reverence for life on earth, for the organic whole, for the physical realm in which human civilization is situated" (7). What we typically consider ethical values, such as truth telling, human dignity, and nonviolence, develop out of a primordial sense of the sacredness of life. Variations in how people from different cultures practice truth telling and recognize human dignity, or in how they practice nonviolence would find a common, primordial ground in the protonorm of the sacredness of life which transcends both time and culture.

Minimalist values and protonorms provide alternative ways to think about the ethical practices of intercultural communication that do not rely upon absolutism and relativism. Minimalist values and protonorms are not your typical theoretically well-developed ethical concepts. They are simple (not simplistic), yet fundamental. Some would consider them wise. Study of comparative religion points to the potential of these two approaches for crossing cultural boundaries. Religious scholar Huston Smith notes that the **Golden Rule**, of thinking about the interests of others as a guide for your own action rather than solely focusing on your interests, finds diverse expression in major world religions (228–30). Karen Armstrong shows how culturally different religious sages, emerging from the experience of warfare and terror in the "Axial Age" in ancient China, India, Judea, and Greece, developed different religious programs "designed to eradicate the egotism that is largely responsible for our violence, and promoted the empathic spirituality of the Golden Rule" (391). The Golden Rule is a minimalist ethical practice of communication that may provide a common ground in intercultural discussions. As a minimalist ethical practice, the Golden Rule applies to local intercultural issues, such as the conflict in the chapter's opening case, or global issues such as climate change and poverty. The existence of a Golden Rule in so many different cultures encourages us to consider using it as part of our personal ethical standard. Its existence also encourages us to consider that there may be other minimalist ethical practices, values, or protonorms.

Textbox 10.3

Golden Rules

Huston Smith's scholarship on the Golden Rule provides evidence supporting Sissela Bok's claim that minimalist values cross cultural boundaries. The Golden Rule's practice of acknowledging and taking into account the interests of others developed in culturally diverse ways in different religions.

Buddhism—*metta* and *karuna,* boundless heart toward all beings
Christianity—Do unto others as you would have them do unto you
Confucianism—human-hearted *jen*
Hinduism—high [yogin] who judges pleasure or pain everywhere by the same standard as he applies to himself
Islam—who "gives his wealth . . . to kinsfolk and orphans and to the needy and to the wayfarer . . . who sets slaves free and payeth the poor"
Jainism—*ahimsa* and *aparigraha*

> **Judaism**—What doth the Lord require of thee but to do justice, love mercy. . . .
> **Sikhism**—humility to serve

Point to Ponder

❖ *Examine an expression of the Golden Rule that is culturally different from your own. What are the similarities and differences?*

Philosopher **Kwame Anthony Appiah** claims there is enough overlap in different cultures of what he calls the "vocabulary of values" to begin conversations about significant issues of human survival (57). Development of the United Nations' Universal Declaration of Human Rights illustrates Appiah's point. While the Declaration has been criticized as an artifact of Western culture or promoting Western biases, the contributions of Chinese diplomat Peng Chun Chang points to overlapping Western and Eastern values that form a common basis for human rights, particularly in the first article "All men [sic] are created free" (Roth). Chang worked to justify human rights using several different ethical traditions, especially French Enlightenment philosophy and Confucian ethical traditions.

Appiah suggests that when we practice **cosmopolitanism** we recognize that cultures overlap in minimal or fundamental ways, while culturally distinct practices differ. This recognition offers the potential for intercultural understanding. A **communication ethics practice of cosmopolitanism** is a process of understanding others more than a process for creating agreement for future action. Appiah claims that cosmopolitans have a realistic understanding of universalism that recognizes the limitations of agreement about values that guide ethical practice. This is not relativism, because it recognizes the need for agreement and encourages conversation about similarities and differences. But Appiah's concept of cosmopolitanism is not absolutist. If our goal is to discover a practice of ethics based upon a universal truth that everyone should agree without variation, we create a universalism without toleration of differences (140–3). Universalism without toleration is a form of absolutism that can create bloodbaths, as we first exclude then eliminate those who disagree with our viewpoints. Appiah notes that this is the lesson of the violence that led to the Enlightenment and the development of modernism (141). Jonathan Sacks develops this insight further in his argument that at different points in history, the lack of toleration of difference within Abrahamic religions threatened to destroy Judaism and Christianity, and is now threatening to destroy Islam. A lack of toleration among religious believers combined with a desire for political power creates a form of **altruistic evil** in which perpetrators of extreme violence see themselves as "doing good" in the name of what they believe.

Textbox 10.4

Religious Extremist Violence

Theologian and philosopher Jonathan Sacks, former chief rabbi of Great Britain, argues that efforts to end extremist religious violence committed in the name of God must come from within the religious tradition. Secular responses are insufficient to end religious altruistic evil. Altruistic evil is committed in the name of high ideals that are religious, political, or some combination (9–18). Sacks acknowledges the human tendency toward violence, what some called the "crooked timber of humanity" school of thinking. While all monotheisms believe in human nature as a mix of good and bad, each monotheism must overcome the doctrine that "a person must share our faith to be fully human." This doctrine becomes the basis for violence against nonbelievers. Sacks presents a careful reading of the Genesis narratives, shared by all three Abrahamic religions, " . . . that the one *outside* the covenant . . . is also human, also loved, also blessed by God" (183). Most simply, the mystery of God is reflected in the idea that both the believer and those who are different from the believer are made in God's image (200–6). *All* are human and should be treated fairly with basic human dignity.

The historical legacy of Abrahamic religions in practicing this theological tenet is tragic. Each has experienced religiously motivated terror for political gain. Judaism and Christianity learned through violent experience, in which each religion lost almost everything, that religion can survive without political power. For Judaism, this occurred during the failed rebellions against Rome in the late first and early second centuries CE, during which extremist Jewish factions killed other Jews who did not exhibit "right thinking." For Christianity, this occurred in the 16th and 17th century religious wars between Catholics and Protestants in Europe, which also provided an impetus for immigration to North America and the modern era. Today, Islam is facing this crisis. "The primary victims of Islamist violence are Muslims themselves, across the dividing lines of Sunni and Shia, modernist and neo-traditionalists, moderate against radical, and sometimes simply sect against sect" (225). Sacks argues that while no religion relinquishes power voluntarily, you cannot impose religious truth by force. Violence happens when a religion tries to resolve a religious dispute with power. Only when religious adherents find themselves fighting violently with their fellow believers do they come to realize the futility of violence and power in the name of religion.

Cosmopolitans recognize that minimalist universal values allow for local variation (Appiah 46–57). Alternative ways of organizing family life in different cultures create culturally different practices of universal, minimalist values such as fairness and care. While culturally different practices can challenge our understanding of these values, they do not disprove the truth of fairness and care as universal minimalist values. Cosmopolitanism encourages us to practice toleration as a method for understanding the ethical practices of other cultures in a search for understanding the universal nature of those values. For Appiah, a distinctive commitment to pluralism (a form of diversity) guides the practice of cosmopolitanism, "that there are many values worth living by and *that you cannot live by all of them*" (144, emphasis added). Because it is not possible for an individual to practice all values worth living by, it is important that our conversations about practicing ethics search for understanding, not necessarily agreement about what is good, right, or virtuous.

Point to Ponder

❖   *How could you practice the idea "there are many values worth living by and I cannot live by all of them"?*

Disagreements about ethics have an important role in Appiah's cosmopolitanism. Practice of ethics involves individual discernment and judgment about how to apply values and principles to new situations. Because there are many ways to apply values and principles, we are meant to argue about the individual practice of ethics. The practice of ethics is "contestable" (57–9). Appiah reminds us that we do not avoid disagreement, argument, and even conflict about ethics when we share the same values with others. In fact, conflicts about values often focus on how to apply a shared value (78–9). Our most intense conflicts involve different viewpoints about how to apply shared values, as illustrated by the repeated human experience of civil war and the intense and often violent conflicts within religious traditions. We may become the most intolerant of those who share our values but understand and apply them differently.

Appiah's point that the practice of ethics is contestable is consistent with the idea that the process of ethical reasoning helps develop the individual practice of communication ethics. An important stage in the process of ethical reasoning that promotes the ethical quality of decision making occurs when decision makers offer their reasoning to others for discussion and critical evaluation. Offering justifications to others provides a decision maker with opportunities to reexamine her reasoning and, if warranted, make changes in her decision. Critical examination by others does not require a decision maker to change her decision simply because objections were raised. It does, however, require that these objections be examined with an open mind. Appiah's concept of cosmopolitanism offers an additional explanation for why it is important to engage in conversations with others who think differently about the practice of communication ethics.

> [C]osmopolitans believe in universal truth, although we are less certain that we have it already. It is not skepticism about the very idea of truth that guides us; it is realism about how hard the truth is to find. One truth we hold, to, however, is that every human being has obligations to every other. Everybody matters: that is our central idea. And it sharply limits the scope of our tolerance.
>
> (144)

Cosmopolitans believe that universal minimalist values exist, but are developed, expressed, and practiced in alternative ways in different cultures. While they accept the existence of universal values and what some of those values are, cosmopolitans also admit that searching for universal values is difficult. It is not possible for any of us to practice the complete truth of a value. We need others who practice values differently, so together we can practice values more completely.

Conclusion

In intercultural communication, we experience dialectical tensions, especially the dialectical tension of similarity and difference. The ethnocentric tendency to notice and accept others who are like us, rather than recognizing and understanding how others are both similar and different, promotes an ethical nearsightedness that limits our moral imaginations. When we do not recognize both cultural difference and similarity, it becomes difficult to be ethically responsive. Not recognizing dialectical tensions of similarity and difference, individuals and culture, static and dynamic, or privilege and disadvantage, for example, limits our capacity to imagine potential benefits and harms of our communication choices. Traditional approaches to practicing ethics in intercultural communication can alternate between absolutism and relativism. Cultural relativists point to human history, which repeatedly shows that when we ignore cultural differences, even well-intentioned actions can create significant harm. In turn, absolutists point to practices of relativism that repeatedly tolerate significant ethical harms or atrocities. A challenge of intercultural practices of communication ethics is making decisions that promote the legitimate interests of others in a way that is also ethically responsive to the dialectical tensions of intercultural communication practice.

Addressing the polarized practices of absolutism and relativism has reached a new level of urgency. Significant global and regional problems of climate change and environmental degradation, poverty, disease, war, and terrorism point to the necessity of meaningful communication across cultural boundaries. Addressing problems like these requires decision makers to communicate ethically their concerns about what is good, right, or virtuous across cultural boundaries and to strive to understand the concerns of others. One approach is to search for ethical universals, not in an absolutist sense, but as a minimalist common ground for communication. This chapter has introduced you to three possible minimalist universals for communication ethics—the protonorm of the sacredness of life, acknowledging the call of the other, and the Golden Rule. If you practice any of these minimalist universals as a cosmopolitan as Appiah proposes, you strive to discern the presence of these and other universal values in culturally different communication practices.

Vocabulary

Altruistic evil 251
Communication ethics practice of cosmopolitanism 251
Cosmopolitanism 251
Cultural contracts theory 245
Cultural identity 240
Culture 237
Golden Rule 250
Identity negotiation theory 240
Intercultural communication 237
Kwame Anthony Appiah 251
Minimalist values 249
Protonorm 249
Sacredness of life 249
Six dialectical tensions of intercultural communication practice 238–9
Value orientation of a culture 247

Cases for Discussion

Directions: Use the process of ethical reasoning to identify an ethical communication response for the recurring decision points of communication. Describe the cultural contracts being negotiated. Identify any potential minimal values of communication that may help in creating an ethical communication response.

1. Raising Biracial Children

Lindsey felt her heart breaking, and not for the first time. She never got used to it, and she hopes she never does. That day she had been at her son Isaac's school and stopped by the lunchroom, just to check on how he was doing. That afternoon after school, she had asked Isaac if he ever ate lunch with white kids. "No," he replied. "They don't think black kids are cool."

Lindsey is a single, white mother. Isaac, age 10, does not know his father or his father's family. Given Lindsey's past troubled relationship with Isaac's father, that is for the best. Her parents are supportive and involved in their grandson's life, but they are white too. Lindsey has dealt with Isaac being called the "N-word" by strangers. Now kids at school think he's not cool, because of the color of his skin and his kinky hair. How can she help him develop a positive identity as an African-American teenage boy and later as a man?

What should Lindsey do?

2. The Campus Exhibit

You are a member of a planning committee for an exhibit on Queen Elizabeth I of England that will be displayed in the campus library. The exhibit, created by an organization internationally recognized for its work on this historical period, consists of six 6- by 15-feet panels of pictures and text. There are portraits of Elizabeth and other major figures, and copies of prints and paintings showing major political and religious conflict, including public executions. There is an entire panel on the English exploration of North America and the first English settlements.

Your committee of faculty, campus library staff, and students is responsible for organizing speakers and activities. The committee has almost finished its work. Angela, a campus librarian, has been bringing copies of pictures used in the exhibit she found in library books. At today's meeting, she opens two books and says, "I think we may have a problem with the exhibit. There are Elizabethan prints showing the native peoples of North America. These pictures accurately show how people in England at the time imagined native peoples, but they do not accurately present the lives of native peoples. I am not aware of any pictures from this time period created by native peoples that present their lives." Angela passes around a third book. "This picture may be very disturbing, particularly for American Indian students and faculty. It shows Indians torturing captives with fire and bows and arrows." Passing around yet another book, she says, "Torture and execution were part of Elizabethan life. Here are pictures from a different panel of the display showing the torture of Protestants and of Catholics. They look very similar to the pictures of Indians." After some discussion of the pictures, Angela tells the group, "I contacted the exhibit's national coordinator to discover if any other campus showing the exhibit has had complaints about these pictures, and especially in depicting American Indians. The coordinator said that this was the first time she has heard anything like this."

Angela then asks, "Should we do anything or just go ahead as planned? And if we decide we need to do something, does anyone have any idea of what we should do?"

As a member of this committee, how would you practice your personal ethical standard of communication? Would minimal ethical values be part of your deliberation and decision making? If so, what would they be?

3. Reaching Out

Matt realized for a long time that he had lived an insulated life. He was home schooled by his mother. He grew up in an evangelical Christian family and is active in the campus evangelical Christian student organization. He knew the importance of diversity as an ideal; after all, God created a diverse universe. But he knew that he had not lived as if diversity was important, at least in a meaningful way: in fact, living what he said he believed is becoming more important to him as he approaches graduation. "Jesus taught that we are to 'love one another.' The one group my church says it loves, but does not act like it does is the LGBTQ community. How could I love LGBTQ people as Jesus taught, actually show that I love them? Do I have the courage to step forward in my church and convince them to show love to LGBTQ people in town? How would I begin?"
What should Matt do?

References

Adams, David Wallace. *Education for Extinction: American Indians and the Boarding School Experience, 1875–1928*. Lawrence, KS: U of Kansas P, 1995.

Albarran, Alan B. and Sylvia M. Chan-Olmsted. *Global Media Economics: Commercialization, Concentration and Integration of World Media Markets*. Ames, IA: U of Iowa P, 1998.

Appiah, Kwame Anthony. *Cosmopolitanism: Ethics in a World of Strangers*. New York: Norton, 2006.

Armstrong, Karen. *The Great Transformation: The Beginning of Our Religious Traditions*. New York: Knopf, 2006.

Arnett, Ronald C. *Levinas's Rhetorical Demand: The Unending Obligations of Communication Ethics*. Carbondale, IL: Southern Illinois UP, 2017.

Barnett, George A. and Meihua Lee. "Issues in Intercultural Communication Research." *Handbook of International and Intercultural Communication*. 2nd ed. Eds. William B. Gudykunst and Bella Mody. Thousand Oaks, CA: Sage, 2002. 275–90.

Bohm, David. *On Dialogue*. Ed. Lee Nichol. New York: Routledge, 1996.

Bok, Sissela. *Common Values*. Columbia, MO: U of Missouri P, 1995.

Chen, Guo-Ming and Xiaodong Dai. "New Media and Asymmetry in Cultural Identity Negotiation." *New Media and Intercultural Communication: Identity, Community and Politics*. Eds. Pauline Hope Cheong, Judith N. Martin, and Leah P. MacFadyen. New York: Peter Lang, 2012. 123–137.

Cheong, Pauline Hope, Judith N. Martin, and Leah P. MacFadyen. *New Media and Intercultural Communication: Identity, Community and Politics*. New York: Peter Lang, 2012.

Christians, Clifford G. and Thomas W. Cooper. "The Search for Universals". *The Handbook of Mass Communication*. Eds. Lee Wilkins and Clifford G. Christians. New York: Routledge, 2009. 55–68.

Friedman, Thomas. *The Lexus and the Olive Tree.* New York: Farrar, Straus, and Giroux, 1999.

Hamelink, Cees J. "Grounding the Human Right to Communicate." Lee 21–33.

Hyde, Michael J. *The Life-Giving Gift of Acknowledgement.* West Lafayette, IN: Purdue UP, 2006.

Jackson II, Ronald L. "Cultural Contracts Theory: Toward an Understanding of Identity Negotiation." *Communication Quarterly* 50.3 and 4 (2002). 359–67.

Jensen, J. Vernon. "Bridging the Millennia: Truth and Trust in Human Communication." *World Communication* 30.2 (2001): 68–92.

Kim, Wang Lay. "Malaysian Women in the Information Society: Opportunities and Challenges." Lee, 113–34.

Kluckhohn, Florence R. and Fred L. Strodtbeck. 1961. *Variations in Value Orientations.* Westport, CT: Greenwood Press, 1973.

Lee, Philip, Ed. *Many Voices, One Vision: The Right to Communicate in Practice.* London: World Association for Christian Communication, 2004.

Levinas, Emmanuel. *Ethics and Infinity.* Trans. Richard A. Cohen. Pittsburg, PA: Duquesne UP, 1985.

Martin, Judith N. and Thomas Nakayama. *Intercultural Communication in Contexts.* 5th ed. Boston, MA: McGraw-Hill, 2010.

Martin, Judith N., Thomas K. Nakayama, and Lisa A. Flores. "A Dialectical Approach to Intercultural Communication." *Readings in Cultural Contexts.* 2nd ed. Eds. Judith N. Martin, Thomas K. Nakayama, and Lisa A. Flores. Boston, MA: McGraw-Hill, 2002. 3–13.

Martinez, Juan. "AI and Digital Self-Service Will Revolutionize Customer Service." *PC Magazine UK.* 4 August 2017. http://uk.pcmag.com/feature/90596/ai-and-digital-self-service-will-revolutionize-customer-serv. Date accessed: 24 August 2017.

McChesney, Robert W. *Rich Media, Poor Democracy: Communication Politics in Dubious Times.* Chicago, IL: U of Illinois P, 1999.

Mieth, Dietmar. "The Basic Norm of Truthfulness: Its Ethical Justification and Universality." *Communication Ethics and Universal Values.* Eds. Clifford Christians and Michael Traber. Thousand Oaks, CA: Safe, 1997. 87–104.

Murray, Jeffrey. "The Other Ethics of Emmanuel Levinas: Communication Beyond Relativism." *Moral Engagement in Public Life: Theorists for Contemporary Ethics.* Eds. Sharon Bracci and Clifford G. Christians. New York: Peter Lang, 2002. 171–95.

Punathambekar, Aswin. *From Bombay to Bollywood: The Making of a Global Media Industry.* New York: New York UP, 2013.

Roth, Hans Ingvar. "Pen Chun Chang, Intercultural Ethics and the Universal Declaration of Human Rights." *Ethics and Communication: Global Perspectives.* London: Rowman & Littlefield, 2016. 95–124

Sacks, Jonathan. *Not in God's Name: Confronting Religious Violence.* New York: Schocken Books, 2015.

Smith, Huston. *Essays on World Religions.* Ed. M. Darrol Bryant. New York: Paragon House, 1992.

Ting-Toomey, Stella. *Communicating Across Cultures.* New York: Guilford Press, 1999.

Tompkins, Paula S. "Communication and Children's Moral Development." *The Children's Communication Sourcebook.* Eds. Thomas Socha and Narissra Punyanunt-Carter. New York: Peter Lang, *in press.*

Vidal-Hall, Judith. "The Right to Communicate: For Whom?" Lee 33–59.

Yun Kim, Young, "Mapping the Domain of Intercultural Communication: An Overview." *Communication Yearbook 24.* Ed. William B. Gudykunst. Thousand Oaks, CA: Sage, 2001. 139–58.

11

YOUR PRACTICE OF
COMMUNICATION ETHICS

Jayson took a sip of coffee. He needs to decide. Carlson, a friend at work, wants him to go on a volunteer vacation travel to South Africa to build homes. The trip would use all of Jayson's vacation. Volunteering would be the first week. The second week he and Carlson would go on safari. Carlson has researched the entire trip and come up with an affordable budget. Jayson thinks, "It would be tight financially, but I can afford it. I've always wanted to travel to Africa. I could go on safari and do some good for others in the same trip. This is a win-win." But Jayson is just not sure about using all his vacation on this trip. He has been dating someone for about two months, and it is becoming serious. Then there is dad. "Dad is improving with this experimental treatment for stage 4 cancer, but if something happens while I'm gone . . . This may not be the best time to leave or use all my vacation. But to miss an opportunity like this . . . " Jayson took another sip of coffee.

By reading this book, you have explored the ethical dimension of your communication and how it matters in your relationships, family, at work, and in the community where you live. You have become more mindful of the ethical dimension of your communication and how your communication influences your social worlds. You may have been thinking about who you are as an ethical communicator, understanding that your communication matters ethically to more people than the receivers of your messages. Each person who receives a verbal or nonverbal message from you is relationally connected to people you will never meet. You communicate within an expanding network of relational connection over which your messages and their impacts travel.

The practice of ethics is entwined with communication from the moment each of us is born, beginning with communication acts of acknowledgment by adults who are present at our birth (Tompkins "Development"). Acknowledgment, a communication act of care and compassion, begins the construction of each of our social worlds (Hyde *Acknowledgement*) where we learn about communication and practices of ethics. In Chapter 2, you read about moral psychology and neuroscience research that shows the importance of moral emotions for any ethical practice, especially communication. Moral emotions of empathy and a bias for equality are hardwired in our brains, working alongside the moral emotion of disgust that we learn at a very young age. Moral emotions create an ethical capacity that provides a foundation for moral development and the practice of ethics (Bloom). How each of us experiences communication, in our relationships with parents, caregivers, friends and peers, teachers, coaches, spiritual or religious teachers, coworkers, and in the social worlds of digital technology and popular culture, influences our moral development and how we practice our personal ethical commitments. Without memorable messages about ethics (Waldron et al.) or self-reflection about personal ethical commitments, many people experience the development of their ethical commitments and practices more mindlessly than with awareness. It becomes difficult for them to recognize that ethical issues exist or to explain or justify decisions and actions to others beyond reference to emotions (and not always moral emotions)—"It felt right" or "I had a gut feeling." When we are unable to explain or discuss how our decisions or actions are good, right, or virtuous, ethics begins to disappear in our relationships, families, workplaces, and communities. When we do not understand our personal ethical commitments or are unable to explain them to others, ethics in our social worlds become "thin and spotty" (Smith et al.). We find it difficult to identify what are appropriate and fitting ethical practices, especially in ambiguous, complex, or confusing situations.

Moral emotions, especially empathy, the equality bias, and disgust, are important for recognizing that an ethical issue may exist. While moral emotions can help us quickly discern possible ethical actions and motivate us to act, in ambiguous, complex, or confusing situations, moral emotions may not offer enough guidance to discern what is the good, right, or virtuous thing to say or do. When we rely *only* on emotions to guide our decision making and action, we may cause harm, rather than do good (Hoffman 22; Kligyte et al.). Over the millennia thoughtful people have developed ideas and theories to help us make better (not necessarily perfect) decisions using ethical reasoning. In this book, you have read some of these ideas about ethical reasoning, applying ethical values, and key concepts of several well-known philosophical theories of ethics.

Philosopher Martha Nussbaum argues that ethically responsive action relies upon *both* emotions and ethical reasoning. Our moral emotions help us identify what is important, demanding our attention and motivating possible action. Sound ethical reasoning, which uses our personal ethical commitments, perhaps along with carefully selected philosophical concepts and theories, helps us think critically and deliberate about the situation our emotions have drawn to our attention. Ethical reasoning helps us thoughtfully choose a good, right, or virtuous response. Ethical reasoning begins with thinking about the facts of a situation, evaluating what is accurate or inaccurate, identifying what we do not know, and clarifying what we cannot find out before we act. It encourages us to critically examine whether our initial thoughts stimulated by our emotions might create more harm than good, if we acted on them. When we reason ethically, we go beyond an initial and solely intuitive response to a situation to carefully consider its facts. We exercise our moral imaginations, using rhetorical listening to imagine potential impacts of our choices on named and unnamed stakeholders. Rhetorical listening helps us overcome our ethical nearsightedness, our tendencies to mindlessly rely on habits or routines or to consider only our self-interest or the interests of those we care about. Once unseen stakeholders are named and recognized, newly engaging our moral emotions of empathy, equality bias, and even disgust, we gain a better understanding of the ethical issues in a situation, including what is at stake for the survival and thriving of unseen stakeholders. Our ethical reasoning shifts because our moral imagination has broadened our thinking.

Ethical reasoning helps us think outside the limitations of polarized categories of good/bad, right/wrong, or black/white. When our thinking is limited to opposing ethical options, we become vulnerable to a paralyzing fear of doing harm by making the wrong decision and, so, we may do nothing. We may think that it is better to *not* act and cause more harm. We may go to the opposite direction of rationalizing as necessary the harmful consequences of a decision that could have been limited or avoided by listening to alternative viewpoints or with creative problem solving. We may think that such harm is unfortunate, but necessary for the greater good. Setting aside polarized thinking during deliberation promotes brainstorming alternative responses to an ethical issue. This can be important when you face ethical dilemmas, where doing good for one person harms another, or ethical tragedies, where the degree of harm for everyone is so great that your goal is simply to do the least amount of harm possible. Another way to stimulate moral imagination and creative problem solving is thinking about how different ethical values, principles, or theories, especially those that are not part of your personal ethical commitments, apply to an ethical issue. Using different ethical values and principles alongside your personal ethical commitments helps identify options you had not considered. You may then more thoroughly evaluate the strengths and weaknesses of each alternative, identifying unexpected benefits or harms that are revealed when you consider a different ethical viewpoint. When we evaluate an emerging decision using values, principles, or theories that are not part of our personal ethical commitments, we are better prepared to recognize when we are rationalizing a decision or being ethically nearsighted.

When our practices of communication ethics become more mindful, engaging both our moral emotions and ethical reasoning, we can become more ethically responsive communicators. Our moral emotions help us initially discern what is important and motivate us to implement our decision. Ethical reasoning mindfully structures our deliberations. We focus our thinking on the nature of the ethical issues we face, the facts of a situation, and its stakeholders. As a practice of mindfulness, ethical reasoning helps lessen the human tendency toward ethical nearsightedness, polarized thinking, and rationalization of self-interested or poorly examined social convention. The final contribution of ethical reasoning to communication ethics is that it provides resources for explaining or justifying our decisions and actions to others. When we explain why we did what we did, we strengthen the place for ethics in our relationships, family, workplace, and community.

Two Additional Challenges to Your Practice of Communication Ethics

As you travel through life, you will face many challenges that can disrupt your intention to be an ethical communicator. You have read about the challenges of ethical nearsightedness and rationalization. This section discusses two additional challenges, special ethical temptations and the human desire for perfection.

Special ethical temptations disrupt our discernment and deliberation by encouraging us to ignore or set aside important facts or stakeholders, because we believe we "know better." **Special ethical temptations** arise from specialized skills or knowledge which give you an advantage over others who lack these. For example, specialized knowledge and skills required in professions such as law, medicine, or teaching create advantages for professionals over those not in these professions. One reason for the development of professional codes of conduct has been social and cultural concerns about the impact of such advantages on individuals and community life (Goldman; Fritz).

Special ethical temptations are not limited to well-recognized professions. Jobs that have access to confidential or private information, such as jobs in the health care, finance, or credit industries, offer special ethical temptations to people who work in those jobs. As a student of communication, your knowledge can create special ethical temptations for you in your friendship or at work. For example, someone with the specialized knowledge of interpersonal communication, with skills in empathic listening and using nonverbal cues, may be tempted to manage the flow and even the intimacy of a conversation to her advantage, especially if the conversational partner is mindlessly communicating. Specialized skill and knowledge can create a temptation to use a conversational partner to achieve a personal goal, rather than respecting her human dignity. You might be tempted to use your specialized knowledge and skill for personal advantage at work (rationalization of self-interest) or for a "good" cause (ethical nearsightedness). When we communicate mindlessly or are ethically nearsighted, we become more vulnerable to special ethical temptations. Mindfulness of your personal ethical standard and skills in ethical reasoning can stimulate awareness of special ethical temptations as they arise. Mindfulness, however, is not a guarantee that you are not ethically nearsighted or have rationalized a special ethical temptation. Discussing your intended decision with people who do not think as you do, for example using Bok's tests of publicity, can help you recognize when you are vulnerable to a special ethical temptation. Such discussions are practices of communication ethics that contribute to the ethical dimension of your relationships and social worlds.

Everyday Communication Ethics

❖   *What are the special ethical temptations of your current job? Your major?*

A second challenge of practicing communication ethics is our desire for perfection. The desire for perfection motivates us to make ethical decisions that do *no* harm. One advantage of doing no harm is that we cannot be criticized. Our desire for perfection also can make us vulnerable to the harmfulness of rigid perfection. Kenneth Burke (21) highlights the rigidity of perfection in his definition of human beings, noting that humans are "rotten with perfection." The **rottenness of perfection** is the rigid imposition of rules that dooms us to failure, so we feel guilt or shame for being imperfect. Burke spent much of his career studying scapegoating and the self-punishment of mortification, which are symbolic efforts to manage the psychological and symbolic effects of rigid perfection. As Burke makes clear, scapegoating and self-punishment merely restart the rotten cycle of rigid perfection. Perfection characterized by rigid rules ultimately condemns us to failure, because humans are imperfect creatures. Rigid perfection also encourages binary thinking—success or failure, good or bad. Rigid perfection may be coupled with the moral emotion of disgust, causing us to distinguish between the pure and perfect as good and the impure and imperfect as disgusting or bad. When this occurs, it becomes logical to develop practices that promote the purity of perfection by avoiding the impurity of imperfection. Because any amount of impurity taints a rigid notion of perfection, any source of impurity must be removed to protect or restore perfection. This cycle of perfection/purity/good and imperfection/impurity/disgust is desirable in food production and pharmaceutical manufacturing to meet standards of purity for food and medicine. However, when people are associated with impurity and, thus, are disgusting, the rigidity of perfection motivates us to exclude, remove, and perhaps even eliminate "impure" people to restore rigid perfection. Rigid perfection combined with disgust makes it emotionally easier to ignore the legitimate interests to survive and thrive of people labeled disgusting. We must be wary of communication practices that encourage us to condemn people as disgusting because they do not meet a rigid standard of perfection, and be ready to challenge these practices.

Yet, perfection can be good, which is why we are attracted to perfection. **Perfection characterized by aspiration** defines and performs excellence in ways that promote stability, security, or completeness in our lives (Hyde *Perfection* 8). Perfection can be ethically good. In fact, an aspiration to perfection as excellence emphasizes the importance of doing good. The prominence of rigid perfection sometimes makes it difficult to understand how the excellence of perfection as aspiration is ethically good. Perfection in nature can help illustrate. In his 2007 Arnold Lecture to the National Communication Association convention, Michael Hyde offered a brief history of the study of perfection in mathematics, nature, and art. He highlighted how perfection is a structure of logarithmic *proportion*. The proportional structure of perfection is found in nature in spirals, such as the nautilus shell and the American Beauty rose. Proportion, balance, and harmony inform our understanding of beauty and excellence (perfection) in nature, visual arts, mathematics, music, and, as Hyde notes, even the human body. The structure of proportion in nature finds diverse not rigid expression, as in the proportion found in flower petals, seed heads, pine cones, shells, spiral galaxies in space, hurricanes, and the human face (Hom; Rafael). Perhaps a motivation for communication is the innately human search for and appreciation of proportion, which we can satisfy as we gaze at a human face whenever we speak and listen.

Communication Ethics as a Practice of Hope

One of the definitions of ethics offered in Chapter 1 is discerning the proper weight to place on our legitimate interest to survive and thrive, relative to the legitimate interests of others to survive and thrive, a weight that is good, right, or virtuous. The practice of ethics is a search for harmony or proportion in balancing our self-interests with the self-interests of others, a harmony or proportion that is good, right, or virtuous for everyone involved. Aristotle defines virtue as an excellence or point of harmony between the vices of excess and deficiency of an emotion or domain of action. Virtue is a point of harmony, a display of excellence that is not rigid or permanent, because a fixed point would lose its harmony as people or situations change. The excellence or harmony of virtue shifts from person to person because the capabilities of each of us differ. The practice of ethics is a search for harmony or proportion in balancing our legitimate self-interests and the legitimate self-interests of others that varies as the point of harmony or proportion varies with the situation and its stakeholders. Unlike rigid perfection, perfection is an aspiration to be responsive to people, circumstances, and situations, because it is a search for how to achieve harmony or proportion rather than a rigid application of rules. Perfection as aspiration is a search for harmony or proportion in our relationships with others that is good, right, or virtuous. When each of us mindfully practices our personal ethical commitments in processes of ethical discernment, deliberation, and decision making, we are searching for harmony or proportion in our personal relationships, families, workplaces, and communities. Discerning what these points of harmony are will change as people, circumstances, situations, relationships, and communities change. The search for the excellence of what is good, right, or virtuous is one reason why the practice of communication ethics is a lifelong endeavor.

Everyday Communication Ethics

❖ *How have you experienced both the rottenness and aspiration of perfection?*

Just as there is no communication without a listener, we cannot aspire to the excellence of perfection as harmony without openness to the interruption of others in our lives, especially those who are different from ourselves (Arnett; Hyde *Acknowledgement*). Without the existence of others and their legitimate interests, harmony, proportion, excellence, even perfection in ethics is impossible. The concept of harmony in music can help us understand perfection's harmonic quality. Musical harmony *requires* difference or there is no harmony. Musical harmony requires continuous adjustment that allows for creativity within a specific musical act, adjustment that is in some way proportionate to other notes so that a musical relationship between the notes is sustained. Just as different and continual adjustment or attunement is necessary for musical harmony, so it is necessary for the practice of communication ethics (Tompkins "Justice"). Our openness to the legitimate interests of others to survive and thrive, alongside consideration of our own legitimate interests, creates the opportunity for each of us to aspire to the harmony of perfection as we live our lives. According to Hyde, our openness to the legitimate interests of others to survive and thrive is what makes each of us potential heroes—"We *are* beings of heroic potential who must face the fact that our fate is to be open and to listen to a constant calling that challenges us with the ethical and moral struggle of coming to know and to speak the good, the just, and the truth" (*Perfection* 173). In your aspiration to perfection of what is good, right, and virtuous, your communication matters.

Even when we understand perfection as an aspiration for harmony, proportion, and balance in our lives, we can become vulnerable to the rottenness of the perfection whenever we substitute rigid rules and standards for ethically responsive discernment and deliberation. This is not a rejection of absolutism in the practice of ethics, but a warning about the emotions of certainty and self-righteousness that leads to thinking that we already know everything we need to know. If we believe that we have found perfection, we may become arrogant about our knowledge or technique. We may be tempted to impose this discovered practice of perfection in situations where its practice is not harmonious or proportional. We may impose a rigid practice of perfection on ourselves or others, demanding the impossible and then condemning those who inevitably fail, as they must because humans are imperfect beings. This cycle of rigid perfection, failure, condemnation, and punishment is the rottenness of perfection Burke warned us about in the iron law of history. To avoid the rottenness of perfection, we must be wary of pride in our knowledge and abilities that may slip into self-righteousness and certainty that is rotten with perfection.

You may be wondering how to watch for the self-righteous belief that you have a sure technique for ethical communication. Humility is a companion practice in ethical communication that helps us aspire to the harmony of perfection without becoming self-righteous. **Humility** seeks to cultivate mindfulness about our personality and character that controls the arrogance and rigidity of self-righteousness. Mark Button proposes that we understand humility as a social, not an individualistic virtue, so humility is understood "less as a private, self-referencing quality and more as an active civic virtue and political ethos geared toward facilitating attentiveness, listening, and mutual understanding" (849). Button's understanding of humility clearly links ethically responsive communication to humility. Whenever our practice of communication ethics stimulates our moral imagination to recognize and understand others we encourage our humility, because we turn our attention away from ourselves to others to understand their legitimate interests to survive and thrive. Practices of humility also help us separate our aspirations for the harmony and proportion of perfection from our emotions of disgust or pride, especially when human frailty or failure misses the mark of perfection. Aspiration to perfection is not a demand, but a goal, a telos. We learn more from our failures than from our successes, if we are willing to listen with humility. Imperfection, while not ethically pure, can be ethically good. When practices of humility are coupled with practices of aspiring to perfection as harmony or proportion, we are better prepared to be ethically responsive to ourselves and others as we face life's opportunities, successes, setbacks, and failures.

Aspiring to the harmony of perfection with humility is an act of hope. It may seem odd that this book ends encouraging you to practice hope. Yet, hope is how this book began with the claim that your communication matters, that your communication is not trivial. Each time you practice your personal ethical standard, you practice hope. Each time you respond as an ethically responsive communicator, you practice hope. In their study of communicating hope and resilience across the lifespan, Gary Beck and Thomas

Socha note that communication and the relationships that our communication creates are vital to hope. They outline a **practice of hope** that converges with what you have been learning about practicing communication ethics. "Hopeful outcomes can be achieved by a clear sense of our goals, awareness of pathways or options toward achieving those goals, agency or belief and motivation that our efforts will push us toward those outcomes" (6). You have clarified your ethical goals whenever you reflected on your personal ethical standard. Clarifying your personal ethical standard helps you identify how you want to live your life, including your goal to be an ethical communicator in your friendships, family, workplace, and community. Your personal ethical standard is a practice of hope that provides you with resources for responding to life's challenges, problems, and opportunities. Your practice of ethical reasoning is a pathway for applying your personal ethical standard as you deliberate and make decisions in challenging and difficult situations. What you have learned about the moral imagination, ethical nearsightedness, rhetorical listening, and rationalization not only help you identify roadblocks in this pathway, they also offer resources for overcoming these roadblocks as you aspire to live your life ethically and creatively. Your practice of communication ethics—your personal ethical commitments, moral imagination, skills in ethical reasoning, and skills in recognizing rationalizations—are resources for your resilience and hope. There is one more reason to be hopeful. When you use these resources in your practice of communication ethics, you contribute to the ethical dimension of your relationships, workplaces, and the communities where you live, because your communication and my communication help construct the social worlds in which we live.

Remember . . .
you never know how far the good you do will go.

Vocabulary

Humility 266
Perfection characterized by aspiration 264
Practice of hope 267
Rottenness of perfection 263
Special ethical temptations 262

References

Aristotle. *The Ethics of Aristotle: The Nicomachean Ethics.* 1955. Trans. J.A.K. Thomson and Hugh Tredennick. New York: Penguin Books, 1976.

Arnett, Ronald C. *Levinas's Rhetorical Demand: The Unending Obligations of Communication Ethics.* Carbondale, IL: Southern Illinois UP, 2017.

Beck, Gary A. and Thomas J. Socha. "Embracing the Insights of 'Murphy': New Frontiers of Communication, Hope, and Resilience Across the Lifespan." *Communicating Hope and Resilience Across the Lifespan.* Eds. Gary A. Beck and Thomas J. Socha. New York: Peter Lang, 2015. 1–12.

Bloom, Paul. *Just Babies: The Origins of Good and Evil.* New York: Crown Publishers, 2013.

Bok, Sissela. *Lying: Moral Choice in Public and Private Life.* 1978. New York: Vintage Books, 1989.

Burke, Kenneth. *Language as Symbolic Action: Essays on Life, Literature, and Method.* Berkeley, CA: U of California P, 1966.

Button, Mark. "A Monkish Kind of Virtue." *Political Theory* 33.6 (2005): 840–68.

Fritz, Janie M. Harden. *Professional Civility: Communicative Virtue at Work.* New York: Peter Lang, 2013.

Goldman, Alan H. *The Moral Foundations of Professional Ethics.* Totowa, NJ: Rowman and Littlefield, 1980.

Hoffman, Martin. *Empathy and Moral Development: Implications for Caring and Justice.* New York: Cambridge UP, 2001.

Hom, Elaine J. "What is the Golden Ratio? *LiveScience.* 24 June 2013. www.livescience. com/37704-phi-golden-ratio.html. Date accessed: 14 September 2017.

Hyde, Michael J. *The Life-Giving Gift of Acknowledgement.* West Lafayette, IN: Purdue UP, 2006.

Hyde, Michael J. *Perfection, Postmodern Culture, and the Biotechnology Debate.* National Communication Association Arnold Distinguished Lecture. Boston: Pearson, 2008. www.natcom.org/sites/default/files/annual-convention/NCA_Convention_Video_ Archive_2007_Arnold_Lecture.pdf. Date accessed: 1 December 2017.

Hyde, Michael J. *Perfection: Coming to Terms with Being Human.* Waco, TX: Baylor UP, 2010.

Kligyte, Vykinta, Shane Connelly, Chase Thiel, and Lynn Devenport. "The Influence of Anger, Fear, and Emotion Regulation on Ethical Decision Making." *Human Performance* 26 (2013): 297–326.

Nussbaum, Martha C. *Upheavals of Thought: The Intelligence of Emotions.* Cambridge: Cambridge UP, 2001.

Rafael, Lance. "How to Draw a Face (Proportions Made Easy)." *Instructables.* 23 March 2014. www.instructables.com/id/How-To-Draw-a-Face-Proportions-Made-Easy/. Date accessed: 30 October 2017.

Smith, Christian, Kari Christoffersen, Hilary Davidson, and Patricia Snell Herzog. *Lost in Transition: The Dark Side of Emerging Adulthood.* New York: Oxford UP, 2011.

Tompkins, Paula S. "Communication and Children's Moral Development." *The Children's Communication Sourcebook.* Eds. Thomas Socha and Narissra Punyanunt-Carter. New York: Peter Lang, *in press.*

Tompkins, Paula S. "Acknowledgment, Justice, and Communication Ethics." *Review of Communication* 15 (2015): 240–57.

Waldron, Vincent, Joshua Danaher, Carmen Goman, Nicole Piemonte, and Dayna Kloeber. "Which Parent Messages about Morality Are Accepted by Emerging Adults?" *Moral Talk Across the Lifespan: Creating Good Relationships.* Eds. Vince Waldron and Douglas Kelley. New York: Peter Lang. 35–54.

INDEX